AMERICA'S FAVORITE BRAND NAME

ONE-DISH MEALS

PiL

Publications International, Ltd.

Microwave Cooking: Microwave ovens vary in wattage. Use the cooking times as guidelines and check for doneness before adding more time.

The HEALTHY CHOICE® recipes contained in this book have been tested by the manufacturers and have been carefully edited by the publisher. The publisher and the manufacturers cannot be held responsible for any ill effects caused by errors in the recipes, or by spoiled ingredients, unsanitary conditions, incorrect preparation procedures or any other cause.

AMERICA'S FAVORITE BRAND NAME
ONE-DISH MEALS

PRIME TIME MEATS

Beef "Chow Fun" Stir-Fry

½ pound boneless tender beef steak
    (sirloin, rib eye or top loin)
7 tablespoons KIKKOMAN® Stir-Fry
    Sauce, divided
6 ounces uncooked extra wide egg
    noodles
6 tablespoons beef broth
¼ teaspoon white pepper
2 tablespoons vegetable oil, divided
1 clove garlic, minced
1 teaspoon minced fresh ginger root
1 onion, chunked
1 pound romaine lettuce, washed and
    cut crosswise into 1-inch strips

Cut beef across grain into thin slices 1 inch wide; coat with 1 tablespoon stir-fry sauce. Let stand 30 minutes. Meanwhile, cook noodles according to package directions in lightly salted water; drain. Combine remaining 6 tablespoons stir-fry sauce, beef broth and pepper in small bowl; set aside. Heat 1 tablespoon oil in hot wok or large skillet. Add beef and stir-fry 1 minute; remove. Heat remaining 1 tablespoon oil in same pan. Add garlic and ginger; stir-fry 10 seconds, or until fragrant. Add onion; stir-fry 2 minutes. Add romaine; stir-fry 2 minutes longer. Reduce heat to medium. Add

noodles and stir-fry sauce mixture; cook and stir until noodles are thoroughly heated, about 2 minutes. Stir in beef; heat through. Serve immediately. *Makes 4 servings*

Chili Stew

1 box (10 ounces) BIRDS EYE® frozen
    Sweet Corn
2 cans (15 ounces each) chili
1 can (14 ounces) stewed tomatoes
    Chili powder

• In large saucepan, cook corn according to package directions; drain.

• Stir in chili and tomatoes; cook until heated through.

• Stir in chili powder to taste.
Makes 4 servings

Serving Suggestion: Serve with your favorite corn bread or sprinkle with shredded Cheddar cheese.

Prep Time: 2 minutes
Cook Time: 7 to 10 minutes

Beef "Chow Fun" Stir-Fry

Beef Stew in Red Wine

1½ pounds boneless beef round, cut into
    1-inch cubes
1½ cups dry red wine
2 teaspoons olive oil
    Peel of half an orange
2 large cloves garlic, thinly sliced
1 bay leaf
½ teaspoon dried thyme leaves
⅛ teaspoon pepper
8 ounces fresh mushrooms, quartered
8 sun-dried tomatoes, quartered
1 can (about 14 ounces) fat-free
    reduced-sodium beef broth
6 small potatoes, unpeeled, cut into
    wedges
1 cup baby carrots
1 cup fresh pearl onions, outer skins
    removed
1 tablespoon cornstarch mixed with
    2 tablespoons water

1. Combine beef, wine, oil, orange peel, garlic, bay leaf, thyme and pepper in large glass bowl. Refrigerate, covered, at least 2 hours or overnight.

2. Place beef mixture, mushrooms and tomatoes in large nonstick skillet or Dutch oven. Add enough beef broth to just cover ingredients. Bring to a boil over high heat. Cover; reduce heat to low. Simmer 1 hour. Add potatoes, carrots and onions; cover and cook 20 to 25 minutes or until vegetables are tender and meat is no longer pink. Remove meat and vegetables from skillet with slotted spoon; cover and set aside. Discard orange peel and bay leaf.

3. Stir cornstarch mixture into skillet with sauce. Increase heat to medium; cook and stir until sauce is slightly thickened. Return meat and vegetables to sauce; heat thoroughly. *Makes 6 servings*

Countdown Casserole

1 jar (8 ounces) pasteurized process
    cheese spread
¾ cup milk
2 cups (12 ounces) cubed cooked roast
    beef
1 bag (16 ounces) frozen vegetable
    combination (broccoli, corn, red
    pepper), thawed and drained
4 cups frozen hash brown potatoes,
    thawed
1⅓ cups FRENCH'S® French Fried Onions,
    divided
½ teaspoon seasoned salt
¼ teaspoon freshly ground black
    pepper
½ cup (2 ounces) shredded Cheddar
    cheese

Preheat oven to 375°F. Spoon cheese spread into 12×8-inch baking dish; place in oven just until cheese melts, about 5 minutes. Using fork, stir milk into melted cheese until well blended. Stir in beef, vegetables, potatoes, ⅔ cup French Fried Onions and the seasonings. Bake, covered, at 375°F 30 minutes or until heated through. Top with Cheddar cheese; sprinkle remaining ⅔ cup onions down center. Bake, uncovered, 3 minutes or until onions are golden brown. *Makes 4 to 6 servings*

Microwave Directions: In 12×8-inch microwave-safe dish, combine cheese spread and milk. Cook, covered, on HIGH 3 minutes; stir. Add ingredients as directed. Cook, covered, 14 minutes or until heated through, stirring beef mixture halfway through cooking time. Top with Cheddar cheese and remaining ⅔ cup onions as directed. Cook, uncovered, 1 minute or until cheese melts. Let stand 5 minutes.

Beef Stew in Red Wine

Beef Enchiladas

Red Chili Sauce (recipe follows)
1½ pounds lean boneless beef chuck, cut into 1-inch cubes
½ teaspoon salt
2 tablespoons vegetable oil
½ cup finely chopped white onion
¾ cup beef broth
¼ cup raisins
1 clove garlic, minced
½ teaspoon ground cloves
¼ teaspoon anise seeds, crushed
12 corn tortillas (6-inch diameter)
1 cup (4 ounces) shredded mild Cheddar cheese
¾ cup sour cream
⅓ cup sliced pitted black olives
Basil sprig and tomato wedge for garnish

1. Prepare Red Chili Sauce.

2. Sprinkle beef with salt. Brown half of beef in hot oil in large skillet over medium-high heat 10 to 12 minutes, turning frequently. Remove with slotted spoon to plate. Repeat with remaining beef.

3. Reduce heat to medium. Add onion; cook and stir 4 minutes or until onion is softened. Return beef to skillet. Stir in broth, raisins, garlic, cloves, anise seeds and ¼ cup Red Chili Sauce. Bring to a boil over medium-high heat. Reduce heat to low. Cover and simmer 1½ to 2 hours until beef is very tender. Using 2 forks, pull beef into coarse shreds in skillet. Remove from heat.

4. Preheat oven to 375°F. Heat remaining Red Chili Sauce in medium skillet over medium heat until hot; remove from heat.

5. Dip 1 tortilla in sauce with tongs a few seconds or until limp. Remove, draining off excess sauce. Spread about 3 tablespoons meat filling down center of tortilla. Roll up; place in 13×9-inch baking dish. Repeat with remaining tortillas, sauce and meat filling. Pour remaining sauce over enchiladas.

6. Sprinkle cheese over top. Bake 25 minutes or until bubbly and cheese is melted. To serve, spoon sour cream down center of enchiladas. Sprinkle with olives. Garnish, if desired. *Makes 4 to 6 servings*

Red Chili Sauce

3 ounces dried ancho chilies (about 5), seeded, deveined and rinsed
2½ cups boiling water
2 tablespoons vegetable oil
2 tablespoons tomato paste
1 clove garlic, minced
½ teaspoon salt
½ teaspoon dried oregano leaves
¼ teaspoon ground cumin
¼ teaspoon ground coriander

1. Place chilies in medium bowl; cover with boiling water. Let stand 1 hour.

2. Place chilies along with soaking water in blender; blend until smooth.

3. Pour into 2-quart saucepan; whisk in remaining ingredients. Bring to a boil over medium-high heat. Reduce heat to very low. Cover and simmer 10 minutes, stirring occasionally. *Makes about 2½ cups*

Note: Sauce can be refrigerated, covered up to 3 days or frozen up to 1 month.

Beef Enchiladas

Kublai Khan's Stir-Fry with Fiery Walnuts

Fiery Walnuts (recipe follows)
1 pound boneless tender beef steak (sirloin, rib eye or top loin) or lamb sirloin
2 tablespoons KIKKOMAN® Stir-Fry Sauce
1 teaspoon cornstarch
2 large cloves garlic, minced
2 tablespoons vegetable oil, divided
1 medium onion, cut into ¾-inch chunks
2 large carrots, cut into julienne strips
1 pound fresh spinach, washed and drained
½ pound fresh mushrooms, sliced
⅓ cup KIKKOMAN® Stir-Fry Sauce

Prepare Fiery Walnuts. Cut beef across grain into thin slices, then into narrow strips. Combine 2 tablespoons stir-fry sauce, cornstarch and garlic in medium bowl; stir in beef. Heat 1 tablespoon oil in hot wok or large skillet over medium-high heat. Add beef and stir-fry 1½ minutes; remove. Heat remaining 1 tablespoon oil in same pan. Add onion; stir-fry 2 minutes. Add carrots; stir-fry 1 minute. Add spinach and mushrooms; stir-fry 2 minutes, or until spinach is wilted. Add beef and ⅓ cup stir-fry sauce; cook and stir only until beef and vegetables are coated with sauce and heated through. Remove from heat; stir in Fiery Walnuts and serve immediately.

Makes 6 servings

Fiery Walnuts: Combine 2 teaspoons vegetable oil, ¼ teaspoon ground red pepper (cayenne) and ⅛ teaspoon salt in small skillet; heat over medium heat until hot. Add ¾ cup walnut halves or large pieces. Cook, stirring, 1 minute, or until walnuts are coated. Turn out onto small baking sheet; spread out in single layer. Bake in 350°F oven 7 minutes, or until golden. Cool.

Oven-Easy Beef & Potato Dinner

4 cups frozen hash brown potatoes, thawed
3 tablespoons vegetable oil
⅛ teaspoon pepper
1 pound ground beef
1 cup water
1 package (about ¾ ounce) brown gravy mix
½ teaspoon garlic salt
1 package (10 ounces) frozen mixed vegetables, thawed and drained
1 cup (4 ounces) shredded Cheddar cheese
1⅓ cup FRENCH'S® French Fried Onions, divided

Preheat oven to 400°F. In 12×8-inch baking dish, combine potatoes, oil and pepper. Firmly press potato mixture evenly across bottom and up sides of dish to form a shell. Bake, uncovered, at 400°F for 15 minutes. Meanwhile, in large skillet, brown ground beef; drain. Stir in water, gravy mix and garlic salt; bring to a boil. Add mixed vegetables; reduce heat to medium and cook, uncovered, 5 minutes. Remove from heat and stir in ½ cup cheese and ⅔ cup French Fried Onions; spoon into hot potato shell. Reduce oven temperature to 350°F. Bake, uncovered, at 350°F for 15 minutes or until heated through. Top with remaining cheese and ⅔ cup onions; bake, uncovered, 5 minutes or until onions are golden brown.

Makes 4 to 6 servings

Kublai Khan's Stir-Fry with Fiery Walnuts

Fiesta Corn Casserole

1 tablespoon butter
3 cups cornflakes, divided
1 pound ground beef
1 can (8 ounces) tomato sauce
1 package (1.0 ounce) LAWRY'S® Taco
 Spices & Seasonings
½ teaspoon LAWRY'S® Seasoned Salt
1 can (17 ounces) whole kernel corn,
 drained (reserve ¼ cup liquid)
2 cups (8 ounces) shredded cheddar
 cheese

Microwave Directions: In 1½-quart shallow glass casserole, place butter and microwave on HIGH 30 seconds. Sprinkle 2 cups cornflakes over butter. Crush remaining 1 cup cornflakes and set aside. In separate baking dish, microwave ground beef on HIGH 5 minutes, stirring to crumble after 3 minutes. Drain fat and crumble beef. Add tomato sauce, Taco Spices & Seasonings, Seasoned Salt and ¼ cup corn liquid; mix well. Layer half of corn, meat mixture and cheese over buttered cornflakes; repeat layers. Sprinkle remaining 1 cup crushed cornflakes over top in diagonal strips. Microwave on HIGH 12 to 15 minutes.

Conventional Oven Directions: In large skillet, melt butter. Add 2 cups cornflakes; mix well. Remove buttered cornflakes and set aside. Wipe skillet clean. In same skillet, brown ground beef over medium-high heat until crumbly; drain fat. Add tomato sauce, Taco Spices & Seasonings, Seasoned Salt and ¼ cup corn liquid; mix well. In 1½-quart casserole, layer half buttered cornflakes, corn, meat mixture and cheese; repeat layers. Sprinkle remaining 1 cup crushed cornflakes over top in diagonal strips. Bake in 350°F oven 15 to 20 minutes until heated through.

Makes 4 to 6 servings

Serving Suggestion: Serve with sliced tomatoes, cucumbers and fresh fruit.

Hint: May use 2 cups broken taco shell pieces and 1 cup crushed taco shells.

Steak Pot Pie

1 cup chopped onion
2 tablespoons PARKAY® 70% Vegetable
 Oil Spread
3 tablespoons all-purpose flour
1½ cups beef broth
½ cup A.1.® Original or A.1.® Bold &
 Spicy Steak Sauce
3 cups cubed cooked steak (about
 1½ pounds)
1 (16-ounce) package frozen broccoli,
 cauliflower & carrot mixture
 Prepared pastry for 1-crust pie
1 egg, beaten

In 2-quart saucepan, over medium-high heat, cook onion in spread until tender. Blend in flour; cook 1 minute more. Add broth and steak sauce; cook and stir until mixture thickens and begins to boil. Stir in steak and vegetables. Spoon mixture into 8-inch square glass baking dish. Roll out and cut pastry crust to fit over dish. Seal crust to edge of dish; brush with egg. Slit top of crust to vent. Bake at 400°F 25 minutes or until crust is golden brown. Serve immediately. Garnish as desired.

Makes 4 servings

Steak Pot Pie

Meatball Stroganoff with Rice

MEATBALLS

  1 egg, lightly beaten
1½ pounds ground beef round
  ⅓ cup plain dry bread crumbs
  1 tablespoon Worcestershire sauce
  1 teaspoon salt
  ¼ teaspoon pepper
  2 tablespoons CRISCO® Vegetable Oil

SAUCE

  1 tablespoon CRISCO® Vegetable Oil
  ½ pound mushrooms, sliced
  2 tablespoons all-purpose flour
  1 teaspoon ketchup
  1 can (10½ ounces) condensed, double
     strength beef broth (bouillon),
     undiluted*
  ½ (1-ounce) envelope dry onion soup
     mix (about 2 tablespoons)
  1 cup sour cream
  4 cups hot cooked rice

*1¼ cups reconstituted beef broth made with double amount of very low sodium beef broth granules may be substituted for beef broth (bouillon).

1. For meatballs, combine egg, meat, bread crumbs, Worcestershire sauce, salt and pepper in large bowl. Mix until well blended. Shape into eighteen 2-inch meatballs.

2. Heat 2 tablespoons Crisco® Oil in large skillet on medium heat. Add meatballs. Brown on all sides. Reduce heat to low. Cook 10 minutes. Remove meatballs from skillet.

3. For sauce, add 1 tablespoon Crisco® Oil to skillet. Add mushrooms. Cook and stir 4 minutes. Remove skillet from heat.

4. Stir in flour and ketchup until blended. Stir in broth gradually. Add soup mix. Return to heat. Bring to a boil on medium heat. Reduce heat to low. Simmer 2 minutes. Return meatballs to skillet. Heat thoroughly, stirring occasionally.

5. Stir in sour cream. Heat but do not bring to a boil. Serve over hot rice. Garnish, if desired. *Makes 6 servings*

Spicy Quick and Easy Chili

  1 pound ground beef
  1 large clove garlic, minced
  1 can (15¼ ounces) DEL MONTE®
     Golden Sweet Whole Kernel Corn,
     drained
  1 can (16 ounces) kidney beans,
     drained
1½ cups salsa, mild, medium or hot
  1 can (4 ounces) diced green chiles,
     undrained

1. Brown meat with garlic in large saucepan; drain.

2. Add remaining ingredients. Simmer, uncovered, 10 minutes, stirring occasionally. Sprinkle with chopped green onions, if desired. *Makes 4 servings*

Prep and Cook Time: 15 minutes

Spicy Quick and Easy Chili

All-in-One Burger Stew

1 pound lean ground beef
2 cups frozen Italian vegetables
1 can (14½ ounces) chopped tomatoes with basil and garlic
1 can (about 14 ounces) beef broth
2½ cups uncooked medium egg noodles
Salt
Black pepper

1. Cook meat in Dutch oven or large skillet over medium-high heat until no longer pink, breaking meat apart with wooden spoon. Drain drippings.

2. Add vegetables, tomatoes and broth; bring to a boil over high heat.

3. Add noodles; reduce heat to medium. Cover and cook 12 to 15 minutes or until noodles have absorbed liquid and vegetables are tender. Add salt and pepper to taste.

Makes 6 servings

Tip: To complete this meal, serve with breadsticks or a loaf of Italian bread and a mixed green and tomato salad.

Prep and Cook Time: 25 minutes

Spaghetti Rolls

1 package (8 ounces) manicotti shells
2 pounds ground beef
1 tablespoon onion powder
1 teaspoon salt
½ teaspoon pepper
2 cups spaghetti sauce, divided
1 cup (4 ounces) shredded pizza-flavored cheese blend or mozzarella cheese

1. Cook pasta according to package directions. Place in colander, then rinse under warm running water. Drain well.

2. Preheat oven to 350°F. Grease 13×9-inch baking pan.

3. Cook beef in large skillet over medium-high heat until brown; drain drippings. Stir in onion powder, salt and pepper. Stir in 1 cup spaghetti sauce; set aside.

4. Reserve ½ cup ground beef mixture. Combine remaining beef mixture with cheese in large bowl. Fill shells with remaining beef mixture using spoon.

5. Arrange shells in prepared pan. Combine remaining 1 cup spaghetti sauce with reserved beef mixture in small bowl; blend well. Pour over shells. Cover with foil. Bake 20 to 30 minutes or until hot. Garnish as desired. *Makes 4 servings*

Classic Hamburger Casserole

1 pound ground beef
1 package (9 ounces) frozen cut green beans, thawed and drained
1 can (10¾ ounces) condensed tomato soup
¼ cup water
½ teaspoon seasoned salt
⅛ teaspoon pepper
2 cups hot mashed potatoes
1⅓ cups FRENCH'S® French Fried Onions, divided
½ cup (2 ounces) shredded Cheddar cheese

Preheat oven to 350°F. In medium skillet, brown ground beef; drain. Stir in green beans, soup, water and seasonings; pour into 1½-quart casserole. In medium bowl, combine mashed potatoes and ⅔ cup French Fried Onions. Spoon potato mixture in mounds around edge of casserole. Bake, uncovered, at 350°F for 25 minutes or until heated through. Top potatoes with cheese and remaining ⅔ cup onions; bake, uncovered, 5 minutes or until onions are golden brown. *Makes 4 to 6 servings*

Spaghetti Rolls

Texas-Style Deep-Dish Chili Pie

- 1 pound beef stew meat, cut into ½-inch cubes
- 1 tablespoon vegetable oil
- 2 cans (14½ ounces each) Mexican-style stewed tomatoes, undrained
- 1 medium green bell pepper, diced
- 1 package (1.0 ounce) LAWRY'S® Taco Spices & Seasonings
- 1 tablespoon yellow cornmeal
- 1 can (15¼ ounces) kidney beans, drained
- 1 package (15 ounces) flat refrigerated pie crusts
- ½ cup (2 ounces) shredded cheddar cheese, divided

In Dutch oven, brown beef in oil; drain fat. Add stewed tomatoes, bell pepper, Taco Spices & Seasonings and cornmeal. Bring to a boil over medium-high heat; reduce heat to low and cook, uncovered, 20 minutes. Add kidney beans. In 10-inch pie plate, unfold 1 crust and fill with chili mixture and ¼ cup cheese. Top with remaining crust, fluting edges. Bake, uncovered, in 350°F oven 30 minutes. Sprinkle remaining cheese over crust; return to oven and bake 10 minutes longer.   *Makes 6 servings*

Serving Suggestion: Serve with an orange and red onion salad.

Beef Teriyaki Stir-Fry

- 1 cup uncooked rice
- 1 pound beef sirloin, thinly sliced
- ½ cup teriyaki marinade, divided
- 2 tablespoons vegetable oil, divided
- 1 medium onion, halved and sliced
- 2 cups frozen green beans, rinsed and drained

1. Cook rice according to package directions, omitting salt.

2. Combine beef and ¼ cup marinade in medium bowl; set aside. Heat ½ tablespoon oil in wok or large skillet over medium-high heat until hot. Add onion; stir-fry 3 to 4 minutes or until crisp-tender. Remove from wok to medium bowl.

3. Heat ½ tablespoon oil in wok. Stir-fry beans 3 minutes or until crisp-tender and hot. Drain off excess liquid. Add beans to onions in bowl.

4. Heat remaining 1 tablespoon oil in wok. Drain beef, discarding marinade. Stir-fry beef about 3 minutes or until browned. Stir in vegetables and remaining ¼ cup marinade; cook and stir just until heated through. Serve with rice.   *Makes 4 servings*

Beefy Bean & Walnut Stir-Fry

- 1 teaspoon vegetable oil
- 3 cloves garlic, minced
- 1 pound lean ground beef or ground turkey
- 1 bag (16 ounces) BIRDS EYE® frozen Cut Green Beans, thawed
- 1 teaspoon salt
- ½ cup walnut pieces

• In large skillet, heat oil and garlic over medium heat about 30 seconds.

• Add beef and beans; sprinkle with salt. Mix well.

• Cook 5 minutes or until beef is well browned, stirring occasionally.

• Stir in walnuts; cook 2 minutes more.
Makes 4 servings

Serving Suggestion: Serve over hot cooked egg noodles or rice.

Prep Time: 5 minutes

Cook Time: 7 to 10 minutes

Beef Teriyaki Stir-Fry

Beef Mole Tamale Pie

1½ pounds ground chuck
1 medium onion, chopped
1 green bell pepper, chopped
2 cloves garlic, minced
1¼ cups medium-hot salsa
1 package (10 ounces) frozen whole kernel corn, partially thawed
1 tablespoon unsweetened cocoa powder
2 teaspoons ground cumin
1 teaspoon dried oregano leaves
1½ teaspoons salt, divided
¼ teaspoon ground cinnamon
2 cups (8 ounces) shredded Monterey Jack or Cheddar cheese
⅓ cup chopped fresh cilantro
1 cup all-purpose flour
¾ cup yellow cornmeal
3 tablespoons sugar
2 teaspoons baking powder
⅔ cup milk
3 tablespoons butter, melted
1 egg, beaten
Cilantro leaves, chili pepper and sour cream for garnish

Preheat oven to 400°F. Spray 11×7-inch baking dish with nonstick cooking spray. Brown ground chuck with onion, bell pepper and garlic in large deep skillet or Dutch oven over medium heat until meat just loses its pink color. Pour off drippings. Stir in salsa, corn, cocoa, cumin, oregano, 1 teaspoon salt and cinnamon. Bring to a boil. Reduce heat to medium-low; simmer, uncovered, 8 minutes, stirring occasionally. Remove from heat; stir in cheese and cilantro. Spread in prepared dish.

Combine flour, cornmeal, sugar, baking powder and remaining ½ teaspoon salt in large bowl. Add milk, butter and egg; stir just until dry ingredients are moistened. Drop by spoonfuls evenly over meat mixture; spread batter evenly with spatula.

Bake 15 minutes. *Reduce oven temperature to 350°F. Bake 20 minutes or until topping is light brown and filling is bubbly. Let stand 5 minutes before serving. Garnish, if desired.*
Makes 6 servings

Bistro Burgundy Stew

1 pound boneless beef sirloin, cut into 1½-inch pieces
3 tablespoons all-purpose flour
6 slices bacon, cut into 1-inch pieces (about ¼ pound)
2 cloves garlic, crushed
3 carrots, peeled and cut into 1-inch pieces (about 1½ cups)
¾ cup Burgundy or other dry red wine
½ cup GREY POUPON® Dijon Mustard
½ cup beef broth or lower sodium beef broth
12 small mushrooms
1½ cups green onions, cut into 1½-inch pieces
Tomato rose and parsley, for garnish
Breadsticks, optional

Coat beef with flour, shaking off excess; set aside.

In large skillet, over medium heat, cook bacon just until done; pour off excess fat. Add beef and garlic; cook until browned. Add carrots, wine, mustard and beef broth. Heat to a boil; reduce heat. Cover; simmer 30 minutes or until carrots are tender, stirring occasionally. Stir in mushrooms and green onions; cook 10 minutes more, stirring occasionally. Garnish with tomato rose and parsley. Serve with breadsticks, if desired.
Makes 4 servings

Beef Mole Tamale Pie

Three-Pepper Steak

1 pound boneless beef top round or
　flank steak
3 tablespoons reduced-sodium soy
　sauce
1 tablespoon cornstarch
1 tablespoon brown sugar
1½ teaspoons sesame oil
¼ teaspoon red pepper flakes
1 small green bell pepper
1 small red bell pepper
1 small yellow bell pepper
1 medium onion
2 cloves garlic
3 tablespoons vegetable oil, divided
　Hot cooked rice

• Cut beef across grain into ¼-inch-thick
slices. Combine soy sauce, cornstarch,
brown sugar, sesame oil and red pepper
flakes in medium bowl; stir until smooth.
Add beef and toss to coat; set aside.

• Cut green, red and yellow peppers
lengthwise in half. Remove stems and seeds.
Rinse, dry and cut into ½-inch strips. Cut
onion in half then into 1-inch pieces. Finely
chop garlic. Set aside.

• Heat wok over high heat about 1 minute
or until hot. Drizzle 1 tablespoon vegetable
oil into wok and heat 30 seconds. Add
pepper strips; stir-fry until crisp-tender.
Remove to large bowl. Add 1 tablespoon
vegetable oil and heat 30 seconds. Add
half of beef mixture to wok; stir-fry until
well browned. Remove beef to bowl with
peppers. Repeat with remaining 1
tablespoon vegetable oil and beef mixture.
Reduce heat to medium.

• Add onion; stir-fry about 3 minutes or until
softened. Add garlic; stir-fry 30 seconds.
Return peppers, beef and any accumulated
juices to wok; cook until heated through.
Spoon rice into serving dish; top with beef
and vegetable mixture.　*Makes 4 servings*

Heartland Shepherd's Pie

¾ pound ground beef
1 medium onion, chopped
1 can (14½ ounces) DEL MONTE®
　Original Recipe Stewed Tomatoes
1 can (8 ounces) DEL MONTE® Tomato
　Sauce
1 can (14½ ounces) DEL MONTE®
　Mixed Vegetables, drained
　Instant mashed potato flakes plus
　ingredients to prepare (enough
　for 6 servings)
3 cloves garlic, minced

1. Preheat oven to 375°F. In large skillet,
brown meat and onion over medium-high
heat; drain.

2. Add tomatoes and tomato sauce; cook
over high heat until thickened, stirring
frequently. Stir in mixed vegetables. Season
with salt and pepper, if desired.

3. Spoon into 2-quart baking dish; set aside.
Prepare 6 servings mashed potatoes
according to package directions, first
cooking garlic in specified amount of butter.

4. Top meat mixture with potatoes. Bake 20
minutes or until heated through. Garnish
with chopped parsley, if desired.

Makes 4 to 6 servings

Prep Time: 5 minutes
Cook Time: 30 minutes

Three-Pepper Steak

Beef Benihana

1 pound boneless beef sirloin, cut
    1 inch thick
2 medium zucchini
1 large onion
1 tablespoon sesame seeds
2 tablespoons vegetable oil, divided
½ pound sliced mushrooms
3 tablespoons teriyaki sauce
1 teaspoon sugar
½ teaspoon salt
¼ teaspoon black pepper
    Hot cooked rice

• Trim fat from beef; discard. Slice beef across grain into ¼-inch-thick slices. Scrub zucchini; cut off ends. Cut each zucchini crosswise and lengthwise in half. Cut pieces lengthwise into ½-inch strips. Cut onion lengthwise in half; slice crosswise into ¼-inch slices. Set aside.

• Heat wok over high heat about 1 minute or until hot. Add sesame seeds; cook and stir until lightly browned. Remove to small bowl. Drizzle 1 tablespoon oil into wok and heat 30 seconds. Add beef; stir-fry about 2 minutes or until well browned on outside and rare on inside. Remove beef to large bowl. Reduce heat to medium.

• Add remaining 1 tablespoon oil to wok and heat 30 seconds. Add mushrooms, zucchini and onion; stir-fry about 5 minutes or until vegetables are crisp-tender. Stir in teriyaki, sugar, salt and black pepper. Return beef and any accumulated juices to wok; cook until heated through. Spoon rice onto serving plate; top with beef mixture. Sprinkle with sesame seeds.

Makes 4 servings

Texas Beef Stew

1 pound lean ground beef
1 small onion, chopped
1 can (28 ounces) crushed tomatoes
    with roasted garlic
1½ cups BIRDS EYE® frozen Farm Fresh
    Mixtures Broccoli, Cauliflower &
    Carrots
1 can (14½ ounces) whole new
    potatoes, halved
1 cup BIRDS EYE® frozen Sweet Corn
1 can (4½ ounces) chopped green
    chilies, drained
½ cup water

• In large saucepan, cook beef and onion over medium-high heat until beef is well browned, stirring occasionally.

• Stir in tomatoes, vegetables, potatoes with liquid, corn, chilies and water; bring to boil.

• Reduce heat to medium-low; cover and simmer 5 minutes or until heated through.

Makes 4 servings

Serving Suggestion: Serve over rice and with warm crusty bread.

Birds Eye Idea: The smell of onions and garlic can penetrate into your cutting boards. Keep a separate cutting board exclusively for these vegetables.

Prep Time: 5 minutes

Cook Time: 15 minutes

Texas Beef Stew

Potato-Crusted Meat Loaf

1 large yellow onion
1 large green bell pepper
1 large red bell pepper
3 large cloves garlic
1 pound lean ground beef
1 pound ground veal
¼ cup egg substitute or 1 large egg, beaten
½ cup bottled chili sauce
1 cup seasoned dry bread crumbs, divided
½ cup (2 ounces) shredded ALPINE LACE® Fat Free Pasteurized Process Skim Milk Cheese Product—For Cheddar Lovers
½ teaspoon freshly ground black pepper
1 pound russet baking potatoes, peeled, cooked, kept hot (2 large)
1 cup (4 ounces) shredded ALPINE LACE® Fat Free Pasteurized Process Skim Milk Cheese Product—For Cheddar Lovers
¼ cup minced chives
2 tablespoons unsalted butter substitute, melted

1. Preheat the broiler. Place the onion, bell peppers and garlic cloves on a baking sheet. Broil 3 inches from heat for 7 minutes or until blackened, turning frequently. Transfer to a paper bag, close tightly and let stand 15 minutes or until soft. Scrape off outside skins. Chop the onion and garlic; seed and chop the peppers. (You will have about 2 cups vegetables.)

2. Preheat the oven to 350°F and spray a 13×9×3-inch baking dish with nonstick cooking spray. In a large bowl, mix the beef, veal, vegetables, egg substitute (or the whole egg), chili sauce, bread crumbs, the ½ cup of the cheese and the black pepper. Mix with your hands until well combined.

Transfer to the baking dish and pat into a 12×7-inch loaf, mounding it slightly in the center.

3. In a small bowl, with an electric mixer set on medium-high, whip the hot potatoes with the 1 cup of cheese, the chives and the butter until fluffy. Pipe or spoon on top and sides of the loaf. Bake for 1 hour or until a meat thermometer inserted into the center of the meat loaf registers 145°F. Let stand for 10 minutes, then serve.

Makes 12 servings

Cowpoke Enchiladas

1⅓ cups tomato salsa
1 cup HEINZ® Tomato Ketchup
½ pound lean ground beef
½ cup chopped onion
½ cup chopped green bell pepper
1 can (15½ ounces) pinto or kidney beans, drained
6 (8-inch) flour tortillas, warmed
1¼ cups shredded Cheddar cheese, divided

In small bowl, combine salsa and ketchup. Pour ½ cup salsa mixture into bottom of 13×9-inch baking pan; set remainder aside. In large nonstick skillet, brown beef with onion and bell pepper; drain fat. Add beans and ⅓ cup salsa mixture; mix well. Spoon ½ cup beef mixture onto each tortilla; sprinkle with 2 tablespoons cheese. Roll tortillas; place seam-side down in prepared baking pan. Spoon remaining salsa mixture over tortillas; sprinkle with remaining ½ cup cheese. Cover; bake in 350°F oven, 35 to 40 minutes or until hot. *Makes 6 servings*

Potato-Crusted Meat Loaf

Five-Spice Beef and Bok Choy

    1 boneless beef sirloin steak (about
        1 pound)
    ¼ cup soy sauce
    2 tablespoons dry sherry
    2 teaspoons minced fresh ginger
    2 cloves garlic, minced
    1 teaspoon sugar
    ½ teaspoon Chinese five-spice powder*
    ¼ teaspoon red pepper flakes
        (optional)
    1 large head bok choy
    2 teaspoons cornstarch
    2 tablespoons peanut oil or vegetable
        oil, divided
      Hot cooked Chinese egg noodles

*Five-spice powder is a cocoa-colored blend of five
ground spices, usually anise seeds, fennel seeds, cloves,
cinnamon and ginger or black pepper. It has a slightly
sweet, pungent flavor and should be used sparingly.

• Trim fat from beef; discard. Cut beef across
grain into ⅛-inch-thick slices; cut each slice
into 2-inch pieces. Combine soy sauce,
sherry, ginger, garlic, sugar, five-spice
powder and red pepper in medium bowl.
Add beef and toss to coat; set aside.

• Separate bok choy leaves from stems; rinse
and pat dry. Stack leaves and cut crosswise
into 1-inch slices. Cut stems diagonally into
½-inch slices. Keep leaves and stems
separate.

• Drain beef, reserving marinade. Stir
reserved marinade into cornstarch in small
bowl; stir until smooth. Set aside.

• Heat wok over medium-high heat 1
minute or until hot. Drizzle 1 tablespoon oil
into wok and heat 30 seconds. Add beef;
stir-fry 2 minutes or until beef is barely pink
in center. Remove beef to large bowl.

• Add remaining 1 tablespoon oil and heat
30 seconds. Add bok choy stems; stir-fry 3
minutes. Add bok choy leaves; stir-fry 2
minutes.

• Stir marinade mixture until smooth; add to
wok. Stir-fry 1 minute or until sauce boils
and thickens.

• Return beef and any accumulated juices to
wok; cook until heated through. Serve over
noodles. Garnish, if desired.

Makes 4 servings

Old-Fashioned Beef Pot Pie

    1 pound ground beef
    1 can (11 ounces) condensed beef with
        vegetables and barley soup
    ½ cup water
    1 package (10 ounces) frozen peas and
        carrots, thawed and drained
    ½ teaspoon seasoned salt
    ⅛ teaspoon garlic powder
    ⅛ teaspoon ground black pepper
    1 cup (4 ounces) shredded Cheddar
        cheese
    1⅓ cups FRENCH'S® French Fried Onions,
        divided
    1 package (7.5 ounces) refrigerated
        biscuits

Preheat oven to 350°F. In large skillet, brown
ground beef in large chunks; drain. Stir in
soup, water, vegetables and seasonings;
bring to a boil. Reduce heat and simmer,
uncovered, 5 minutes. Remove from heat;
stir in ½ cup cheese and ⅔ cup French Fried
Onions.

Pour mixture into 12×8-inch baking dish.
Cut each biscuit in half; place, cut side
down, around edge of casserole. Bake,
uncovered, 15 to 20 minutes or until biscuits
are done. Top with remaining cheese and ⅔
cup onions; bake, uncovered, 5 minutes or
until onions are golden brown.

Makes 4 to 6 servings

Five-Spice Beef and Bok Choy

Mandarin Tomato Beef

1 boneless beef sirloin steak, cut 1 inch thick (about 1 pound)
½ cup reduced-sodium teriyaki sauce
2 teaspoons minced fresh ginger
2 teaspoons cornstarch
2 cups fresh snow peas *or* 1 package (6 ounces) frozen snow peas, thawed
2 tablespoons peanut oil or vegetable oil, divided
1 medium onion, cut into ½-inch wedges
2 medium tomatoes, cut into ½-inch wedges
Hot cooked rice
Freshly ground black pepper (optional)

• Trim fat from beef; discard. Cut beef across grain into ⅛-inch-thick slices; cut each slice into 2-inch pieces. Combine teriyaki and ginger in medium bowl. Add beef and toss to coat. Marinate beef 10 minutes.

• Drain beef, reserving marinade. Stir reserved marinade into cornstarch in small bowl; stir until smooth. Set aside.

• Pinch off stem end from fresh snow peas, pulling strings down to remove if present. Rinse snow peas and pat dry. Set aside. (Omit step if using frozen.)

• Heat wok over medium-high heat 2 minutes or until hot. Drizzle 1 tablespoon oil into wok and heat 30 seconds. Add half of beef; stir-fry 2 to 3 minutes or until beef is barely pink in center. Remove beef to large bowl. Repeat with remaining beef.

• Drizzle remaining 1 tablespoon oil into wok and heat 30 seconds. Add onion; cook 3 minutes or until browned, stirring occasionally. Add snow peas; stir-fry 3 minutes for fresh snow peas or 1 minute for frozen.

• Stir marinade mixture until smooth and add to wok. Stir-fry 30 seconds or until sauce boils and thickens.

• Return beef, any accumulated juices and tomatoes to wok; cook until heated through. Serve over rice. Sprinkle with black pepper and garnish, if desired. *Makes 4 servings*

Beef à la Stroganoff

1¼ pounds boneless beef sirloin
1 large onion
1 tablespoon butter
8 ounces sliced mushrooms
2 tablespoons water
2 tablespoons all-purpose flour
1 cup beef broth
¼ cup dry red wine
¼ teaspoon salt
1 cup low-fat sour cream
¼ teaspoon dried dill weed
Hot cooked noodles

• Trim fat from beef; discard. Slice beef across grain into thin slices. Cut onion lengthwise in half and slice crosswise into ¼-inch slices.

• Heat wok over medium-high heat 1 minute or until hot. Add butter and swirl to coat bottom. Add beef; stir-fry about 2 minutes or until well browned. Remove beef to large bowl. Reduce heat to medium.

• Add mushrooms, onion and water to wok; stir-fry about 2 minutes or until onion is tender. Add flour; mix well. Gradually stir in broth, wine and salt. Bring to a boil. Simmer 5 minutes. Stir in sour cream and dill weed. Return beef and any accumulated juices to wok; cook until heated through. Serve over noodles. *Makes 4 servings*

Mandarin Tomato Beef

Beef Bourguignon

1 boneless beef sirloin steak, ½ inch
    thick, trimmed and cut into ½-inch
    pieces (about 3 pounds)
½ cup all-purpose flour
4 slices bacon, diced
3 cups Burgundy wine or beef broth
2 medium carrots, diced
1 teaspoon dried marjoram leaves
½ teaspoon dried thyme leaves
½ teaspoon salt
    Black pepper to taste
1 bay leaf
2 tablespoons vegetable oil
20 to 24 fresh pearl onions
8 small new red potatoes, cut into
    quarters
8 to 10 mushrooms, sliced
3 cloves garlic, minced

Coat beef with flour, shaking off excess. Set aside.

Cook and stir bacon in 5-quart Dutch oven over medium-high heat until partially cooked. Brown half of beef with bacon in Dutch oven over medium-high heat. Remove with slotted spoon; set aside. Brown remaining beef. Pour off drippings. Return beef and bacon to Dutch oven.

Stir in wine, carrots, marjoram, thyme, salt, pepper and bay leaf. Bring to a boil over high heat. Reduce heat to low. Cover and simmer 10 minutes.

Meanwhile, heat oil in large saucepan over medium-high heat. Cook and stir onions, potatoes, mushrooms and garlic about 10 minutes. Add to Dutch oven. Cover and simmer 50 minutes or until meat is fork-tender. Discard bay leaf before serving.
Makes 10 to 12 servings

Patchwork Casserole

2 pounds ground beef
2 cups chopped green bell pepper
1 cup chopped onion
2 pounds frozen Southern-style hash-
    brown potatoes, thawed
2 cans (8 ounces each) tomato sauce
1 cup water
1 can (6 ounces) tomato paste
1 teaspoon salt
½ teaspoon dried basil, crumbled
¼ teaspoon ground black pepper
1 pound pasteurized process American
    cheese, thinly sliced

Preheat oven to 350°F.

Cook and stir beef in large skillet over medium heat until crumbled and brown, about 10 minutes; drain off fat.

Add bell pepper and onion; cook and stir until tender, about 4 minutes. Stir in potatoes, tomato sauce, water, tomato paste, salt, basil and black pepper.

Spoon half of mixture into 13×9×2-inch baking pan or 3-quart baking dish; top with half of cheese. Spoon remaining meat mixture evenly on top of cheese. Cover pan with aluminum foil. Bake 45 minutes.

Cut remaining cheese into decorative shapes; place on top of casserole. Let stand loosely covered until cheese melts, about 5 minutes.
Makes 8 to 10 servings

Beef Bourguignon

Spicy Beef Stir-Fry

1 boneless beef sirloin, top loin or tenderloin steak, cut 1 inch thick (about 1 pound)
5 tablespoons reduced-sodium teriyaki sauce, divided
1 teaspoon hot chili oil *or* ½ teaspoon crushed Szechuan peppercorns
1 tablespoon cornstarch
1 tablespoon dry sherry
2 tablespoons peanut oil or vegetable oil, divided
2 cups sliced fresh mushrooms
1 small onion, cut into 1-inch pieces
Hot cooked angel hair pasta

• Trim fat from beef; discard. Cut beef across grain into ⅛-inch-thick slices; cut each slice into 1½-inch pieces. Combine 1 tablespoon teriyaki sauce and chili oil in medium bowl. Add beef and toss to coat; set aside.

• Combine cornstarch, remaining 4 tablespoons teriyaki sauce and sherry in small bowl; stir until smooth. Set aside.

• Heat wok over high heat about 1 minute or until hot. Drizzle 1 tablespoon peanut oil into wok and heat 30 seconds. Add half the beef mixture; stir-fry 2 minutes or until beef is barely pink in center. Remove beef to large bowl. Repeat with remaining beef mixture. Reduce heat to medium-high.

• Add remaining 1 tablespoon peanut oil to wok and heat 30 seconds. Add mushrooms and onion; stir-fry 5 minutes or until vegetables are tender.

• Stir cornstarch mixture until smooth and add to wok. Stir-fry 30 seconds or until sauce boils and thickens.

• Return beef and any accumulated juices to wok; cook until heated through. Serve over pasta. Garnish, if desired.

Makes 4 servings

Family Favorite Hamburger Casserole

1 tablespoon CRISCO® Vegetable Oil
1 cup chopped onion
1 pound ground beef round
1 package (9 ounces) frozen cut green beans
3 cups frozen southern style hash brown potatoes
1 can (10¾ ounces) zesty tomato soup
½ cup water
1 teaspoon dried basil leaves
¾ teaspoon salt
¼ teaspoon pepper
¼ cup plain dry bread crumbs

1. Heat oven to 350°F. Oil 11¾×7½×2-inch baking dish lightly.

2. Heat Crisco® Oil in large skillet on medium-high heat. Add onion. Cook and stir until tender. Add meat. Cook until browned, stirring occasionally. Add beans. Cook and stir 5 minutes or until thawed. Add potatoes.

3. Combine tomato soup and water in small bowl. Stir until well blended. Stir into skillet. Stir in basil, salt and pepper. Spoon into baking dish. Sprinkle with bread crumbs.

4. Bake at 350°F for 30 minutes or until potatoes are tender. Let stand 5 minutes before serving. *Makes 4 servings*

Spicy Beef Stir-Fry

Mexican Stuffed Shells

12 pasta stuffing shells, cooked in
    unsalted water and drained
1 pound ground beef
1 jar (12 ounces) mild or medium
    picante sauce
½ cup water
1 can (8 ounces) tomato sauce
1 can (4 ounces) chopped green
    chilies, drained
1 cup (4 ounces) shredded Monterey
    Jack cheese
1⅓ cups FRENCH'S® French Fried Onions

Preheat oven to 350°F. In large skillet, brown
ground beef; drain. In small bowl, combine
picante sauce, water and tomato sauce. Stir
½ cup sauce mixture into beef along with
chilies, ½ cup cheese and ⅔ cup French
Fried Onions; mix well. Spread half the
remaining sauce mixture in bottom of
10-inch round baking dish. Stuff cooked
shells with beef mixture. Arrange shells in
baking dish; top with remaining sauce. Bake,
covered, at 350°F for 30 minutes or until
heated through. Top with remaining ⅔ cup
onions and cheese; bake, uncovered, 5
minutes or until cheese is melted.

Makes 6 servings

Microwave Directions: Crumble ground
beef into medium microwave-safe bowl.
Cook, covered, on HIGH (100%) 4 to 6
minutes or until beef is cooked. Stir beef
halfway through cooking time. Drain well.
Prepare sauce mixture as above; spread ½
cup in 12×8-inch microwave-safe dish.
Prepare beef mixture as above. Stuff cooked
shells with beef mixture. Arrange shells in
dish; top with remaining sauce. Cook,
covered, 10 to 12 minutes or until heated
through. Rotate dish halfway through
cooking time. Top with remaining onions
and cheese; cook, uncovered, 1 minute or
until cheese is melted. Let stand 5 minutes.

Teriyaki Beef

¾ pound sirloin tip steak, cut into thin
    strips
½ cup teriyaki sauce
¼ cup water
1 tablespoon cornstarch
1 teaspoon sugar
1 bag (16 ounces) BIRDS EYE® frozen
    Farm Fresh Mixtures Broccoli,
    Carrots and Water Chestnuts

• Spray large skillet with nonstick cooking
spray; cook beef strips over medium-high
heat 7 to 8 minutes, stirring occasionally.

• Combine teriyaki sauce, water, cornstarch
and sugar; mix well.

• Add teriyaki sauce mixture and vegetables
to beef. Bring to boil; quickly reduce heat to
medium.

• Cook 7 to 10 minutes or until broccoli is
heated through, stirring occasionally.

Makes 4 to 6 servings

Prep Time: 5 to 10 minutes
Cook Time: 20 minutes

Chili & Potato Casserole

1 pound HILLSHIRE FARM® Yard-O-
    Beef, cut into small cubes
1 cup chopped yellow onion
1 egg, lightly beaten
¼ cup bread crumbs
1 tablespoon chili powder
    Salt to taste
3 cups prepared mashed potatoes
1 can (11 ounces) succotash, drained
¼ cup thinly sliced green onions
1 cup (4 ounces) shredded taco-
    flavored cheese

Preheat oven to 375°F.

Combine Yard-O-Beef, yellow onion, egg, bread crumbs, chili powder and salt in large bowl; mix thoroughly. Pour beef mixture into medium baking dish, pressing mixture firmly onto bottom of dish. Bake 20 minutes. Pour off any juices.

Mix potatoes, succotash and green onions in medium bowl. Spread potato mixture over beef mixture; sprinkle top with cheese. Broil 3 to 4 inches from heat source 3 to 5 minutes or until top is lightly browned.

Makes 4 to 6 servings

Farm Fresh Tip: Frozen casseroles should be reheated in a 350°F oven. Add some liquid during cooking if the food seems dry.

Ranch Stroganoff

1½ **pounds flank steak or top sirloin steak**
2 **packages (1 ounce each) HIDDEN VALLEY® Milk Recipe Original Ranch® Salad Dressing mix**
¼ **cup all-purpose flour**
¼ **cup vegetable oil**
¼ **cup minced onion**
1 **clove garlic, minced**
½ **pound fresh mushrooms, thinly sliced**
1½ **cups milk**
8 **ounces wide egg noodles, cooked and buttered**
1 **tablespoon poppy seeds**

Cut steak diagonally into 2×½-inch strips; set aside. Combine salad dressing mix and flour in plastic bag. Add steak and dredge with flour mixture. Place steak on platter; reserve extra coating mixture. In large skillet, heat oil over medium heat until hot. Add onion and garlic; sauté 1 minute. Add steak and mushrooms and continue cooking until steak is lightly browned, 4 to 5 minutes. Stir

in milk and remaining coating mixture and continue cooking over low heat, stirring constantly, until thickened. Serve over noodles tossed with poppy seeds.

Makes 4 servings

Korean Beef

1 **pound beef flank steak**
¼ **cup reduced-sodium soy sauce**
2 **tablespoons sugar**
1 **tablespoon sesame oil**
1 **teaspoon ground ginger**
¼ **teaspoon red pepper flakes**
¼ **small head napa cabbage**
3 **tablespoons vegetable oil**
1 **can (14½ ounces) beef broth**
1 **cup peeled baby carrots**
2 **cups frozen cauliflowerets, thawed**
1 **cup frozen green bean cuts, thawed Hot cooked rice noodles**

• Slice beef across grain into ¼-inch-thick slices. Combine soy sauce, sugar, sesame oil, ginger and red pepper flakes in medium bowl. Add beef and toss to coat. Cut cabbage crosswise into 1-inch slices. Set aside.

• Heat wok over high heat about 1 minute or until hot. Drizzle half of vegetable oil into wok and heat 30 seconds. Drain beef, reserving marinade. Add half of beef to wok; stir-fry until browned. Remove to large bowl. Repeat with remaining vegetable oil and beef.

• Add reserved marinade and broth to wok. Cover; bring to a boil. Add carrots; cook, uncovered, 5 minutes or until crisp-tender. Stir in cabbage, cauliflowerets and beans; cook until tender. Return beef to wok; heat through. Serve over noodles in bowls.

Makes 4 servings

Zucchini Lasagna

1½ pounds ground beef
¾ pound sweet Italian sausage, casing removed
3 tablespoons FILIPPO BERIO® Olive Oil
1½ cups coarsely chopped mushrooms
1 large onion, chopped
1 large clove garlic, minced
1 can (14½ ounces) tomatoes, chopped, undrained
1 jar (15 ounces) marinara sauce
1 teaspoon salt
1 teaspoon dried basil leaves, crushed
½ teaspoon Italian herb seasoning
1 container (24 ounces) ricotta cheese
1 package (8 ounces) mozzarella cheese, cubed, divided
2 eggs, beaten
¼ cup chopped Italian parsley
6 unpeeled zucchini, cut lengthwise into thin slices about 8 inches long

Cook beef and sausage in hot oil in large skillet over medium-high heat until meats are no longer pink. Add mushrooms, onion and garlic. Cook several minutes, stirring frequently. Add tomatoes with juice, marinara sauce, salt, basil and Italian seasoning. Combine ricotta, ¾ of the mozzarella, eggs and parsley in medium bowl. Spoon 1 cup of the sauce onto bottom of 13×9-inch baking dish. Top with ⅓ of the zucchini, ⅓ of the cheese mixture and then 1 cup of the sauce. Repeat layers twice, ending with sauce. Cover with foil. Bake at 350°F for 45 minutes. Sprinkle with remaining mozzarella. Bake, uncovered, 10 minutes more or until cheese melts. Let stand 10 minutes before cutting. Heat remaining sauce and serve with lasagna.

Makes 8 servings

Sherried Beef

¾ pound boneless beef top round steak
1 cup water
¼ cup dry sherry
3 tablespoons soy sauce
2 large carrots, cut into diagonal slices
1 large green pepper, cut into strips
1 medium onion, cut into chunks
2 tablespoons vegetable oil, divided
1 tablespoon cornstarch
2 cups hot cooked rice

Partially freeze steak; slice across the grain into ⅛-inch strips. Combine water, sherry, and soy sauce. Pour over beef in dish; marinate 1 hour. Stir-fry vegetables in 1 tablespoon oil in large skillet over medium-high heat. Remove from skillet; set aside. Drain beef; reserve marinade. Brown beef in remaining 1 tablespoon oil. Combine cornstarch with marinade in bowl. Add vegetables and marinade to beef. Cook, stirring, until sauce is thickened; cook 1 minute longer. Serve over rice.

Makes 4 servings

*Favorite recipe from **USA Rice Federation***

Sherried Beef

Pork Chops O'Brien

1 tablespoon vegetable oil
6 pork chops, ½ to ¾ inch thick
  Seasoned salt
1 can (10¾ ounces) condensed cream
  of celery soup
½ cup milk
½ cup sour cream
¼ teaspoon pepper
1 bag (24 ounces) frozen O'Brien or
  hash brown potatoes, thawed
1 cup (4 ounces) shredded Cheddar
  cheese, divided
1⅓ cups FRENCH'S® French Fried Onions,
  divided

Preheat oven to 350°F. In large skillet, heat oil. Brown pork chops on both sides; drain. Sprinkle chops with seasoned salt; set aside. In large bowl, combine soup, milk, sour cream, pepper and ½ teaspoon seasoned salt. Stir in potatoes, ½ cup cheese and ⅔ cup French Fried Onions. Spoon mixture into 13×9-inch baking dish; arrange pork chops on top. Bake, covered, at 350°F for 35 to 40 minutes or until pork chops are done. Top chops with remaining cheese and ⅔ cup onions; bake, uncovered, 5 minutes or until onions are golden brown.

Makes 6 servings

Microwave Directions: Omit oil. Prepare soup-potato mixture as above; spoon into 12×8-inch microwave-safe dish. Cook, covered, on HIGH 5 minutes. Stir well. Arrange unbrowned pork chops on top with meatiest parts toward edges of dish. Cook, covered, on MEDIUM (50-60%) 15 minutes. Turn chops over; sprinkle with seasoned salt. Stir potatoes and rotate dish. Cook, covered, on MEDIUM 12 to 15 minutes or until pork chops are done. Top chops with remaining cheese and ⅔ cup onions; cook, uncovered, on HIGH 1 minute or until cheese melts. Let stand 5 minutes.

Sweet & Sour Mustard Pork

1 pound boneless pork, cut into strips
¼ cup GREY POUPON® Dijon Mustard,
  divided
3 teaspoons soy sauce, divided
1 (3-ounce) package chicken-flavored
  ramen noodles
1 (8-ounce) can pineapple chunks,
  drained, reserving juice
½ cup water
2 tablespoons firmly packed light
  brown sugar
1 tablespoon cornstarch
½ teaspoon grated fresh ginger
2 cups broccoli flowerettes
½ cup chopped red or green cabbage
½ cup chopped red bell pepper
½ cup coarsely chopped onion
2 tablespoons vegetable oil

In medium bowl, combine pork strips, 2 tablespoons mustard and 1 teaspoon soy sauce. Refrigerate for 1 hour.

In small bowl, combine remaining mustard and soy sauce, chicken flavor packet from noodles, reserved pineapple juice, water, brown sugar, cornstarch and ginger; set aside. Cook ramen noodles according to package directions; drain and set aside.

In large skillet, over medium-high heat, stir-fry vegetables in oil until tender-crisp; remove from skillet. Add pork mixture; stir-fry for 3 to 4 minutes or until done. Return vegetables to skillet with pineapple chunks and cornstarch mixture; heat until mixture thickens and begins to boil. Add cooked noodles, tossing to coat well. Garnish as desired. Serve immediately.

Makes 4 servings

Sweet & Sour Mustard Pork

Pork Curry

2 tablespoons vegetable oil, divided
1 pound boneless pork tenderloin, cut
 into ¾-inch cubes
1 large onion, cut in half lengthwise
 and thinly sliced
1 small carrot, shredded
1 clove garlic, minced
1 tablespoon curry powder
1 package (8 ounces) frozen sugar
 snap peas
1 Granny Smith or McIntosh apple, cut
 into thin wedges
1 can (6 ounces) frozen apple juice
 concentrate, thawed
2 tablespoons FRANK'S® Original
 REDHOT® Cayenne Pepper Sauce
¼ cup nonfat sour cream
 Cooked white rice (optional)

1. Heat 1 tablespoon oil in large nonstick skillet over medium-high heat. Add pork; cook and stir 5 minutes or until browned. Transfer to platter; set aside. Heat remaining 1 tablespoon oil in same skillet. Add onion, carrot and garlic; cook and stir until tender. Stir in curry powder; cook 1 minute.

2. Return pork to skillet; stir in sugar snap peas, apple, juice and RedHot® sauce. Bring to a boil. Reduce heat to low; cook, uncovered, 5 minutes or until pork is no longer pink and sugar snap peas and apple are tender. Stir in sour cream. Serve with rice, if desired.   *Makes 4 servings*

Prep Time: 20 minutes

Cook Time: 20 minutes

Ham and Potato au Gratin

3 tablespoons butter or margarine
3 tablespoons all-purpose flour
2 cups milk
1½ cups (6 ounces) shredded Cheddar
 cheese
1 tablespoon Dijon mustard
2 cups HILLSHIRE FARM® Ham, cut into
 thin strips
1 package (24 ounces) frozen
 shredded hash brown potatoes,
 thawed
1 package (10 ounces) frozen chopped
 spinach, thawed and drained

Preheat oven to 350°F.

Melt butter in large saucepan over medium heat; stir in flour. Add milk. Cook and stir until bubbly; cook 1 minute more. Remove from heat. Stir in cheese and mustard; set aside.

Place ½ of Ham into ungreased medium casserole. Top ham with ½ of potatoes and ½ of milk mixture. Spoon spinach over top. Repeat layers with remaining ham, potatoes and milk mixture.

Bake, uncovered, 30 minutes or until heated through.   *Makes 8 servings*

Farm Fresh Tip: When buying new baking dishes or pans, choose pieces you can use for more than one job. Baking dishes should be freezer-to-oven capable and skillets should be able to go into the oven. Make sure the item you buy is easy to clean.

Ham and Potato au Gratin

Taco Soup

1 pound BOB EVANS® Original Recipe
   or Zesty Hot Roll Sausage
1½ tablespoons olive oil
½ small Spanish onion, diced
1 jalapeño pepper, seeded and diced
1½ cups beef broth
1 cup peeled, seeded, diced fresh or
   canned tomatoes
1 cup vegetable juice
½ tablespoon ground cumin
½ tablespoon chili powder
¼ teaspoon salt
⅓ cup shredded Cheddar cheese
12 tortilla chips, broken into pieces

Crumble and cook sausage in olive oil in
Dutch oven until no longer pink but not yet
browned. Add onion and pepper; cook until
onion is tender. Add remaining ingredients
except cheese and chips; bring to a boil over
high heat. Reduce heat to low and simmer,
uncovered, 15 minutes. Ladle soup into
bowls; garnish with cheese and chips.
Refrigerate leftovers.   *Makes 6 servings*

Cajun Pork Skillet Dinner

1 tablespoon vegetable oil
4 rib-cut pork chops* (about 1 pound),
   cut ¾ inch thick
1 jar (16 ounces) chunky medium salsa
1⅓ cups FRENCH'S® French Fried Onions,
   divided
½ teaspoon dried thyme leaves
   Cooked white rice (optional)

*Or, substitute 1 pound boneless skinless chicken breasts
for pork chops.*

Heat oil in large nonstick skillet. Add pork
chops; cook about 5 minutes or until
browned on both sides.

Stir in salsa, ⅔ cup French Fried Onions and
thyme. Bring to a boil over high heat.
Reduce heat to medium-low. Cover; cook 10
minutes or until pork is no longer pink near
bone, stirring occasionally. Sprinkle
remaining ⅔ cup onions over pork. Serve
with rice, if desired.   *Makes 4 servings*

Tip: For a Mediterranean flare, substitute
½ teaspoon oregano for ½ teaspoon thyme.

Prep Time: 5 minutes
Cook Time: 15 minutes

Quick Cassoulet

2 slices bacon, cut into ½-inch pieces
¾ pound boneless pork chops, sliced
   crosswise ¼ inch thick
1 medium onion, chopped
1 clove garlic, minced
1 teaspoon dried thyme, crushed
1 can (14½ ounces) DEL MONTE®
   Original Recipe Stewed Tomatoes
½ cup dry white wine
1 can (15 ounces) white or pinto
   beans, drained

1. Cook bacon in large skillet over medium-
high heat until almost crisp.

2. Stir in meat, onion, garlic and thyme.
Season with salt and pepper, if desired.

3. Cook 4 minutes. Add tomatoes and wine;
bring to boil. Cook, uncovered, over
medium-high heat 10 minutes or until
thickened, adding beans during last 5
minutes.   *Makes 4 servings*

Prep and Cook Time: 30 minutes

Taco Soup

Polish Reuben Casserole

2 cans (10¾ ounces each) condensed
   cream of mushroom soup
1⅓ cups milk
½ cup chopped onion
1 tablespoon prepared mustard
2 cans (16 ounces each) sauerkraut,
   rinsed and drained
1 package (8 ounces) uncooked
   medium-width noodles
1½ pounds Polish sausage, cut into
   ½-inch pieces
2 cups (8 ounces) shredded Swiss
   cheese
¾ cup whole wheat bread crumbs
2 tablespoons butter, melted

Combine soup, milk, onion and mustard in
medium bowl; blend well. Spread sauerkraut
into greased 13×9-inch pan. Top with
uncooked noodles. Spoon soup mixture
evenly over noodles; cover with sausage.
Top with cheese. Combine bread crumbs
and butter in small bowl; sprinkle over
cheese. Cover pan tightly with foil. Bake
in preheated 350°F oven 1 hour or until
noodles are tender. Garnish as desired.
Makes 8 to 10 servings

Sweet and Sour Ham

1 tablespoon butter or margarine
1½ pounds HILLSHIRE FARM® Ham, cut
   into ½-inch cubes
3 tomatoes, cut into sixths
1 green bell pepper, cut into chunks
1 onion, chopped
½ cup apricot preserves
1 tablespoon cornstarch
1 tablespoon vinegar
1 tablespoon soy sauce
½ teaspoon ground ginger
2 cups drained pineapple chunks
   Hot cooked rice

Melt butter in large skillet over medium-high
heat. Sauté Ham, tomatoes, bell pepper and
onion 5 minutes.

Combine preserves, cornstarch, vinegar, soy
sauce and ginger in small bowl. Pour
preserves mixture into skillet; stir to mix
thoroughly. Cook over low heat until sauce
thickens. Mix in pineapple; cook until
pineapple is heated through. Serve over rice.
Makes 6 servings

Farm Fresh Tip: Be prepared for unexpected
company: keep plenty of Hillshire Farm
products in your freezer.

Corn, Bacon & Rice Chowder

1 package (7.2 ounces) RICE-A-RONI®
   Rice Pilaf
2 tablespoons margarine or butter
1 can (13¾ ounces) reduced-sodium
   or regular chicken broth
1½ cups frozen corn *or* 1 can (16 or
   17 ounces) whole kernel corn,
   drained
1 cup milk
1 cup water
½ cup sliced green onions
2 slices crisply cooked bacon, crumbled

1. In 3-quart saucepan, sauté rice-pasta mix
in margarine over medium heat, stirring
frequently until pasta is lightly browned.

2. Stir in chicken broth and contents of
seasoning packet; bring to a boil over high
heat.

3. Cover; reduce heat. Simmer 8 minutes.

4. Stir in corn, milk, water and onions.
Simmer, uncovered, 10 to 12 minutes,
stirring occasionally. Stir in bacon before
serving. *Makes 4 servings*

Polish Reuben Casserole

Mandarin Pork Stir-Fry

1½ cups DOLE® Pineapple Orange or
     Pineapple Juice, divided
     Vegetable cooking spray
12 ounces lean pork tenderloin, chicken
     breast or turkey tenderloin, cut
     into thin strips
 1 tablespoon finely chopped fresh
     ginger *or* ½ teaspoon ground
     ginger
 2 cups DOLE® Shredded Carrots
 ½ cup chopped DOLE® Pitted Prunes or
     Chopped Dates
 4 DOLE® Green Onions, cut into 1-inch
     pieces
 2 tablespoons low-sodium soy sauce
 1 teaspoon cornstarch

• Heat 2 tablespoons juice over medium-high heat in large nonstick skillet sprayed with vegetable cooking spray until juice bubbles.

• Add pork; cook and stir 3 minutes or until pork is no longer pink. Remove pork from skillet.

• Heat 3 more tablespoons juice in skillet; add carrots, prunes and green onions. Cook and stir 3 minutes.

• Stir soy sauce and cornstarch into remaining juice; add to carrot mixture. Stir in pork; cover and cook 2 minutes until heated through.   *Makes 4 servings*

Prep time: 15 minutes

Cook time: 15 minutes

Lean Picadillo Pie

1½ pounds lean ground pork
 ½ cup *each* chopped onion and green
     bell pepper
 1 clove garlic, minced
 1 can (14½ ounces) whole tomatoes,
     undrained, cut up
 ¾ cup chopped dried apricots or raisins
12 pimiento-stuffed green olives, sliced
 3 tablespoons chili powder
 2 tablespoons chopped almonds
 2 cans (14½ ounces each) chicken
     broth
 2 cups cornmeal

Heat large nonstick skillet over medium heat; cook and stir pork, onion, green pepper and garlic 5 minutes or until pork is lightly browned. Pour off any drippings. Stir in tomatoes, dried apricots, olives, chili powder and almonds. Cover and simmer 10 minutes. Bring chicken broth to a boil in large saucepan. Gradually stir in cornmeal; mix well. Spoon cornmeal mixture into 13×9-inch baking dish sprayed with nonstick cooking spray. Top with pork mixture. Cover with foil. Bake at 350°F for 30 minutes. Cut into squares to serve.

Makes 12 servings

Prep Time: 20 minutes

Cook Time: 30 minutes

Favorite recipe from **National Pork Producers Council**

Mandarin Pork Stir-Fry

Mexicali Cornbread Casserole

2½ cups frozen mixed vegetables, thawed
1½ cups cubed HILLSHIRE FARM® Ham
1 package (10 ounces) cornbread stuffing mix
2 cups milk
3 eggs, lightly beaten
Salt and black pepper to taste
½ cup (2 ounces) shredded taco-flavored cheese

Preheat oven to 375°F.

Combine mixed vegetables, Ham and stuffing mix in small casserole; set aside. Combine milk, eggs, salt and pepper in medium bowl; pour over ham mixture. Bake, covered, 45 minutes. Top with cheese; bake, uncovered, 3 minutes or until cheese is melted. *Makes 4 servings*

Ham and Cauliflower Chowder

1 bag (16 ounces) BIRDS EYE® frozen Cauliflower
2 cans (10¾ ounces each) cream of mushroom or cream of celery soup
2½ cups milk or water
½ pound ham, cubed
⅓ cup shredded colby cheese (optional)

• Cook cauliflower according to package directions.

• Combine cauliflower, soup, milk and ham in saucepan; mix well.

• Cook over medium heat 4 to 6 minutes, stirring occasionally. Top individual servings with cheese. *Makes 4 to 6 servings*

Prep Time: 2 minutes

Cook Time: 10 to 12 minutes

Savory Pork Chop Supper

6 medium potatoes, thinly sliced (about 5 cups)
1⅓ cups FRENCH'S® French Fried Onions, divided
1 jar (2 ounces) sliced mushrooms, drained
2 tablespoons butter or margarine
¼ cup soy sauce
1½ teaspoons ground mustard
½ teaspoon FRANK'S® Original REDHOT® Cayenne Pepper Sauce
⅛ teaspoon garlic powder
1 tablespoon vegetable oil
6 pork chops, ½ to ¾ inch thick

Preheat oven to 350°F. In 12×8-inch baking dish, layer half the potatoes and ⅔ cup French Fried Onions. Top with mushrooms and remaining potatoes. In small saucepan, melt butter; stir in soy sauce, mustard, RedHot® sauce and garlic powder. Brush half the soy sauce mixture over potatoes. In large skillet, heat oil. Brown pork chops on both sides; drain. Arrange chops over potatoes and brush with remaining soy sauce mixture. Bake, covered, at 350°F for 1 hour. Bake, uncovered, 15 minutes or until pork chops and potatoes are done. Top chops with remaining ⅔ cup onions; bake, uncovered, 5 minutes or until onions are golden brown. *Makes 4 to 6 servings*

Mexicali Cornbread Casserole

White Sausage Chili

2 tablespoons vegetable oil
1 pound HILLSHIRE FARM® Smoked
    Sausage, cut into ½-inch pieces
1 onion, diced
1 can (15 ounces) navy beans, rinsed
    and drained
1 can (15 ounces) chick-peas, rinsed
    and drained
1 can (15 ounces) white kernel corn,
    drained
1 can (about 14 ounces) chicken broth
1 cup cooked wild rice
1 can (4 ounces) diced green chilies,
    drained
1½ teaspoons ground cumin
¼ teaspoon garlic powder
⅛ teaspoon hot pepper sauce
    Chopped parsley

Heat oil in large saucepan over medium-
high heat. Sauté Smoked Sausage and onion
until onion is soft and sausage is lightly
browned, about 5 minutes. Stir in all
remaining ingredients, except parsley.
Simmer, covered, 20 minutes. Spoon into
6 individual serving bowls; garnish with
parsley. *Makes 6 servings*

Farm Fresh Tip: Did you know?—If you
don't have a clove of garlic, you can
substitute with ⅛ teaspoon of garlic powder
or minced dry garlic.

Szechuan Pork & Vegetables

4 butterflied pork loin chops, ½ inch
    thick (1 to 1¼ pounds)
¼ cup plus 1 tablespoon stir-fry sauce,
    divided
¾ teaspoon bottled minced ginger *or*
    ½ teaspoon ground ginger
1 package (16 ounces) frozen Asian-
    style vegetables, thawed
1 can (5 ounces) crisp chow mein
    noodles
2 tablespoons chopped green onion

1. Heat large, deep nonstick skillet over
medium heat until hot. Add pork. Spoon 1
tablespoon stir-fry sauce over pork; sprinkle
with ginger. Cook 3 minutes. Turn pork;
cook 3 minutes. Transfer chops to plate; set
aside.

2. Add vegetables and remaining ¼ cup stir-
fry sauce to skillet. Cook over medium-low
heat 3 minutes; add pork. Cook 3 minutes
or until pork is no longer pink in center,
stirring vegetables and turning chops once.

3. While pork is cooking, arrange chow mein
noodles around edges of 4 serving plates.
Transfer chops to plates. Top noodles with
vegetable mixture. Sprinkle with green
onion. *Makes 4 servings*

Prep and Cook Time: 12 minutes

Szechuan Pork & Vegetables

Ham Paella with Sun-Dried Tomatoes and Pine Nuts

¼ cup extra-virgin olive oil
2 pounds HILLSHIRE FARM® Ham,
    sliced into 2×½-inch strips
1 onion, chopped
12 sun-dried tomatoes packed in olive
    oil
3 tablespoons pine nuts
4 cloves garlic, minced
2 cups uncooked rice
4 cups chicken broth, heated
½ cup chopped parsley
¼ cup sliced pitted green olives
1 teaspoon ground cumin
    Salt and freshly ground black pepper
    to taste

Heat oil in medium saucepan over medium-high heat. Brown Ham in hot oil, about 30 seconds on each side. Remove ham from saucepan; set aside. Add onion to saucepan; reduce heat to medium and sauté 10 minutes. Add tomatoes, pine nuts and garlic; sauté 5 minutes. Add rice; sauté, stirring constantly, 3 to 4 minutes. Stir in chicken broth, parsley, olives, cumin and ham. Season with salt and pepper. Reduce heat to low; simmer, covered, 30 to 40 minutes or until rice is tender and liquid is absorbed.

Makes 6 servings

Sausage Ham Jambalaya

6 ounces spicy smoked sausage links,
    sliced
6 ounces cooked ham, diced
2 cans (14½ ounces each) DEL
    MONTE® Cajun Recipe Stewed
    Tomatoes
1 cup uncooked long grain white rice
1 large clove garlic, minced
1 tablespoon chopped fresh parsley
1 bay leaf

1. Brown sausage and ham in heavy 4-quart saucepan. Drain tomatoes, reserving liquid; pour liquid into measuring cup. Add water to measure 1½ cups.

2. Add reserved liquid, tomatoes and remaining ingredients to sausage mixture.

3. Cover and simmer 30 to 35 minutes, stirring occasionally. Remove bay leaf. Garnish with additional chopped parsley, if desired. *Makes 4 to 6 servings*

Prep Time: 10 minutes

Cook Time: 40 minutes

Pork Chops with Apples and Stuffing

4 pork chops, ½ inch thick
    Salt and pepper
1 tablespoon oil
2 medium apples, cored, cut into
    8 wedges
1 cup apple juice
2 cups STOVE TOP® Cornbread Stuffing
    Mix in the Canister
¼ cup chopped pecans

SPRINKLE chops with salt and pepper. Heat oil in large skillet on medium-high heat. Add chops and apples; cook until chops are browned on both sides.

STIR in apple juice. Bring to boil. Reduce heat to low; cover and simmer 8 minutes or until chops are cooked through. Remove chops from skillet.

STIR stuffing mix and pecans into skillet. Return chops to skillet; cover. Remove from heat. Let stand 5 minutes.

Makes 4 servings

Prep Time: 10 minutes

Cook Time: 20 minutes

Sausage Ham Jambalaya

Sunday Supper Stuffed Shells

1 package (12 ounces) jumbo pasta
    shells
1 package (10 ounces) frozen chopped
    spinach
2 tablespoons olive oil
3 cloves garlic, peeled
¾ pound ground veal
¾ pound ground pork
1 cup parsley, finely chopped
1 cup fresh bread crumbs
2 eggs, beaten
3 cloves garlic, minced
3 tablespoons grated Parmesan cheese
    Salt to taste
3 cups spaghetti sauce, divided
    Sautéed zucchini slices (optional)

1. Cook pasta according to package
directions. Place in colander and rinse under
warm running water. Drain well.

2. Cook spinach according to package
directions. Place in colander to drain. Let
stand until cool enough to handle. Squeeze
spinach between hands to remove excess
moisture. Set aside.

3. Heat oil in large skillet over medium heat.
Cook and stir whole garlic cloves in hot oil
until garlic is lightly browned. Discard garlic.
Add veal and pork. Cook until lightly
browned, stirring to separate meat; drain
drippings. Cool slightly.

4. Preheat oven to 375°F. Grease 12×8-inch
baking pan.

5. Combine spinach, parsley, bread crumbs,
eggs, minced garlic and cheese in large
bowl; blend well. Season to taste with salt.
Add cooled meat mixture; blend well. Fill
shells with meat mixture.

6. Spread about 1 cup of spaghetti sauce
over bottom of prepared pan. Arrange shells
in pan. Pour remaining sauce over shells.
Cover with foil.

7. Bake 35 to 45 minutes or until bubbly.
Serve with zucchini. Garnish as desired.

Makes 8 to 9 servings

Sausage & Zucchini Soup

1 pound BOB EVANS® Italian Roll
    Sausage
1 medium onion, diced
1 (28-ounce) can stewed tomatoes
2 (14-ounce) cans beef broth
2 medium zucchini, diced or sliced
    (about 2 cups)
2 small carrots, diced
2 stalks celery, diced
4 large mushrooms, sliced
    Grated Parmesan cheese for garnish

Crumble and cook sausage and onion in
large saucepan over medium heat until
sausage is browned. Drain off any drippings.
Add remaining ingredients except cheese;
simmer, uncovered, over low heat about 40
minutes or until vegetables are tender.
Garnish with cheese. Refrigerate leftovers.

Makes 8 servings

Sausage & Zucchini Soup

Wonton Soup

¼ pound lean ground pork
2 ounces medium-size raw shrimp,
   peeled, deveined and minced
2 tablespoons minced green onions
   and tops
4 teaspoons KIKKOMAN® Soy Sauce,
   divided
½ teaspoon cornstarch
¼ teaspoon grated fresh ginger root
24 wonton wrappers
4 cups water
3 cans (about 14 ounces each) chicken
   broth
¼ cup dry sherry
½ pound bok choy cabbage
2 tablespoons chopped green onions
   and tops
½ teaspoon Oriental sesame oil

Combine pork, shrimp, minced green onions, 2 teaspoons soy sauce, cornstarch and ginger in medium bowl; mix well. Arrange several wonton wrappers on clean surface; cover remaining wrappers to prevent drying out. Place 1 teaspoonful pork mixture in center of each wrapper. Fold wrapper over filling to form a triangle. Gently fold center point down and moisten left corner with water. Twist and overlap opposite corner over moistened corner; press firmly to seal. Repeat with remaining wrappers. Bring water to boil in large saucepan. Add wontons. Boil gently 3 minutes; remove with slotted spoon. Discard water. Pour broth and sherry into same saucepan. Cut bok choy crosswise into ½-inch slices, separating stems from leaves. Add stems to broth mixture; bring to boil. Add cooked wontons; simmer 1 minute. Add bok choy leaves and chopped green onions; simmer 1 minute longer. Remove from heat; stir in remaining 2 teaspoons soy sauce and sesame oil. Serve immediately.

Makes 6 servings

Country-Style Lasagna

9 lasagna noodles (2 inches wide)
2 cans (14½ ounces each) DEL
   MONTE® Diced Tomatoes with
   Garlic & Onion
   Milk
2 tablespoons butter or margarine
3 tablespoons all-purpose flour
1 teaspoon dried basil, crushed
1 cup diced cooked ham
2 cups (8 ounces) shredded mozzarella
   cheese

1. Cook noodles according to package directions; rinse, drain and separate noodles.

2. Meanwhile, drain tomatoes, reserving liquid; pour liquid into measuring cup. Add milk to measure 2 cups.

3. Melt butter in large saucepan; stir in flour and basil. Cook over medium heat 3 minutes, stirring constantly. Stir in reserved liquid; cook until thickened, stirring constantly. Season to taste with salt and pepper, if desired. Stir in tomatoes.

4. Spread thin layer of sauce on bottom of 11×7-inch or 2-quart baking dish. Top with 3 noodles and ⅓ each of sauce, ham and cheese; repeat layers twice, ending with cheese.

5. Bake uncovered at 375°F, 25 minutes. Serve with grated Parmesan cheese and garnish, if desired. *Makes 6 servings*

Prep Time: 15 minutes
Cook Time: 25 minutes

Wonton Soup

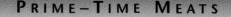

Skillet Pork & Vegetables

1 pound pork tenderloin, trimmed and cut into 1-inch cubes
2 tablespoons soy sauce
1 clove garlic, minced
1 tablespoon olive oil
2 zucchini (about ¾ pound), quartered and sliced
1 red bell pepper, cut into strips
1⅓ cups FRENCH'S® French Fried Onions, divided
1 can (11 ounces) whole kernel corn, drained
½ cup balsamic vinaigrette salad dressing
2 tablespoons chopped fresh cilantro or parsley
1 teaspoon cornstarch dissolved in 2 tablespoons water
Cooked white rice (optional)

Combine pork, soy sauce and garlic in large bowl. Cover; marinate in refrigerator 20 minutes.

Heat oil in large nonstick skillet over medium-high heat. Add pork; cook about 5 minutes or until browned. Add zucchini and bell pepper strips; cook 3 minutes or until vegetables are crisp-tender.

Add ⅔ cup French Fried Onions, corn, salad dressing, cilantro and cornstarch mixture. Bring to a boil. Cook 2 minutes or until sauce thickens. Sprinkle with remaining ⅔ cup onions. Serve with cooked rice, if desired. *Makes 4 to 6 servings*

Prep Time: 20 minutes

Marinate Time: 20 minutes

Cook Time: 10 minutes

Ham & Potato Scallop

1 package (5 ounces) scalloped potatoes plus ingredients as package directs
1 bag (16 ounces) BIRDS EYE® frozen Broccoli Cuts
½ pound cooked ham, cut into ½-inch cubes
½ cup shredded Cheddar cheese (optional)

• Prepare potatoes according to package directions for stove top method, adding broccoli and ham when adding milk and butter.

• Stir in cheese just before serving.
Makes 4 servings

Serving Suggestion: Spoon mixture into shallow casserole dish. Sprinkle with cheese; broil until lightly browned.

Prep Time: 5 minutes

Cook Time: 25 minutes

Skillet Pork & Vegetables

Hunan Pork & Tofu Stir-Fry

1 block (14 to 16 ounces) firm tofu, drained
½ pound ground pork
1 tablespoon dry sherry
1 teaspoon minced fresh ginger root
1 clove garlic, minced
½ cup chicken broth
1 tablespoon cornstarch
3 tablespoons KIKKOMAN® Soy Sauce
1 tablespoon vinegar
½ teaspoon crushed red pepper
1 tablespoon vegetable oil
1 onion, cut into ¾-inch pieces
1 green bell pepper, cut into ¾-inch pieces

Cut tofu into ½-inch cubes; drain well on paper towels. Meanwhile, combine pork, sherry, ginger and garlic; let stand 10 minutes. Blend chicken broth, cornstarch, soy sauce, vinegar and crushed red pepper; set aside. Heat wok or large skillet over medium-high heat; add pork. Cook, stirring to separate pork, about 3 minutes, or until lightly browned; remove. Heat oil in same pan. Add onion and bell pepper; stir-fry 4 minutes. Add pork and soy sauce mixture. Cook and stir until mixture boils and thickens. Gently fold in tofu; heat through.

Makes 4 servings

Bratwurst Skillet

1 pound bratwurst links, cut into ½-inch slices
1½ cups green bell pepper strips
1½ cups red bell pepper strips
1½ cups sliced onions
1 teaspoon paprika
1 teaspoon caraway seeds

1. Heat large skillet over medium heat until hot. Add bratwurst; cover and cook about 5 minutes or until browned and no longer pink in center. Transfer bratwurst to plate. Cover and keep warm.

2. Drain all but 1 tablespoon drippings from skillet. Add bell peppers, onions, paprika and caraway seeds. Cook and stir about 5 minutes or until vegetables are tender.

3. Combine bratwurst and vegetables. Serve immediately.   *Makes 4 servings*

Serving Suggestion: For a special touch, garnish dish with cherry tomato halves and celery leaves.

Tip: To make this even speedier, purchase a packaged stir-fry pepper and onion mix and use in place of the bell peppers and onions.

Prep and Cook Time: 18 minutes

Baked Cabbage with Smoked Sausage

1 head cabbage
¼ pound HILLSHIRE FARM® Bacon, sliced
Salt and black pepper to taste
1 onion, finely chopped
½ cup white wine
½ cup beef broth
1 pound HILLSHIRE FARM® Smoked Sausage, cut into ¼-inch slices

Preheat oven to 350°F.

Clean and quarter cabbage; soak in salted water. Line large casserole with Bacon; add cabbage. Season cabbage with salt and pepper; sprinkle with onion. Pour wine and beef broth over cabbage; top with Smoked Sausage. Bake, covered, 1 hour or until cooked through.   *Makes 4 servings*

Bratwurst Skillet

Paprika Pork with Spinach

1 pound boneless pork loin or leg
3 tablespoons all-purpose flour
3 tablespoons vegetable oil
1 cup frozen pearl onions, thawed
1 tablespoon paprika
1 can (14½ ounces) vegetable or
    chicken broth
8 ounces medium curly egg noodles,
    uncooked
1 package (10 ounces) frozen leaf
    spinach, thawed and well drained
½ cup sour cream

• Trim fat from pork; discard. Cut pork into 1-inch cubes. Place flour and pork in resealable plastic food storage bag; shake until well coated.

• Heat wok over high heat about 1 minute or until hot. Drizzle oil into wok and heat 30 seconds. Add pork; stir-fry about 5 minutes or until well browned on all sides. Remove pork to large bowl.

• Add onions and paprika to wok; stir-fry 1 minute. Stir in broth, noodles and pork. Cover and bring to a boil. Reduce heat to low; cook about 8 minutes or until noodles and pork are tender, stirring occasionally.

• Stir thawed spinach into pork and noodles. Cover and cook until heated through. Add additional water if needed. Add sour cream; mix well. Transfer to serving dish. Garnish, if desired. *Makes 4 servings*

Italian Sausage Soup

2 boxes (10 ounces each) BIRDS EYE®
    frozen Italian Style Vegetables
2 cans (14 ounces each) beef broth
1 pound cooked Italian sausage, cubed
1 can (8 ounces) tomato sauce

• In large saucepan, place vegetables and broth; bring to boil over high heat. Reduce heat to medium; cover and simmer 7 to 10 minutes or until vegetables are crisp-tender.

• Stir in cooked sausage and tomato sauce; cook until heated through.
Makes 4 servings

Prep Time: 2 minutes
Cook Time: 10 to 12 minutes

Ham Starburst Casserole

1 can (10¾ ounces) condensed cream
    of potato soup
¾ cup sour cream
1 can (16 ounces) sliced potatoes,
    drained
1 package (10 ounces) frozen peas,
    thawed and drained
1⅓ cups FRENCH'S® French Fried Onions,
    divided
2 tablespoons diced pimiento
    (optional)
8 to 12 ounces cooked ham or turkey
    ham, unsliced

Preheat oven to 350°F. In medium bowl, combine soup, sour cream, potatoes, peas, ⅔ cup French Fried Onions and the pimiento; stir well. Spoon into 10-inch round baking dish. Cut ham into 3 thick slices; cut each slice crosswise into halves. Press ham slices into potato mixture, rounded-side up in spoke-fashion, to form a starburst. Bake, covered, at 350°F for 30 minutes or until heated through. Top with remaining ⅔ cup onions; bake, uncovered, 5 minutes or until onions are golden brown.
Makes 4 servings

Paprika Pork with Spinach

Hearty Hot Dish

⅓ cup honey
¼ cup spicy brown mustard
¼ cup vegetable oil
1 tablespoon soy sauce
2 cloves garlic, minced
1 teaspoon ground ginger
1 pound HILLSHIRE FARM® Beef
   Smoked Sausage,* sliced
2 onions, cut into quarters
1 cup chopped carrots
1 cup chopped celery
1 cup sliced mushrooms

*Or use any variety Hillshire Farm® Smoked Sausage.

Combine honey, mustard, oil, soy sauce, garlic and ginger in large bowl; blend thoroughly. Add Smoked Sausage, onions, carrots, celery and mushrooms. Sauté sausage mixture in large skillet over medium-high heat until sausage is lightly browned.   *Makes 4 to 6 servings*

Southwest Pork and Dressing

1 pound boneless pork, cut into 1-inch
   strips
2 teaspoons chili powder
¼ cup margarine or butter
½ cup diagonally sliced green onions
1½ cups water
1 cup frozen sweet corn, thawed
1 can (4 ounces) chopped green
   chilies, drained
3 cups STOVE TOP® Cornbread Stuffing
   Mix in the Canister
1¼ cups (5 ounces) shredded Monterey
   Jack cheese, divided

TOSS meat with chili powder. Melt margarine in large skillet on medium-high heat. Add meat and onions; cook and stir until meat is browned.

STIR in water, corn and chilies. Bring to boil. Stir in stuffing mix and ¾ cup of the cheese. Remove from heat. Sprinkle with remaining ½ cup cheese. Cover. Let stand 5 minutes.
     Makes 4 to 6 servings

Prep Time: 10 minutes
Cook Time: 15 minutes

Dijon Ham and Lentil Soup

1 cup finely chopped onion
¾ cup finely chopped green bell
   pepper
½ cup finely chopped carrot
1 clove garlic, minced
1 bay leaf
2 (14½-fluid ounce) cans chicken broth
   or lower sodium chicken broth
1 (14½-ounce) can stewed tomatoes
1¼ cups water
1 cup diced ham
¾ cup dry lentils
½ cup GREY POUPON® COUNTRY
   DIJON® Mustard

In large saucepan, combine all ingredients except mustard. Heat to a boil over medium-high heat. Reduce heat; simmer, uncovered, for 1 hour. Stir in mustard. Serve hot.   *Makes 6 servings*

Hearty Hot Dish

Ravioli Soup

8 ounces sweet Italian sausage, casing removed
1 clove garlic, crushed
2 (13¾-fluid ounce) cans lower-sodium chicken broth
2 cups water
1 (9-ounce) package frozen miniature cheese-filled ravioli
1 (15-ounce) can garbanzo beans, drained
1 (14½-ounce) can stewed tomatoes
⅓ cup GREY POUPON® Dijon Mustard
½ teaspoon dried oregano leaves
¼ teaspoon coarsely ground black pepper
1 cup torn fresh spinach leaves
Grated Parmesan cheese

In 4-quart heavy pot, over medium heat, brown sausage and cook garlic until tender, stirring to break up sausage, about 5 minutes. Pour off excess fat; remove sausage mixture from pot and set aside.

In same pot, over medium-high heat, heat chicken broth and water to a boil. Add ravioli; cook for 4 to 5 minutes or until tender. Stir in beans, stewed tomatoes, sausage mixture, mustard, oregano and pepper; heat through. Stir in spinach and cook until wilted, about 1 minute. Serve topped with Parmesan cheese.

Makes 8 servings

Black Bean Sausage Skillet

2 tablespoons olive oil
1 cup chopped red onion
1 cup chopped green bell pepper
1 pound BOB EVANS® Special Seasonings Roll Sausage
3 (15-ounce) cans black beans, undrained
1 teaspoon dried oregano leaves
½ teaspoon garlic powder
¼ teaspoon ground cumin
⅛ teaspoon ground cinnamon
   Salt and black pepper to taste
   Cooked rice
   Flour tortillas, cut into wedges (optional)
   Sour cream and salsa for garnish

Heat olive oil in deep skillet; cook and stir onion and bell pepper until tender. Remove from skillet. Crumble sausage into skillet and cook until browned. Drain off any drippings. Return onion and bell pepper to skillet with beans, oregano, garlic, cumin, cinnamon, salt and pepper; simmer 20 minutes. Serve over rice with tortillas, if desired. Garnish with sour cream and salsa. Refrigerate leftovers.

Makes 6 servings

Black Bean Sausage Skillet

Greek Lamb Braised with Vegetables

¼ cup FILIPPO BERIO® Olive Oil
2½ pounds lean boneless lamb, cut into 1½-inch cubes
1 cup chicken broth
½ cup dry white wine
2 medium carrots, diagonally cut into 1-inch pieces
2 ribs celery, diagonally cut into 1-inch pieces
½ medium bulb fennel, cut into ¼-inch-thick slices lengthwise through stem
1 (14-ounce) can artichoke hearts, drained and cut into quarters lengthwise
3 green onions, trimmed and cut into 1½-inch pieces
Salt and freshly ground black pepper
8 ounces uncooked orzo pasta
Chopped fresh parsley

In Dutch oven, heat olive oil over medium-high heat until hot. Add lamb; cook and stir 5 minutes or until lightly browned. Add broth and wine; cover. Bring mixture to a boil. Reduce heat to low; simmer 1½ hours. Add carrots, celery, fennel, artichokes and green onions. Simmer 15 to 20 minutes or until lamb and vegetables are tender.

Season to taste with salt and pepper. Meanwhile, cook orzo according to package directions until al dente (tender but still firm). Drain. Serve lamb mixture over orzo. Top with parsley. *Makes 6 servings*

Garlic Lamb and Eggplant Stir-Fry

½ pound boneless lamb
1 tablespoon KIKKOMAN® Stir-Fry Sauce
1½ teaspoons minced garlic, divided
1 pound eggplant, trimmed
4 tablespoons vegetable oil, divided
⅛ teaspoon salt
1 onion, thinly sliced
1 red bell pepper, cut into matchsticks
1 crookneck squash, cut into matchsticks
⅓ cup KIKKOMAN® Stir-Fry Sauce
⅛ teaspoon crushed red pepper

Cut lamb into thin strips. Coat lamb in medium bowl with mixture of 1 tablespoon stir-fry sauce and ½ teaspoon garlic; let stand 30 minutes. Meanwhile, peel eggplant lengthwise to form stripes; then cut into matchsticks. Heat 1 tablespoon oil in hot wok or large skillet over high heat. Add lamb and stir-fry 1 minute; remove. Heat 2 tablespoons oil in same pan; reduce heat to medium-high. Add remaining 1 teaspoon garlic; stir-fry 10 seconds. Add eggplant and salt; stir-fry 6 minutes. Push eggplant to edge of pan; add remaining 1 tablespoon oil, onion, bell pepper and squash; stir-fry with eggplant 5 minutes. Add ⅓ cup stir-fry sauce and crushed red pepper; cook, stirring constantly, 2 minutes longer. Stir in lamb; heat through. *Makes 4 servings*

Greek Lamb Braised with Vegetables

Navajo Lamb Stew with Cornmeal Dumplings

2 pounds lean lamb stew meat with bones, cut into 2-inch pieces, *or* 1½ pounds lean boneless lamb, cut into 1½-inch cubes
1 teaspoon salt
½ teaspoon black pepper
2 tablespoons plus 1½ teaspoons vegetable oil, divided
1 large onion, chopped
1 clove garlic, minced
4 cups water
2 tablespoons tomato paste
2 teaspoons chili powder
1 teaspoon ground coriander
3 small potatoes, cut into 1½-inch chunks
2 large carrots, cut into 1-inch pieces
1 package (10 ounces) frozen whole kernel corn
⅓ cup coarsely chopped celery leaves
Cornmeal Dumplings (recipe follows)

Sprinkle meat with salt and pepper. Heat 2 tablespoons oil in 5-quart Dutch oven over medium-high heat. Add meat, a few pieces at a time; cook until browned, stirring occasionally. Transfer meat to medium bowl. Heat remaining 1½ teaspoons oil in Dutch oven over medium heat. Add onion and garlic; cook and stir until onion is tender. Stir in water, tomato paste, chili powder and coriander. Return meat to Dutch oven. Add potatoes, carrots, corn and chopped celery leaves. Bring to a boil. Cover; reduce heat to low. Simmer 1 hour and 15 minutes or until meat is tender. During last 15 minutes of cooking, prepare Cornmeal Dumplings. Drop dough onto stew to make 6 dumplings. Cover and simmer 18 minutes or until dumplings are firm to the touch and toothpick inserted into centers comes out clean. To serve, spoon stew onto individual plates; serve with dumplings.
Makes 6 servings

Cornmeal Dumplings

½ cup yellow cornmeal
½ cup all-purpose flour
1 teaspoon baking powder
¼ teaspoon salt
2½ tablespoons cold butter or margarine
½ cup milk

Combine cornmeal, flour, baking powder and salt in medium bowl. Cut in butter with fingers, pastry blender or 2 knives until mixture resembles coarse crumbs; make a well in center. Pour in milk all at once; stir with fork until mixture forms dough.
Makes 6 dumplings

French Veal Casserole

1 pound veal steaks
2 tablespoons salad oil
1 cup rice
1 tablespoon chopped onion
2¼ cups water
2 teaspoons salt
2 tablespoons chopped pimiento
½ cup BLUE DIAMOND® Slivered Almonds, toasted

Cut veal into ½-inch cubes. Brown lightly in oil. Remove meat from pan. Combine rice and onion in same pan and cook, stirring, until rice is golden brown. Add water and salt and bring to boil. Stir in veal. Turn into casserole dish; cover. Bake at 300°F 50 to 60 minutes or until rice and veal are tender. Just before serving, add pimiento and almonds; fluff rice with fork.
Makes 6 servings

Navajo Lamb Stew with Cornmeal Dumplings

CHICKEN & TURKEY
FAVORITES

Chicken Rice Casserole

4 tablespoons butter, divided
4 boneless skinless chicken breasts
1½ cups uncooked converted rice
6 ounces HILLSHIRE FARM® Lit'l
    Smokies
1 can (about 14 ounces) cream of
    chicken soup
1 can (about 14 ounces) cream of
    celery soup
1 cup sliced mushrooms
½ cup dry sherry
    Bread crumbs
    Cheddar cheese
    Slivered almonds

Preheat oven to 275°F.

Melt 2 tablespoons butter in large skillet over medium-high heat. Add chicken; sauté until cooked through, about 7 minutes on each side. Remove chicken and cut into bite-size pieces.

Place rice on bottom of medium casserole; add chicken, Lit'l Smokies, soups, ¾ cup water, mushrooms, sherry and remaining 2 tablespoons butter. Bake, covered, 2½ hours. Top casserole with bread crumbs, cheese and almonds. Broil until golden brown and cheese is melted.

Makes 6 to 8 servings

Tip: Be sure to avoid overcooking—it's the major pitfall of casseroles destined for the freezer. A simple way is to undercook any pasta or rice; it will cook through when the casserole is reheated.

Mediterranean Carrots with Chicken

2 boxes (10 ounces each) BIRDS EYE®
    frozen Deluxe Baby Whole Carrots
2 cups cubed, cooked chicken breast
3 tablespoons brown sugar
2 tablespoons lemon juice
1 teaspoon cumin

• In large saucepan, combine all ingredients. Cover; cook over medium-low heat 20 minutes or until heated through and carrots are tender. *Makes 4 servings*

Prep Time: 5 minutes
Cook Time: 20 minutes

Chicken Rice Casserole

Asparagus Chicken

1 pound chicken breast tenders
1 egg white
2 tablespoons cornstarch, divided
5 teaspoons soy sauce, divided
2 teaspoons dry sherry
2 large carrots, peeled
1 green onion with tops
1 package (10 ounces) frozen
    asparagus, partially thawed
½ cup fat-free reduced-sodium chicken
    broth
1 teaspoon sesame oil
3 tablespoons vegetable oil, divided
    Hot cooked rice

• Rinse chicken and pat dry with paper towels. Cut each chicken tender crosswise in half. Combine egg white, 1 tablespoon cornstarch, 2 teaspoons soy sauce and sherry in large bowl; stir until smooth. Add chicken and toss to coat; set aside.

• Slice carrots crosswise into 2-inch lengths. Slice carrot pieces lengthwise; stack slices and cut lengthwise into julienne strips. Cut onion diagonally into ½-inch slices. Cut asparagus spears diagonally into 1½-inch lengths.

• Stir broth, remaining 3 teaspoons soy sauce and sesame oil into remaining 1 tablespoon cornstarch in cup until smooth. Set aside.

• Heat wok over high heat about 1 minute or until hot. Drizzle 2 tablespoons vegetable oil into wok and heat 30 seconds. Add chicken; stir-fry about 4 minutes or until chicken is no longer pink in center. Remove to medium bowl. Reduce heat to medium.

• Drizzle remaining 1 tablespoon vegetable oil into wok and heat 30 seconds. Add carrots to wok; stir-fry about 3 minutes or until crisp-tender. Add asparagus; stir-fry 1 minute. Stir broth mixture until smooth and add to wok. Cook until sauce boils and thickens. Stir in onion, chicken and any accumulated juices to wok; cook until heated through. Serve over rice.

Makes 4 servings

Chicken Gumbo

3 tablespoons vegetable oil
1 pound boneless skinless chicken
    breasts, cut into 1-inch pieces
½ pound smoked sausage,* cut into
    ¾-inch slices
1 bag (16 ounces) BIRDS EYE® frozen
    Farm Fresh Mixtures Broccoli, Corn
    and Red Peppers
1 can (14½ ounces) stewed tomatoes
1½ cups water

For a spicy gumbo, use andouille sausage. Any type of kielbasa or turkey kielbasa can also be used.

• Heat oil in large saucepan over high heat. Add chicken and sausage; cook until browned, about 8 minutes.

• Add vegetables, tomatoes and water; bring to boil. Reduce heat to medium; cover and cook 3 minutes.

Makes 4 to 6 servings

Prep Time: 5 minutes
Cook Time: 20 minutes

Chicken Gumbo

Coq au Vin

2 slices bacon, cut into ½-inch pieces
1 chicken, cut up (3½ pounds)
1 medium onion, coarsely chopped
1 cup mushrooms, halved
1 red bell pepper, coarsely chopped
¾ cup red wine or dry white wine
1 cup chicken broth, divided
2 cloves garlic, minced
1 teaspoon dried thyme leaves
¼ teaspoon black pepper
¼ cup all-purpose flour
    Hot cooked rice or noodles

Cook bacon in large skillet or Dutch oven over medium heat until crisp. Remove with slotted spoon; set aside.

Add chicken pieces to skillet; cook 10 minutes or until golden brown, turning occasionally to brown evenly.

Add onion, mushrooms, bell pepper, wine, ¾ cup chicken broth, garlic, thyme and black pepper; bring to a boil. Reduce heat; simmer covered 25 minutes.

Combine remaining ¼ cup broth and flour; stir until smooth. Stir into chicken mixture. Continue simmering, uncovered, 5 minutes or until thickened. Season to taste with salt and black pepper. Top with reserved bacon and chopped parsley, if desired. Serve with rice.

Makes 4 servings

Chicken-Mac Casserole

1½ cups elbow macaroni, cooked in unsalted water and drained
6 slices bacon, fried crisp and crumbled
2 cups (10 ounces) cubed cooked chicken
1⅓ cups FRENCH'S® French Fried Onions, divided
1 can (10¾ ounces) condensed cream of mushroom soup
1 cup sour cream
1 package (10 ounces) frozen chopped spinach, thawed and well drained
⅛ teaspoon garlic powder
1½ cups (6 ounces) shredded Cheddar cheese, divided

Preheat oven to 375°F. Return cooked macaroni to saucepan; stir in bacon, chicken and ⅔ cup French Fried Onions. In medium bowl, combine soup, sour cream, spinach, garlic powder and 1 cup Cheddar cheese. Spoon half the macaroni mixture into greased 12×8-inch baking dish; cover with half the spinach mixture. Repeat layers. Bake, covered, at 375°F for 30 minutes or until heated through. Top with remaining cheese and ⅔ cup onions. Bake, uncovered, 3 minutes or until onions are golden brown.

Makes 6 to 8 servings

Coq au Vin

Home-Style Chicken and Sweet Potato Stew

4 boneless, skinless chicken breasts
  Garlic salt and pepper
½ cup all-purpose flour
¼ cup WESSON® Vegetable Oil
2 cups cubed, peeled sweet potatoes
1 cup chopped onion
1 (14.5-ounce) can HUNT'S® Stewed
  Tomatoes, lightly crushed
¾ cup homemade chicken stock or
  canned chicken broth
¾ cup apple cider
½ teaspoon dried dill weed
1 chicken bouillon cube
  Dash or two of GEBHARDT® Hot
  Pepper Sauce
  Salt to taste

Rinse chicken and pat dry; cut into ½-inch pieces. Sprinkle with garlic salt and pepper. Place flour in plastic bag. Add chicken; shake until chicken is well coated. In large stockpot, heat Wesson® Oil. Add chicken; cook on both sides until golden brown. Remove chicken; set aside. In same pot, add sweet potatoes and onion; sauté until onion is tender. Stir in *remaining* ingredients *except* salt; blend well. Add browned chicken; bring to a boil. Reduce heat; cover and simmer 25 to 30 minutes or until chicken is no longer pink in center and potatoes are tender, stirring often. Salt to taste.

Makes 4 servings

Pure Wesson®: For a sweeter stew, substitute yams for sweet potatoes.

Sweet & Sour Cashew Chicken

1 can (16 ounces) cling peach slices in
  syrup
1 cup KIKKOMAN® Sweet & Sour Sauce
2 boneless, skinless chicken breast
  halves
1 tablespoon cornstarch
1 tablespoon KIKKOMAN® Soy Sauce
1 tablespoon minced fresh ginger root
½ teaspoon sugar
2 tablespoons vegetable oil, divided
1 onion, chunked
1 green bell pepper, chunked
1 small carrot, cut diagonally into thin
  slices
⅓ cup roasted cashews

Reserving ⅓ cup syrup, drain peaches; cut slices in half. Blend reserved syrup and sweet & sour sauce; set aside. Cut chicken into 1-inch-square pieces. Combine cornstarch, soy sauce, ginger and sugar in medium bowl; stir in chicken. Heat 1 tablespoon oil in hot wok or large skillet over high heat. Add chicken and stir-fry 4 minutes; remove. Heat remaining 1 tablespoon oil in same pan. Add onion, bell pepper and carrot; stir-fry 4 minutes. Stir in chicken, sweet & sour sauce mixture, peaches and cashews; heat through. Serve immediately.

Makes 4 servings

Sweet & Sour Cashew Chicken

Chicken Casserole Supreme

STUFFING

2 cups unseasoned dry bread crumbs
1 cup chopped green onions
⅓ cup margarine or butter, melted
2 tablespoons chopped fresh parsley

CHICKEN

¼ cup all-purpose flour
¼ cup cornmeal
¼ teaspoon pepper
6 boneless chicken breast halves
   (about 1½ pounds)
1 egg, beaten
⅓ cup margarine or butter

SAUCE

¼ cup margarine or butter
3 cups sliced fresh mushrooms
1 can (14½ ounces) chicken broth,
   divided
⅓ cup all-purpose flour
¾ cup HOLLAND HOUSE® Vermouth
   Cooking Wine
½ cup whipping cream

In medium bowl, combine all stuffing ingredients; mix well. Place stuffing in 6 mounds in ungreased 13×9-inch baking dish. In shallow dish, combine ¼ cup flour, cornmeal and pepper. Dip chicken in beaten egg, then coat with flour mixture. Melt ⅓ cup margarine in large skillet. Cook chicken 7 to 8 minutes on each side or until browned. Remove chicken; place on top of stuffing.

Heat oven to 375°F. Melt ¼ cup margarine in large saucepan. Add mushrooms; cook until tender. Remove from pan. Stir in 1 cup chicken broth and ⅓ cup flour; mix well. Add remaining chicken broth, cooking wine and whipping cream. Cook until slightly thickened, stirring constantly. Stir in mushrooms. Pour over chicken; cover. Bake at 375°F for 1 to 1¼ hours or until chicken is tender and no longer pink.

Makes 6 servings

Savory Chicken and Biscuits

1 pound boneless, skinless chicken
   thighs or breasts, cut into 1-inch
   pieces
1 medium potato, cut into 1-inch
   pieces
1 medium yellow onion, cut into 1-inch
   pieces
8 ounces fresh mushrooms, quartered
1 cup fresh baby carrots
1 cup chopped celery
1 (14½-ounce) can chicken broth
3 cloves garlic, minced
1 teaspoon dried rosemary leaves
1 teaspoon salt
1 teaspoon black pepper
3 tablespoons cornstarch blended with
   ½ cup cold water
1 cup frozen peas, thawed
1 (4-ounce) jar sliced pimentos,
   drained
1 package BOB EVANS® Frozen
   Buttermilk Biscuit Dough

Preheat oven to 375°F. Combine chicken, potato, onion, mushrooms, carrots, celery, broth, garlic, rosemary, salt and pepper in large saucepan. Bring to a boil over high heat. Reduce heat to low and simmer, uncovered, 5 minutes. Stir in cornstarch mixture; cook 2 minutes. Stir in peas and pimentos; return to a boil. Transfer chicken mixture to 2-quart casserole dish; arrange frozen biscuits on top. Bake 30 to 35 minutes or until biscuits are golden brown. Refrigerate leftovers.

Makes 4 to 6 servings

Savory Chicken and Biscuits

Chicken Skillet Supper

1 teaspoon salt
¼ teaspoon black pepper
¼ teaspoon ground paprika
⅛ teaspoon garlic powder
1 whole chicken (about 3 pounds), cut
    into serving pieces
1 tablespoon vegetable oil
2 tablespoons water
1 medium onion, chopped
1 medium potato, peeled and cut into
    2¼-inch strips
1 tablespoon slivered almonds
    (optional)
1 can (8 ounces) tomato sauce
1 cup chicken broth
1 teaspoon sugar
1 package (10 ounces) frozen
    French-cut green beans or
    mixed vegetables

Mix salt, pepper, paprika and garlic powder in small bowl; rub over chicken. Heat oil in large skillet over medium heat; add chicken, skin-side down. Cover and cook 10 minutes. Add water to chicken; cover and cook 30 minutes, turning chicken over every 10 minutes. Remove chicken from skillet; set aside.

Add onion, potato and almonds to pan juices; cook until onion is tender, about 3 minutes. Add tomato sauce, broth and sugar to onion mixture; cook until liquid comes to a boil. Add beans and chicken pieces to tomato mixture; cover and cook until beans are tender, about 10 minutes. Serve hot.

Makes 4 to 6 servings

Arroz Con Pollo

1 (3-pound) broiler-fryer chicken, cut
    up
½ teaspoon ground cumin
1 tablespoon vegetable oil
1 can (14½ ounces) DEL MONTE®
    Mexican Recipe Stewed Tomatoes
1 cup uncooked long grain white rice
1 can (14 ounces) chicken broth
1 large onion, thinly sliced
2 cloves garlic, minced
1 to 1½ teaspoons minced jalapeño
    chile

1. Sprinkle chicken with cumin. Season with salt and pepper, if desired.

2. Brown chicken in oil in 4-quart heavy saucepan over medium-high heat; drain. Drain tomatoes, reserving ⅓ cup liquid.

3. Add reserved liquid, tomatoes and remaining ingredients to saucepan.

4. Cover and cook over low heat about 30 minutes or until chicken is no longer pink and rice is tender.   *Makes 6 servings*

Prep and Cook Time: 45 minutes

Arroz Con Pollo

Chicken Enchiladas

1¾ cups fat free sour cream
½ cup chopped green onions
⅓ cup minced fresh cilantro
1 tablespoon minced fresh jalapeño chili pepper
1 teaspoon ground cumin
1 tablespoon vegetable oil
12 ounces boneless, skinless chicken breasts, cut into 3×1-inch strips
1 teaspoon minced garlic
8 flour tortillas (8-inch)
1 cup (4 ounces) shredded ALPINE LACE® Reduced Fat Cheddar Cheese
1 cup bottled chunky salsa (medium or hot)
1 small ripe tomato, chopped
Sprigs of cilantro (optional)

1. Preheat the oven to 350°F. Spray a 13×9×3-inch baking dish with nonstick cooking spray.

2. In a small bowl, mix together the sour cream, green onions, cilantro, jalapeño pepper and cumin.

3. Spray a large nonstick skillet with the cooking spray, pour in the oil and heat over medium-high heat. Add the chicken and garlic and sauté for 4 minutes or until the juices run clear when the chicken is pierced with a fork.

4. Divide the chicken strips among the 8 tortillas, placing them down the center of the tortillas. Top with the sour cream mixture, then roll them up and place them, seam side down, in the baking dish.

5. Sprinkle with the cheese, cover with foil and bake for 30 minutes or until bubbly. Spoon the salsa in a strip down the center and sprinkle the salsa with the tomato. Garnish with the sprigs of cilantro, if you wish. Serve hot!   *Makes 8 servings*

Curried Chicken with Couscous

1 package (5.7 ounces) curry flavor couscous mix
1 tablespoon butter or margarine
1 pound boneless, skinless chicken breasts, cut into thin strips
1½ cups BIRDS EYE® frozen Farm Fresh Mixtures Broccoli, Cauliflower & Red Peppers
1⅓ cups water
½ cup raisins

• Remove seasoning packet from couscous mix; set aside.

• In large nonstick skillet, melt butter over medium-high heat. Add chicken; cook until browned on all sides.

• Stir in vegetables, water, raisins and seasoning packet; bring to boil. Reduce heat to medium-low; cover and simmer 5 minutes or until chicken is no longer pink in center.

• Stir in couscous; cover. Remove from heat; let stand 5 minutes. Stir before serving.
Makes 4 servings

Serving Suggestion: Serve with toasted pita bread rounds.

Birds Eye Idea: To add flavor to chicken breasts, simply rub them with lemon juice before cooking.

Prep Time: 5 minutes
Cook Time: 15 minutes

Chicken Enchiladas

Chicken Soup au Pistou

Olive oil-flavored nonstick cooking spray
½ pound boneless skinless chicken breasts, cut into ½-inch pieces
1 large onion, diced
3 cans (14½ ounces each) chicken broth
1 can (15 ounces) whole tomatoes, undrained
1 can (14 ounces) great Northern beans, rinsed and drained
2 medium carrots, sliced
1 large potato, diced
¼ teaspoon salt
¼ teaspoon black pepper
1 cup frozen Italian green beans
¼ cup prepared pesto
Grated Parmesan cheese (optional)

Spray large saucepan with cooking spray; heat over medium-high heat until hot. Add chicken; cook and stir about 5 minutes or until chicken is browned. Add onion; cook and stir 2 minutes.

Add chicken broth, tomatoes with juice, great Northern beans, carrots, potato, salt and pepper. Bring to a boil, stirring to break up tomatoes. Reduce heat to low. Cover and simmer 15 minutes, stirring occasionally. Add green beans; cook about 5 minutes more or until vegetables are tender.

Ladle soup into bowls. Top each serving with 1½ teaspoons pesto and sprinkle with Parmesan cheese, if desired.

Makes about 12 cups (about 8 servings)

Home-Style Chicken Casserole

2 bags SUCCESS® Rice
Vegetable cooking spray
2 tablespoons olive oil
1 pound skinless, boneless chicken breasts, cut into strips
3 cloves garlic, minced
¾ cup spaghetti sauce
¾ cup prepared brown gravy
½ cup plain nonfat yogurt
¼ cup (1 ounce) grated Parmesan cheese
1 teaspoon dried oregano leaves, crushed
½ teaspoon dried rosemary leaves, crushed
1 teaspoon pepper
1 cup (4 ounces) shredded mozzarella cheese

Prepare rice according to package directions.

Preheat oven to 350°F.

Spray 1½-quart baking dish with cooking spray; set aside. Heat oil in large skillet. Add chicken and garlic; cook and stir until chicken is no longer pink in center. Add all remaining ingredients except rice and mozzarella cheese; mix lightly. Place rice in bottom of prepared baking dish; cover with chicken mixture. Sprinkle with mozzarella cheese. Bake until mixture is thoroughly heated and cheese is melted, about 15 minutes.

Makes 8 servings

Chicken Soup au Pistou

Dairyland Confetti Chicken

1 cup diced carrots
¾ cup chopped onion
½ cup diced celery
¼ cup chicken broth
3 cups cubed cooked chicken
1 can (10½ ounces) cream of chicken
    soup
1 cup dairy sour cream
½ cup (4 ounces) sliced mushrooms
1 teaspoon Worcestershire sauce
1 teaspoon salt
⅛ teaspoon pepper
    Confetti Topping (recipe follows)
¼ cup (1 ounce) shredded Wisconsin
    Cheddar Cheese

For casserole, in saucepan, combine carrots, onion, celery and chicken broth. Simmer 20 minutes. In 3-quart casserole, mix chicken cubes, soup, sour cream, mushrooms, Worcestershire sauce, salt and pepper. Add simmered vegetables and liquid; mix well. Prepare Confetti Topping. Drop tablespoons of Confetti Topping onto casserole. Bake in 350°F oven for 40 to 45 minutes or until golden brown. Sprinkle with cheese and return to oven until melted. Garnish as desired.   *Makes 6 to 8 servings*

Confetti Topping

1 cup sifted all-purpose flour
2 teaspoons baking powder
½ teaspoon salt
2 eggs, slightly beaten
½ cup milk
1 tablespoon chopped green bell
    pepper
1 tablespoon chopped pimiento
1 cup (4 ounces) shredded Wisconsin
    Cheddar cheese

In mixing bowl, combine flour, baking powder and salt. Add eggs, green pepper, pimiento and cheese; mix just until well blended.

Favorite recipe from **Wisconsin Milk Marketing Board**

Peanut Chicken Stir-Fry

1 package (6.1 ounces) RICE-A-RONI®
    With ⅓ Less Salt Fried Rice
½ cup reduced-sodium or regular
    chicken broth
2 tablespoons creamy peanut butter
1 tablespoon reduced-sodium or
    regular soy sauce
1 tablespoon vegetable oil
¾ pound skinless, boneless chicken
    breasts, cut into ½-inch pieces
2 cloves garlic, minced
2 cups frozen mixed carrots, broccoli
    and red pepper vegetable medley,
    thawed, drained
2 tablespoons chopped peanuts
    (optional)

1. Prepare Rice-A-Roni® mix as package directs.

2. While Rice-A-Roni® is simmering, combine chicken broth, peanut butter and soy sauce; mix with fork. Set aside.

3. In second large skillet or wok, heat oil over medium-high heat. Stir-fry chicken and garlic 2 minutes.

4. Add vegetables and broth mixture; stir-fry 5 to 7 minutes or until sauce has thickened. Serve over rice. Sprinkle with peanuts, if desired.   *Makes 4 servings*

Peanut Chicken Stir-Fry

Hearty Chicken Bake

3 cups hot mashed potatoes
1 cup (4 ounces) shredded Cheddar
  cheese, divided
1⅓ cups FRENCH'S® French Fried Onions,
  divided
1½ cups (7 ounces) cubed cooked
  chicken
1 package (10 ounces) frozen mixed
  vegetables, thawed and drained
1 can (10¾ ounces) condensed cream
  of chicken soup
¼ cup milk
½ teaspoon ground mustard
¼ teaspoon garlic powder
¼ teaspoon pepper

Preheat oven to 375°. In medium bowl, combine mashed potatoes, ½ cup cheese and ⅔ cup French Fried Onions; mix thoroughly. Spoon potato mixture into greased 1½-quart casserole. Using back of spoon, spread potatoes across bottom and up sides of dish to form a shell. In large bowl, combine chicken, mixed vegetables, soup, milk and seasonings; pour into potato shell. Bake, uncovered, at 375° for 30 minutes or until heated through. Top with remaining cheese and ⅔ cup onions; bake, uncovered, 3 minutes or until onions are golden brown. Let stand 5 minutes before serving. *Makes 4 to 6 servings*

Country Chicken Dinner

¼ cup milk
2 tablespoons margarine or butter
1 package (4.7 ounces) PASTA RONI®
  Chicken & Broccoli with Linguine
2 cups frozen mixed broccoli,
  cauliflower and carrots vegetable
  medley
2 cups chopped cooked chicken or
  turkey
1 teaspoon dried basil leaves

1. In round 3-quart microwavable glass casserole, combine 1¾ cups water, milk and margarine. Microwave, uncovered, at HIGH 4 to 5 minutes or until boiling.

2. Gradually add pasta while stirring.

3. Stir in contents of seasoning packet, frozen vegetables, chicken and basil.

4. Microwave, uncovered, at HIGH 14 to 15 minutes, stirring gently after 7 minutes. Sauce will be thin, but will thicken upon standing.

5. Let stand 4 to 5 minutes or until desired consistency. Stir before serving.
Makes 4 servings

Country Chicken Dinner

Creamy Chicken & Vegetables with Puff Pastry

2 whole chicken breasts, split (about 2 pounds)
1 medium onion, sliced
4 carrots, coarsely chopped, divided
4 ribs celery with leaves, cut into 1-inch pieces, divided
1 frozen puff pastry sheet, thawed
2 tablespoons butter or margarine
1 medium onion, chopped
½ pound fresh mushrooms, sliced
½ cup all-purpose flour
1 teaspoon dried basil leaves
1 teaspoon salt
¼ to ½ teaspoon white pepper
1 cup milk
1 cup frozen peas, thawed

1. To make chicken stock, place chicken, sliced onion, ⅓ of carrots and ⅓ of celery in Dutch oven. Add enough cold water to cover. Cover and bring to a boil over medium heat. Reduce heat to low. Simmer 5 to 7 minutes or until chicken is no longer pink in center.

2. Remove chicken; cool. Strain stock through large sieve lined with several layers of dampened cheesecloth; discard vegetables. Refrigerate stock; skim off any fat that forms on top. Measure 2 cups stock.

3. When chicken is cool enough to handle, remove skin and bones; discard. Cut chicken into bite-sized pieces.

4. Place remaining carrots, celery and enough water to cover in medium saucepan. Cover; bring to a boil. Reduce heat to medium-low; simmer 8 minutes or until vegetables are crisp-tender. Set aside.

5. Preheat oven to 400°F. Roll puff pastry out on lightly floured surface to 12×8-inch rectangle. Place on ungreased baking sheet; bake 15 minutes. Set aside.

6. Melt butter in large saucepan over medium-high heat. Add chopped onion and mushrooms; cook and stir 5 minutes or until tender. Stir flour, basil, salt and pepper. Slowly pour in reserved chicken stock and milk. Cook until mixture begins to boil. Cook 1 minute longer, stirring constantly.

7. Stir in reserved chicken, peas, carrots and celery. Cook until heated through. Pour mixture into 12×8-inch baking dish; top with hot puff pastry. Bake 5 minutes until puff pastry is brown. Garnish as desired.

Makes 6 servings

Chicken Stir-Fry

½ cup A.1.® Steak Sauce
¼ cup dry white wine
2 tablespoons GREY POUPON® Dijon Mustard
2 tablespoons soy sauce
1 tablespoon sesame oil
2 cloves garlic, crushed
½ teaspoon ground black pepper
1½ pounds boneless chicken breasts, cut into ½-inch strips
1 cup sliced carrots
1 cup thinly sliced red bell pepper
1 cup snow peas
1 cup sliced onion
Hot cooked rice, optional

In medium nonmetal bowl, whisk together steak sauce, wine, mustard, soy sauce, sesame oil, garlic and black pepper; add chicken, stirring to coat. Cover; chill 1 hour, stirring occasionally.

In large skillet, over medium-high heat, cook and stir chicken mixture until no longer pink, about 5 minutes. Add vegetables; cook and stir until tender, about 5 to 7 minutes. Serve over rice if desired.

Makes 6 servings

Creamy Chicken & Vegetables with Puff Pastry

Chicken Chili

- 1 tablespoon vegetable oil
- 1 pound ground chicken or turkey
- 1 medium onion, chopped
- 1 medium green bell pepper, chopped
- 2 fresh jalapeño peppers, chopped*
- 1 can (28 ounces) tomatoes, cut up, undrained
- 1 can (15½ ounces) kidney beans, drained
- 1 can (8 ounces) tomato sauce
- 1 tablespoon chili powder
- 1 teaspoon salt
- 1 teaspoon dried oregano leaves
- 1 teaspoon ground cumin
- ¼ teaspoon ground red pepper
- ½ cup (2 ounces) shredded Cheddar cheese

Chili peppers can sting and irritate the skin; wear rubber gloves when handling peppers and do not touch eyes.

Heat oil in 5-quart Dutch oven or large saucepan over medium-high heat. Cook chicken, onion and bell pepper until chicken is no longer pink and onion is crisp-tender, stirring frequently to break up chicken. Stir in jalapeño peppers, tomatoes with juice, beans, tomato sauce, chili powder, salt, oregano, cumin and red pepper. Bring to a boil over high heat. Reduce heat to medium-low; simmer, uncovered, 45 minutes to blend flavors. To serve, spoon into 6 bowls and top with cheese.

Makes 6 servings

Chicken Provençal

- 1 tablespoon olive oil
- 2 pounds skinless chicken thighs
- ½ cup sliced green bell pepper
- ½ cup sliced onion
- 2 cloves garlic, minced
- 1 pound eggplant, peeled and cut into ¼-inch-thick slices
- 2 medium tomatoes, cut into ¼-inch-thick slices
- ¼ cup chopped fresh parsley *or* 2 teaspoons dried parsley
- ¼ cup chopped fresh basil *or* 2 teaspoons dried basil leaves
- 1 teaspoon salt
- 1 cup fat-free reduced-sodium chicken broth
- ½ cup dry white wine

Heat oil in large skillet over medium-high heat. Add chicken; cook 2 to 3 minutes on each side or until browned. Remove chicken.

Add bell pepper, onion and garlic to same skillet; cook and stir 3 to 4 minutes or until onion is tender.

Return chicken to skillet. Arrange eggplant and tomato slices over chicken. Sprinkle with parsley, basil and salt. Add chicken broth and wine; bring to a boil. Reduce heat; cover and simmer 45 to 50 minutes or until juices from chicken run clear.

Makes 6 servings

Chicken Provençal

Sweet and Sour Stir-Fry

1 tablespoon vegetable oil
1 pound boneless skinless chicken
    breasts, cut into 3-inch strips
1 can (8 ounces) sliced water
    chestnuts, drained
1 cup 2×½-inch red bell pepper strips
¼ cup chopped onion
2 tablespoons cornstarch
2 tablespoons soy sauce
1 tablespoon white vinegar
1 can (8 ounces) pineapple chunks,
    packed in juice, undrained
¼ teaspoon ground ginger
¼ teaspoon salt
1¾ teaspoons EQUAL® MEASURE™ or 6
    packets EQUAL® sweetener or
    ¼ cup EQUAL® SPOONFUL™
1 package (6 ounces) frozen pea pods

• Heat oil in wok or skillet. Add chicken;
cook until chicken is no longer pink, 5 to 6
minutes. Remove and set aside. Add water
chestnuts, pepper and onion to wok; cook
until vegetables are tender, 3 to 4 minutes,
stirring constantly.

• Combine cornstarch, soy sauce and
vinegar in small bowl; stir to dissolve
cornstarch. Add pineapple with juice, ginger
and salt. Add to vegetable mixture; cook
until sauce thickens, 2 to 3 minutes, stirring
constantly.

• Stir in Equal®. Add pea pods and chicken;
cook until pea pods and chicken are heated
through, 2 to 3 minutes.

Makes 4 servings

Chicken-Vegetable Skillet

8 broiler-fryer chicken thighs, skinned,
    fat trimmed
¾ teaspoon salt, divided
1 tablespoon vegetable oil
3 medium red-skinned potatoes,
    scrubbed, cut in ¼-inch slices
1 medium onion, sliced
½ pound mushrooms, quartered
1 large tomato, coarsely chopped
¼ cup chicken broth
¼ cup dry white wine
½ teaspoon dried oregano leaves
¼ teaspoon pepper
1 tablespoon chopped fresh parsley

Sprinkle chicken with ¼ teaspoon salt. In
large nonstick skillet, heat oil to medium-
high temperature. Add chicken and cook,
turning, about 8 minutes or until brown on
both sides. Remove chicken; set aside. In
same pan, layer potatoes, onion, chicken,
mushrooms and tomato. In 1-cup measure,
mix broth and wine. Pour over chicken and
vegetables. Sprinkle with oregano,
remaining ½ teaspoon salt and pepper.
Heat to boiling; cover and reduce heat to
medium-low. Cook about 20 minutes or
until chicken and vegetables are fork-tender.
Sprinkle with parsley before serving.

Makes 4 servings

*Favorite recipe from **Delmarva Poultry Industry, Inc.***

Sweet and Sour Stir-Fry

Chicken and Black Bean Enchiladas

2 jars (16 ounces each) mild picante sauce
¼ cup chopped fresh cilantro
2 tablespoons chili powder
1 teaspoon ground cumin
2 cups (10 ounces) chopped cooked chicken
1 can (15 ounces) black beans, drained and rinsed
1⅓ cups FRENCH'S® French Fried Onions, divided
1 package (about 10 ounces) flour tortillas (7 inches)
1 cup (4 ounces) shredded Monterey Jack cheese with jalapeño peppers

Preheat oven 350°F. Grease 10×15-inch jelly-roll baking pan. Combine picante sauce, cilantro, chili powder and cumin in large saucepan. Bring to a boil. Reduce heat to low; simmer 5 minutes.

Combine 1½ cups sauce mixture, chicken, beans and ⅔ cup French Fried Onions in medium bowl. Spoon a scant ½ cup filling over bottom third of each tortilla. Roll up tortillas enclosing filling and arrange, seam side down, in a single layer in bottom of prepared baking pan. Spoon remaining sauce evenly over tortillas.

Bake, uncovered, 20 minutes or until heated through. Sprinkle with remaining ⅔ cup onions and cheese. Bake 5 minutes or until cheese is melted and onions are golden. Serve immediately.   *Makes 5 to 6 servings (4 cups sauce, 4½ cups filling)*

Tip: This is a great make-ahead party dish.

Prep Time: 45 minutes

Cook Time: 25 minutes

Chicken Bourguignonne

4 pounds skinless chicken thighs and breasts
Flour
Nonstick cooking spray
2 cups defatted low-sodium chicken broth
2 cups dry white wine or defatted low-sodium chicken broth
1 pound whole baby carrots
¼ cup tomato paste
4 cloves garlic, minced
½ teaspoon dried thyme leaves
2 bay leaves
¼ teaspoon salt
¼ teaspoon pepper
8 ounces fresh or thawed frozen pearl onions
8 ounces whole medium mushrooms
2 cups hot cooked white rice
2 cups hot cooked wild rice
¼ cup minced fresh parsley

Preheat oven to 325°F. Coat chicken very lightly with flour. Generously spray nonstick ovenproof Dutch oven or large nonstick ovenproof skillet with cooking spray; heat over medium heat until hot. Cook chicken 10 to 15 minutes or until browned on all sides. Drain fat from Dutch oven.

Add chicken broth, wine, carrots, tomato paste, garlic, thyme, bay leaves, salt and pepper to Dutch oven; heat to a boil. Cover; transfer to oven. Bake 1 hour. Add onions and mushrooms. Uncover; bake about 35 minutes or until vegetables are tender, chicken is no longer pink in center and juices run clear. Remove bay leaves. Combine white and wild rice; serve with chicken. Sprinkle with parsley.

Makes 8 servings

Chicken Bourguignonne

Homestyle Chicken Pot Pie

2 tablespoons margarine or butter, divided
1 pound boneless skinless chicken breasts, cut into 1-inch pieces
½ teaspoon salt
½ teaspoon dried thyme leaves
¼ teaspoon black pepper
1 package (16 ounces) frozen mixed vegetables, such as potatoes, peas and carrots, thawed and drained
1 can (10¾ ounces) condensed cream of chicken or mushroom soup, undiluted
⅓ cup dry white wine or milk
1 refrigerated ready rolled pie crust, at room temperature

1. Preheat oven to 425°F. Melt 1 tablespoon margarine in medium broilerproof skillet over medium-high heat. Add chicken; sprinkle with salt, thyme and pepper. Cook 1 minute, stirring frequently.

2. Reduce heat to medium-low. Stir in vegetables, soup and wine; simmer 5 minutes.

3. While soup mixture is simmering, unwrap pie crust. Using small cookie cutter or apple corer, make 4 decorative cut-outs from pastry to allow steam to escape.

4. Remove chicken mixture from heat; top with pie crust. Melt remaining tablespoon margarine. Brush pie crust with 2 teaspoons melted margarine. Arrange cut-outs attractively over crust, if desired. Brush cut-outs with remaining 1 teaspoon melted margarine. Bake 12 minutes. Turn oven to broil; broil 4 to 5 inches from heat source 2 minutes or until crust is golden brown and chicken mixture is bubbly.

Makes 4 to 5 servings

Prep and Cook Time: 30 minutes

Apple and Chicken Soup

1 sweet potato (8 ounces)
1 tablespoon olive oil
2 ribs celery, thinly sliced
½ medium onion, chopped
1 teaspoon dried thyme leaves
½ teaspoon dried rosemary leaves
¼ teaspoon dried sage leaves
¼ teaspoon ground nutmeg
2 cans (14½ ounces each) chicken broth
1 cup apple juice
1 large McIntosh apple, peeled and chopped
⅔ cup uncooked small pasta shells
¾ pound boneless, skinless chicken breasts

1. Prick sweet potato in several places with fork. Microwave at HIGH 6 to 8 minutes or until crisp-tender; set aside (sweet potato will finish cooking and become tender as it stands).

2. Heat oil in 3-quart saucepan over medium-high heat until hot. Add celery, onion, thyme, rosemary, sage and nutmeg. Cook, covered, 3 to 4 minutes or until onion is tender. Add chicken broth, juice and apple. Bring to a boil over high heat; stir in pasta. Reduce heat to medium-high; boil, uncovered, 8 to 10 minutes.

3. Cut chicken into ¼-inch-wide strips. Pull skin from sweet potato; cut into 1-inch pieces. Add chicken and sweet potato to soup. Reduce heat to medium; simmer 3 to 5 minutes or until chicken is no longer pink in center and pasta is tender.

Makes 4 to 6 servings

Serving Suggestion: Serve with wedges of warm herb-cheese bread.

Prep and Cook Time: 25 minutes

Homestyle Chicken Pot Pie

Creole Chicken Thighs & Rice

  2 tablespoons vegetable oil
2¼ pounds chicken thighs
  ½ teaspoon paprika
  ½ teaspoon dried thyme leaves
  ½ teaspoon salt
  ¼ teaspoon black pepper
  ½ cup chopped celery
  ½ cup chopped green bell pepper
  ½ cup chopped onion
  2 cloves garlic, minced
  1 cup long-grain or converted rice
  1 can (14½ ounces) diced tomatoes,
     undrained
     Hot pepper sauce

Heat oil in large skillet or Dutch oven over medium heat until hot. Add chicken; sprinkle with paprika, thyme, salt and black pepper. Cook 5 to 6 minutes on each side or until golden brown. Remove from skillet.

Add celery, bell pepper, onion and garlic to same skillet; cook 2 minutes. Add rice; cook 2 minutes, stirring to coat rice with oil. Stir in tomatoes with juice, 1 cup water and hot pepper sauce; bring to a boil.

Arrange chicken over rice mixture; reduce heat. Cover; simmer 20 minutes or until chicken is no longer pink in center and liquid is absorbed. *Makes 4 servings*

Chicken Divan

  ⅔ cup milk
  2 tablespoons margarine or butter
  1 package (4.8 ounces) PASTA RONI®
     Four Cheese with Corkscrew Pasta
  2 cups chopped cooked chicken or
     turkey
  2 cups broccoli flowerets
  ½ cup croutons, coarsely crushed

1. In round 3-quart microwaveable glass casserole, combine 1½ cups water, milk and margarine. Microwave, uncovered, on HIGH 4 to 5 minutes or until boiling.

2. Stir in pasta, contents of seasoning packet, chicken and broccoli.

3. Microwave, uncovered, on HIGH 12 to 13 minutes, stirring after 6 minutes.

4. Let stand 4 to 5 minutes or until desired consistency. Sauce will be thin, but will thicken upon standing. Stir before serving.

5. Sprinkle with croutons.

Makes 4 servings

Chicken Carbonara

  1 pound chicken tenders
  1 jar (12 ounces) Alfredo sauce
  1 cup milk
1⅓ cups FRENCH'S® French Fried Onions,
     divided
  ½ of a 10-ounce package frozen peas,
     thawed and drained
  2 tablespoons real bacon bits*
     Hot cooked pasta

Or, substitute 2 strips crumbled, cooked bacon for real bacon bits.

Spray large nonstick skillet with nonstick cooking spray; heat over high heat. Add chicken; cook and stir about 5 minutes or until browned.

Stir in Alfredo sauce and milk. Add ⅔ cup French Fried Onions, peas and bacon bits. Bring to a boil. Reduce heat to low. Cook 5 minutes, stirring occasionally. Serve over pasta. Sprinkle with remaining ⅔ cup onions.
Makes 4 to 6 servings

Prep Time: 10 minutes

Cook Time: 10 minutes

Creole Chicken Thighs & Rice

Thai Chicken with Basil

1 small bunch fresh basil, divided
2 cups vegetable oil
6 large shallots, coarsely chopped
5 cloves garlic, minced
1 piece fresh ginger (about 1 inch square), peeled and cut into thin strips
1 pound ground chicken or turkey
2 fresh Thai or jalapeño chilies (1 red and 1 green or 2 green), cut into thin slices*
2 teaspoons brown sugar
½ teaspoon salt
   Boston lettuce leaves
   Japanese mizuna, cherry tomatoes and additional Thai peppers for garnish

*Chilies can sting and irritate the skin; wear rubber gloves when handling chilies and do not touch eyes.

1. Set aside 8 basil sprigs. Slice remaining basil sprigs into strips; set aside.

2. Heat oil in wok over medium-high heat until oil registers 375°F on deep-fry thermometer. Add 1 basil sprig and deep-fry about 15 seconds or until basil is glossy and crisp. Remove fried sprig with slotted spoon to paper towels; drain. Repeat with remaining 7 sprigs, reheating oil between batches.

3. Let oil cool slightly. Pour off oil, reserving ¼ cup. Return ¼ cup oil to wok and heat over medium-high heat 30 seconds or until hot. Add shallots, garlic and ginger; cook and stir 1 minute. Add chicken and stir-fry about 4 minutes or until lightly browned. Push chicken up side of wok, letting juices remain in bottom.

4. Continue to cook about 5 to 7 minutes or until liquid evaporates. Stir in chili slices, brown sugar and salt; cook 1 minute. Stir in reserved basil strips. Remove from heat.

5. Line serving plate with lettuce. Spoon chicken mixture on top. Garnish, if desired. Top with fried basil and serve immediately.
Makes 4 servings

Ginger Chicken Stir-Fry

1 whole chicken breast, skinned and boned
4 tablespoons KIKKOMAN® Teriyaki Marinade & Sauce, divided
3 teaspoons minced fresh ginger root, divided
1 cup water
2 tablespoons cornstarch
2 tablespoons vegetable oil, divided
2 carrots, cut into julienne strips
1 medium onion, sliced
¾ pound fresh spinach, washed, drained and torn in half

Cut chicken into thin strips. Combine 1 tablespoon teriyaki sauce and 2 teaspoons ginger in small bowl; stir in chicken. Let stand 10 minutes. Meanwhile, combine water, remaining 3 tablespoons teriyaki sauce, 1 teaspoon ginger and cornstarch in small bowl; set aside. Heat 1 tablespoon oil in hot wok or large skillet over high heat. Add chicken and stir-fry 2 minutes; remove. Heat remaining 1 tablespoon oil in same pan. Add carrots and onion; stir-fry 2 minutes. Add chicken and teriyaki sauce mixture; cook and stir until sauce boils and thickens. Stir in spinach; serve immediately.
Makes 4 servings

Ginger Chicken Stir-Fry

Cheesy Chicken Roll-Ups

¼ cup butter
1 medium onion, diced
4 ounces fresh mushrooms, sliced
3 boneless skinless chicken breast
    halves, cut into bite-sized pieces
¾ cup dry white wine
½ teaspoon dried tarragon leaves
½ teaspoon salt
½ teaspoon pepper
6 lasagna noodles, cooked, drained
1 package (8 ounces) cream cheese,
    softened, cubed
½ cup heavy cream
½ cup dairy sour cream
1½ cups (6 ounces) shredded Swiss
    cheese, divided
1 cup (4 ounces) shredded Muenster
    cheese, divided
3 tablespoons sliced almonds, toasted*
    Chopped parsley (optional)

To toast almonds, spread almonds into single layer on baking sheet. Bake in preheated 350°F oven 8 to 10 minutes or until golden brown, stirring frequently.

1. Preheat oven to 325°F. Grease 13×9-inch baking pan; set aside.

2. Melt butter in large skillet over medium-high heat. Add onion and mushrooms; cook and stir until tender. Add chicken, wine, tarragon, salt and pepper; bring to a boil over high heat. Reduce heat to low. Simmer 10 minutes.

3. Cut lasagna noodles in half lengthwise. Curl each half into a circle; arrange in prepared pan. With slotted spoon, fill center of lasagna rings with chicken mixture, reserving liquid in skillet.

4. To remaining liquid in skillet, add cream cheese, heavy cream, sour cream, ¾ cup Swiss cheese and ½ cup Muenster cheese. Cook and stir over medium-low heat until cheese melts. Do not boil. Pour over lasagna rings. Sprinkle remaining cheeses and almonds on top.

5. Bake 35 minutes or until bubbly. Sprinkle with parsley. Garnish as desired.

Makes 6 servings

Chicken Cacciatore

1 pound boneless, skinless chicken
    breasts, cut into strips
1 bag (16 ounces) BIRDS EYE® frozen
    Farm Fresh Mixtures Broccoli,
    Cauliflower and Carrots
1 jar (14 ounces) prepared spaghetti
    sauce
½ cup sliced black olives
¼ cup water
¼ cup grated Parmesan cheese

• Spray large skillet with nonstick cooking spray; cook chicken over medium heat 7 to 10 minutes or until browned, stirring occasionally.

• Add vegetables, spaghetti sauce, olives and water. Cover and cook 10 to 15 minutes or until vegetables are heated through.

• Sprinkle cheese over top before serving.

Makes 4 to 6 servings

Prep Time: 5 to 10 minutes
Cook Time: 20 to 25 minutes

Cheesy Chicken Roll-Ups

Chicken Biscuit Bake

BASE

1 tablespoon CRISCO® Vegetable Oil
1 cup chopped onion
¼ cup all-purpose flour
½ teaspoon salt
¼ teaspoon pepper
¼ teaspoon dried basil leaves
¼ teaspoon dried thyme leaves
2½ cups skim milk
1 tablespoon Worcestershire sauce
1 chicken-flavor bouillon cube *or*
    1 teaspoon chicken-flavor bouillon granules
2 cups chopped cooked chicken
1 bag (16 ounces) frozen mixed vegetables
2 tablespoons grated Parmesan cheese

BISCUITS

1 cup all-purpose flour
1 tablespoon sugar
1½ teaspoons baking powder
1 tablespoon chopped fresh parsley
⅛ teaspoon salt
⅓ cup skim milk
3 tablespoons CRISCO® Vegetable Oil

1. Heat oven to 375°F.

2. For base, heat Crisco® Oil in large saucepan on medium-high heat. Add onion. Cook and stir until tender. Remove from heat. Stir in flour, salt, pepper, basil and thyme. Add milk, Worcestershire sauce and bouillon cube. Return to medium-high heat. Cook and stir until mixture comes to a boil and is thickened. Stir in chicken, vegetables and cheese. Heat thoroughly, stirring occasionally. Pour into 2-quart casserole.

3. For biscuits, combine flour, sugar, baking powder, parsley and salt in medium bowl. Add milk and Crisco® Oil. Stir with fork until dry ingredients are just moistened. Drop dough by well-rounded measuring tablespoonfuls onto hot chicken mixture to form 8 biscuits.

4. Bake at 375°F for 35 to 45 minutes or until chicken mixture is bubbly and biscuits are golden brown. *Makes 8 servings*

Country Chicken Chowder

1 pound chicken tenders
2 tablespoons margarine or butter
1 small onion, chopped
1 rib celery, sliced
1 small carrot, sliced
1 can (10¾ ounces) cream of potato soup
1 cup milk
1 cup frozen corn
½ teaspoon dried dill weed

1. Cut chicken tenders into ½-inch pieces.

2. Melt margarine in large saucepan or Dutch oven over medium-high heat. Add chicken; cook and stir 5 minutes.

3. Add onion, celery and carrot; cook and stir 3 minutes. Stir in soup, milk, corn and dill; reduce heat to low. Cook about 8 minutes or until corn is tender and chowder is heated through. Add salt and pepper to taste. *Makes 4 servings*

Tip: For a special touch, garnish soup with croutons and fresh dill. For a hearty winter meal, serve the chowder in hollowed-out toasted French rolls or small round sourdough loaves.

Prep and Cook Time: 27 minutes

Country Chicken Chowder

Fancy Chicken Puff Pie

4 tablespoons butter or margarine
¼ cup chopped shallots
¼ cup all-purpose flour
1 cup chicken stock or broth
¼ cup sherry
  Salt to taste
⅛ teaspoon white pepper
  Pinch ground nutmeg
¼ pound ham, cut into 2×¼-inch strips
3 cups cooked PERDUE® Chicken, cut
  into 2¼-inch strips
1½ cups fresh asparagus pieces or
  1 (10-ounce) package frozen
  asparagus pieces
1 cup (½ pint) heavy cream
  Chilled pie crust for a 1-crust pie or
  1 sheet frozen puff pastry
1 egg, beaten

In medium saucepan, melt butter over medium-high heat. Add shallots; cook and stir until tender. Stir in flour; cook 3 minutes, stirring constantly. Add broth and sherry. Heat to boiling, stirring constantly; season to taste with salt, pepper and nutmeg. Reduce heat to low; simmer 5 minutes, stirring occasionally. Stir in ham, chicken, asparagus and cream. Pour chicken mixture into ungreased 9-inch pie plate.

Preheat oven to 425°F. Cut 8-inch circle from crust. Cut hearts from extra dough with cookie cutter, if desired. Place circle on cookie sheet moistened with cold water; pierce with fork. Brush with egg. Decorate pastry with hearts; brush hearts with egg.

Bake crust and filled pie plate 10 minutes. Reduce heat to 350°F. Bake additional 10 to 15 minutes or until pastry is golden brown and filling is hot and set. With spatula, place pastry over hot filling and serve immediately.

Makes 4 servings

First Moon Chicken Stir-Fry

3 tablespoons KIKKOMAN® Soy Sauce,
  divided
2 tablespoons cornstarch, divided
2½ teaspoons sugar, divided
1 clove garlic, pressed
2 boneless, skinless chicken breast
  halves, cut into 1-inch squares
¾ cup water
1 teaspoon distilled white vinegar
½ pound fresh broccoli, trimmed
2 tablespoons vegetable oil, divided
1 medium onion, chunked
1 small carrot, cut diagonally into thin
  slices
½ teaspoon crushed red pepper
¼ pound fresh snow peas, trimmed and
  cut diagonally into halves

Combine 1 tablespoon each soy sauce and cornstarch with ½ teaspoon sugar and garlic in medium bowl; stir in chicken. Let stand 15 minutes. Meanwhile, combine water, remaining 2 tablespoons soy sauce, 1 tablespoon cornstarch, 2 teaspoons sugar and vinegar in small bowl; set aside. Remove flowerets from broccoli; cut into bite-size pieces. Peel stalks; cut diagonally into thin slices. Heat 1 tablespoon oil in hot wok or large skillet over high heat. Add chicken and stir-fry 3 minutes; remove. Heat remaining 1 tablespoon oil in same pan. Add broccoli, onion, carrot and crushed red pepper; stir-fry 3 minutes. Add snow peas; stir-fry 2 minutes longer. Add chicken and soy sauce mixture; cook and stir until sauce boils and thickens.

Makes 4 servings

First Moon Chicken Stir-Fry

Down-Home Corn and Chicken Casserole

2 chickens (2 to 3 pounds each), each
cut into 10 pieces
3 tablespoons CHEF PAUL
PRUDHOMME'S Poultry Magic®,
divided
⅓ cup vegetable oil
8 cups fresh corn, cut off cob (about
twelve 8-inch ears), divided
3½ cups finely chopped onions
1½ cups finely chopped green bell
peppers
1 pound tomatoes, peeled, chopped
3½ cups chicken stock or water
2 cups uncooked rice (preferably
converted)

Remove excess fat from chickens; season
chicken pieces with 2 tablespoons Poultry
Magic® and place in plastic bag. Seal and
refrigerate overnight.

Remove chickens from refrigerator; bring
to room temperature. Heat oil in 8-quart
roasting pan over high heat until it begins
to smoke, about 6 minutes. Add 10 largest
pieces of chicken, skin side down; brown 5
minutes on each side. Remove chicken and
reheat oil about 1 minute or until oil stops
sizzling. Brown remaining chicken 5 minutes
on each side. Remove and keep warm.

Add half of corn to hot oil. Scrape bottom
of pan well to incorporate browned chicken
bits; mix well. Cook corn without stirring
about 6 minutes or until brown. Add 1½
teaspoons Poultry Magic® and stir to
combine. Cook, without stirring, about 7
minutes to continue browning. Stir in
onions, bell peppers and remaining 1½
teaspoons Poultry Magic®. Cover with tight-
fitting lid and cook about 5 minutes. Add
remaining corn and tomatoes. Stir to mix
well; cover and cook 10 minutes. Transfer
corn mixture to another pan and keep
warm. Preheat oven to 400°F.

Add stock or water and rice to roasting pan.
Bring to a boil, stirring occasionally. Layer
chicken pieces on top of rice and cover
chicken layer with corn mixture. Cover and
bake 25 minutes.

Remove casserole from oven. Let stand 10
minutes, covered, before serving.

Makes 8 servings

Country Chicken Stew

2 tablespoons butter or margarine
1 pound boneless skinless chicken
breasts, cut into 1-inch cubes
½ pound small red potatoes, cut into
½-inch cubes
2 tablespoons cooking sherry
2 jars (12 ounces each) golden chicken
gravy
1 bag (16 ounces) BIRDS EYE® frozen
Farm Fresh Mixtures Broccoli,
Green Beans, Pearl Onions and Red
Peppers
½ cup water

• Melt butter in large saucepan over high
heat. Add chicken and potatoes; cook about
8 minutes or until browned, stirring
frequently.

• Add sherry; cook until evaporated. Add
gravy, vegetables and water.

• Bring to boil; reduce heat to medium-low.
Cover and cook 5 minutes.

Makes 4 to 6 servings

Prep Time: 5 minutes

Cook Time: 20 minutes

Country Chicken Stew

Chicken Thighs with Peas

8 boneless skinless chicken thighs
2 tablespoons vegetable oil
2 tablespoons reduced-sodium
  soy sauce
2 tablespoons dry sherry
1 teaspoon ground ginger
1 teaspoon sugar
¼ teaspoon garlic powder
½ small head iceberg lettuce
1 cup reduced-sodium chicken broth
2 tablespoons cornstarch
1 package (10 ounces) frozen green
  peas, partially thawed
  Hot cooked rice
  Red onion slices, shredded red
  cabbage and steamed snow peas
  for garnish

• Rinse chicken and pat dry with paper towels. Cut chicken into 1-inch pieces.

• Heat wok over high heat about 1 minute or until hot. Drizzle oil into wok and heat 30 seconds. Add chicken; stir-fry about 4 minutes or until chicken is well browned and no longer pink in center. Reduce heat to low. Stir in soy sauce, sherry, ginger, sugar and garlic powder. Cover and cook 5 minutes.

• Meanwhile, cut lettuce into ½-inch-wide slices. Rinse, drain and pat dry. Stir broth into cornstarch in cup until smooth. Set aside.

• Increase heat to high. Stir peas into chicken mixture. Cover and cook about 2 minutes or until heated through. Stir broth mixture until smooth; stir into chicken mixture. Heat until sauce boils and thickens. Add lettuce; stir-fry until wilted. Transfer to serving dish. Serve with rice. Garnish, if desired.   *Makes 4 to 6 servings*

Bayou-Style Pot Pie

1 tablespoon olive oil
1 large onion, chopped
1 green bell pepper, chopped
1½ teaspoons minced garlic
8 ounces boneless skinless chicken
  thighs, cut into 1-inch pieces
1 can (14½ ounces) stewed tomatoes,
  undrained
8 ounces fully cooked smoked sausage
  or kielbasa, thinly sliced
¾ teaspoon hot pepper sauce or to
  taste
2¼ cups buttermilk baking mix
¾ teaspoon dried thyme leaves
⅛ teaspoon black pepper
⅔ cup milk

1. Preheat oven to 450°F. Heat oil in medium ovenproof skillet over medium-high heat until hot. Add onion, bell pepper and garlic. Cook 3 minutes, stirring occasionally.

2. Add chicken and cook 1 minute. Add tomatoes with juice, sausage and hot pepper sauce. Cook, uncovered, over medium-low heat 5 minutes.

3. While chicken is cooking, combine baking mix, thyme and black pepper. Stir in milk. Drop batter by heaping tablespoonfuls in mounds over chicken mixture. Bake 14 minutes or until biscuits are golden brown and cooked through and chicken mixture is bubbly.   *Makes 4 servings*

Note: You may use any of a variety of fully cooked sausages from your supermarket meat case. Andouille, a fairly spicy Louisiana-style sausage, is perfect for this dish.

Prep and Cook Time: 28 minutes

Chicken Thighs with Peas

Chicken and Zucchini Casserole

3 cups STOVE TOP® Chicken Flavor or Cornbread Stuffing Mix in the Canister
3 tablespoons margarine or butter, divided
1¼ cups hot water
¾ pound boneless skinless chicken breasts, cubed
2 medium zucchini, cut into ½-inch pieces
1½ cups (6 ounces) shredded Cheddar cheese
1 can (8 ounces) water chestnuts, drained, halved (optional)
½ teaspoon dried basil leaves
¼ teaspoon pepper

MIX stuffing mix, 2 tablespoons of the margarine and water in large bowl just until margarine is melted and stuffing mix is moistened.

PLACE chicken, zucchini and remaining 1 tablespoon margarine in 3-quart microwavable casserole. Cover loosely with wax paper.

MICROWAVE on HIGH 4 minutes, stirring halfway through cooking time. Stir in prepared stuffing, cheese, water chestnuts, basil and pepper until well mixed. Cover.

MICROWAVE 10 minutes, stirring halfway through cooking time. Let stand 5 minutes.

Makes 6 servings

Prep Time: 10 minutes
Cook Time: 20 minutes

Polynesian Chicken and Rice

1 can (20 ounces) DOLE® Pineapple Tidbits or Pineapple Chunks
½ cup DOLE® Seedless or Golden Raisins
½ cup sliced DOLE® Green Onions
2 teaspoons finely chopped fresh ginger *or* ½ teaspoon ground ginger
1 garlic clove, finely chopped
3 cups cooked white or brown rice
2 cups chopped cooked chicken breast or turkey breast
2 tablespoons low-sodium soy sauce

• Drain pineapple; reserve 4 tablespoons juice.

• Heat 2 tablespoons reserved juice over medium heat in large, nonstick skillet. Add raisins, green onions, ginger and garlic; cook and stir 3 minutes.

• Stir in pineapple, rice, chicken, soy sauce and remaining 2 tablespoons juice. Cover; reduce heat to low and cook 5 minutes more or until heated through. Garnish with cherry tomatoes and green onions, if desired.

Makes 4 servings

Prep Time: 20 minutes
Cook Time: 10 minutes

Polynesian Chicken and Rice

CHICKEN & TURKEY FAVORITES

Teriyaki Chicken Medley

2 cups cooked white rice (about ¾ cup uncooked)
2 cups (10 ounces) cooked chicken, cut into strips
1⅓ cups FRENCH'S® French Fried Onions, divided
1 package (12 ounces) frozen bell pepper strips, thawed and drained*
1 jar (12 ounces) chicken gravy
3 tablespoons teriyaki sauce

*Or, substitute 2 cups sliced bell peppers for frozen pepper strips.

Preheat oven to 400°F. Grease 2-quart oblong baking dish. Press rice into bottom of prepared baking dish.

Combine chicken, ⅔ cup French Fried Onions, bell pepper strips, gravy and teriyaki sauce in large bowl; mix well. Pour mixture over rice layer. Cover; bake 30 minutes or until heated through. Top with remaining ⅔ cup onions. Bake 1 minute or until onions are golden. *Makes 4 to 6 servings*

Prep Time: 10 minutes
Cook Time: 31 minutes

Golden Chicken and Vegetables

1 boneless, skinless chicken breast half
1 teaspoon KIKKOMAN® Stir-Fry Sauce
3 tablespoons vegetable oil, divided
1 medium onion, thinly sliced
1 large clove garlic, slivered
2 carrots, cut into julienne strips
1 stalk celery, cut diagonally into thin slices
¼ cup KIKKOMAN® Stir-Fry Sauce
1 tablespoon water
1 tablespoon sesame seed, toasted
½ teaspoon Oriental sesame oil

Cut chicken into thin narrow strips; coat with 1 teaspoon stir-fry sauce in small bowl. Heat 1 tablespoon vegetable oil in hot wok or large skillet over medium-high heat. Add chicken and stir-fry 2 minutes; remove. Heat remaining 2 tablespoons oil in same pan. Add onion and garlic; stir-fry 2 minutes. Add carrots and celery; stir-fry 2 minutes longer. Combine ¼ cup stir-fry sauce and water; add to pan with chicken and sesame seed. Cook, stirring, until chicken and vegetables are coated with sauce and heated through. Remove from heat; stir in sesame oil.
Makes 4 servings

"Wildly" Delicious Casserole

1 package (14 ounces) ground chicken
1 package (14 ounces) frozen broccoli with red peppers
1½ cups cooked wild rice
1 can (10¾ ounces) condensed cream of chicken soup
½ cup mayonnaise
½ cup plain yogurt
1 teaspoon lemon juice
½ teaspoon curry powder
¼ cup dry bread crumbs
3 to 4 slices process American cheese, cut in half diagonally

Preheat oven to 375°F. Grease 8-inch square casserole; set aside. In large skillet, cook chicken until no longer pink. Drain; set aside. Cook broccoli and peppers according to package directions; set aside. In large bowl, combine rice, soup, mayonnaise, yogurt, lemon juice and curry. Stir in chicken and broccoli and peppers. Pour into prepared casserole; sprinkle with bread crumbs. Bake 45 to 55 minutes. During last 5 minutes of baking, arrange cheese slices on top of casserole. Remove from oven; let stand 5 minutes. *Makes 6 to 8 servings*

Favorite recipe from **Minnesota Cultivated Wild Rice Council**

Arizona Turkey Stew

3 tablespoons olive oil or vegetable oil
5 medium carrots, cut into thick slices
1 large onion, cut into ½-inch pieces
1 pound sliced turkey breast, cut into 1-inch strips
1 teaspoon LAWRY'S® Garlic Powder with Parsley
3 tablespoons all-purpose flour
8 small red potatoes, cut into ½-inch cubes
1 package (10 ounces) frozen peas, thawed
8 ounces sliced fresh mushrooms
1 cup beef broth
1 can (8 ounces) tomato sauce
1 package (1.48 ounces) LAWRY'S® Spices & Seasonings for Chili

In large skillet, heat oil; cook carrots and onion over medium heat until tender. Stir in turkey strips and Garlic Powder with Parsley; cook additional 3 to 5 minutes or until turkey is just browned. Stir in flour. Pour mixture into 3-quart casserole dish. Stir in remaining ingredients. Bake, covered, in 450°F oven 40 to 45 minutes or until potatoes are tender and turkey is no longer pink in center. Let stand 5 minutes before serving.   *Makes 8 to 10 servings*

Serving Suggestion: Serve with warmed flour tortillas.

Hint: To prepare on the stovetop, use a Dutch oven. Bring mixture to a boil over medium-high heat; reduce heat to low; cover and cook 40 to 45 minutes or until potatoes are tender and turkey is no longer pink in center. Let stand 5 minutes before serving.

Turkey Tetrazzini

½ pound fresh mushrooms, sliced
¼ cup sliced green onions
1 tablespoon margarine
2 tablespoons all-purpose flour
¼ teaspoon black pepper
1 (12-ounce) can light evaporated skim milk
⅓ cup low-sodium chicken broth
2 tablespoons sherry (optional)
8 ounces spaghetti
1 (8-ounce) package HEALTHY CHOICE® Fat Free natural shredded Mozzarella Cheese
1 pound turkey breast, cooked, cut into strips

Heat oven to 375°F. Cook mushrooms and green onions in margarine, stirring occasionally, until mushrooms are tender, about 7 minutes. Stir in flour and pepper. Cook and stir 1 minute. Add evaporated milk, chicken broth and sherry. Cook, stirring occasionally until sauce is thickened. Remove from heat. Cook spaghetti according to package directions. Drain, rinse and keep spaghetti warm. In 2-quart casserole sprayed with nonstick cooking spray, layer half of cooked spaghetti, cheese, turkey strips and sauce. Repeat layers with remaining ingredients. Bake at 375°F for 25 to 30 minutes or until bubbly and hot.
Makes 6 servings

Turkey Vegetable Chili Mac

Nonstick cooking spray
¾ pound ground turkey breast
½ cup chopped onion
2 cloves garlic, minced
1 can (about 15 ounces) black beans,
 rinsed and drained
1 can (14½ ounces) Mexican-style
 stewed tomatoes, undrained
1 can (14½ ounces) no-salt-added
 diced tomatoes, undrained
1 cup frozen whole kernel corn
1 teaspoon Mexican seasoning
½ cup uncooked elbow macaroni
⅓ cup reduced-fat sour cream

1. Spray large nonstick saucepan or Dutch oven with cooking spray; heat over medium heat until hot. Add turkey, onion and garlic; cook 5 minutes or until turkey is no longer pink, stirring to crumble.

2. Stir beans, tomatoes with liquid, corn and Mexican seasoning into saucepan; bring to a boil over high heat. Cover; reduce heat to low. Simmer 15 minutes, stirring occasionally.

3. Meanwhile, cook pasta according to package directions, omitting salt. Rinse and drain pasta; stir into saucepan. Simmer, uncovered, 2 to 3 minutes or until heated through.

4. Top each serving with dollop of sour cream. Garnish as desired.

Makes 6 servings

Turkey Olé

½ cup minced onions
2 tablespoons butter or margarine
1 tablespoon all-purpose flour
1½ cups cubed cooked turkey
1½ cups prepared HIDDEN VALLEY®
 Original Ranch® Salad Dressing
3 ounces rotini (spiral macaroni),
 plain or spinach, cooked
½ (10-ounce) package frozen peas,
 thawed
⅓ cup canned diced green chiles,
 drained
⅛ to ¼ teaspoon black pepper
 (optional)
1 teaspoon dried oregano, crushed
3 tablespoons dry bread crumbs
1 tablespoon butter or margarine,
 melted
Tomato wedges

Preheat oven to 350°F. In skillet, sauté onions in 2 tablespoons butter until tender. Stir in flour and cook until smooth and bubbly; remove from heat. In 1½-quart casserole, combine turkey, salad dressing, rotini, peas, chiles, pepper and oregano; stir in onions. In small bowl, combine bread crumbs with melted butter; sprinkle over casserole. Bake until heated through and bread crumbs are browned, 15 to 20 minutes. Garnish with tomato wedges.

Makes 6 servings

Turkey Vegetable Chili Mac

Turnip Shepherd's Pie

1 pound small turnips,* peeled and
    cut into ½-inch cubes
1 pound lean ground turkey
⅓ cup dry bread crumbs
¼ cup chopped onion
¼ cup ketchup
1 egg
½ teaspoon *each* salt, pepper and beau
    monde seasoning
⅓ cup half-and-half
1 tablespoon butter or margarine
    Salt and pepper
1 tablespoon chopped fresh parsley
¼ cup shredded sharp Cheddar cheese

For Rutabaga Shepherd's Pie, use 1 pound rutabagas in place of turnips.

Preheat oven to 400°F. Place turnips in large saucepan; cover with water. Cover and bring to a boil; reduce heat to medium-low. Simmer 20 minutes or until fork-tender.

Mix turkey, crumbs, onion, ketchup, egg, salt, pepper and seasoning. Pat on bottom and side of 9-inch pie pan. Bake 20 to 30 minutes until turkey is no longer pink. Blot with paper towel to remove any drippings.

Drain cooked turnips. Mash turnips with electric mixer until smooth, blending in half-and-half and butter. Season with salt and pepper to taste. Fill meat shell with turnip mixture; sprinkle with parsley, then cheese. Return to oven until cheese melts. Garnish as desired.   *Makes 4 main-dish servings*

Turkey Cazuela

8 ounces uncooked linguini, broken in
    half*
1⅓ cups FRENCH'S® French Fried Onions,
    divided
2 cups (10 ounces) cubed cooked
    turkey
1 can (10¾ ounces) condensed cream
    of chicken soup
1 jar (8 ounces) picante sauce
½ cup sour cream
1 cup (4 ounces) shredded Cheddar
    cheese

Or, substitute 4 cups cooked pasta for uncooked linguini.

Preheat oven to 350°F. Grease 2-quart shallow baking dish. Cook linguini according to package directions, using shortest cooking time. Layer linguini, ⅔ cup French Fried Onions and turkey in prepared baking dish.

Combine soup, picante sauce and sour cream in large bowl. Pour over turkey.

Cover; bake 40 minutes or until hot and bubbling. Stir gently. Sprinkle with cheese and remaining ⅔ cup onions. Bake 5 minutes or until onions are golden.
                    Makes 4 to 6 servings

Prep Time: 20 minutes
Cook Time: 45 minutes

Turnip Shepherd's Pie

Matchstick Stir Fry

1 package BUTTERBALL® Fresh Boneless Turkey Breast Strips
1 tablespoon cornstarch
1 cup orange juice
1 tablespoon reduced sodium soy sauce
1 clove garlic, minced
2 teaspoons grated orange peel
2 teaspoons minced fresh ginger
1 teaspoon sugar
½ teaspoon salt
¼ teaspoon red pepper flakes
1 tablespoon vegetable oil
¼ pound snow peas, trimmed
2 small carrots, cut into thin strips
1 small onion, cut into strips
1 small red bell pepper, cut into thin strips
2 oranges, peeled and sectioned

Combine cornstarch, orange juice, soy sauce, garlic, orange peel, ginger, sugar, salt and red pepper flakes in small bowl. Stir until mixture is smooth; set aside. Heat oil in large skillet or wok over high heat until hot; add turkey. Cook and stir 4 to 5 minutes or until turkey is no longer pink; remove from skillet. Add snow peas, carrots, onion and bell pepper. Cook and stir 1 minute; remove from skillet. Add cornstarch mixture to skillet. Cook and stir until mixture thickens; add turkey and vegetables. Reduce heat to low; simmer, covered, 1 minute. Add orange sections. Serve with almond rice, if desired.

Makes 6 servings

Note: If short on time, substitute packaged frozen stir-fry blend vegetables for fresh vegetables.

Preparation Time: 20 minutes

Manhattan Turkey à la King

8 ounces wide egg noodles
1 pound boneless turkey or chicken, cut into strips
1 tablespoon vegetable oil
1 can (14½ ounces) DEL MONTE® Pasta Style Chunky Tomatoes
1 can (10¾ ounces) condensed cream of celery soup
1 medium onion, chopped
2 stalks celery, sliced
1 cup sliced mushrooms

1. Cook noodles according to package directions; drain. In large skillet, brown turkey in oil over medium-high heat. Season with salt and pepper, if desired.

2. Add remaining ingredients, except noodles. Cover and cook over medium heat 5 minutes.

3. Remove cover; cook 5 minutes or until thickened, stirring occasionally. Serve over hot noodles. Garnish with chopped parsley, if desired.   *Makes 6 servings*

Hint: Cook pasta ahead; rinse and drain. Cover and refrigerate. Just before serving, heat in microwave or dip in boiling water.

Prep Time: 7 minutes

Cook Time: 20 minutes

Manhattan Turkey à la King

126

Creamy Turkey & Broccoli

1 package (6 ounces) stuffing mix, plus
   ingredients to prepare mix*
1⅓ cups FRENCH'S® French Fried Onions,
   divided
1 package (10 ounces) frozen broccoli
   spears, thawed and drained
1 package (about 1⅛ ounces) cheese
   sauce mix
1¼ cups milk
½ cup sour cream
2 cups (10 ounces) cubed cooked
   turkey or chicken

3 cups leftover stuffing may be substituted for stuffing mix. If stuffing is dry, stir in water, 1 tablespoon at a time, until moist but not wet.

Preheat oven to 350°F. In medium saucepan, prepare stuffing mix according to package directions; stir in ⅔ cup French Fried Onions. Spread stuffing over bottom of greased 9-inch round baking dish. Arrange broccoli spears over stuffing with flowerets around edge of dish. In medium saucepan, prepare cheese sauce mix according to package directions using 1¼ cups milk. Remove from heat; stir in sour cream and turkey. Pour turkey mixture over broccoli stalks. Bake, covered, at 350° for 30 minutes or until heated through. Sprinkle remaining ⅔ cup onions over turkey; bake, uncovered, 5 minutes or until onions are golden brown.

Makes 4 to 6 servings

Microwave Directions: In 9-inch round microwave-safe dish, prepare stuffing mix according to package microwave directions; stir in ⅔ cup onions. Arrange stuffing and broccoli spears in dish as above; set aside. In medium microwave-safe bowl, prepare cheese sauce mix according to package microwave directions using 1¼ cups milk. Add turkey and cook, covered, 5 to 6 minutes, stirring turkey halfway through cooking time. Stir in sour cream. Pour turkey mixture over broccoli stalks. Cook, covered, 8 to 10 minutes or until heated through. Rotate dish halfway through cooking time. Top turkey with remaining ⅔ cup onions; cook, uncovered, 1 minute. Let stand 5 minutes.

Turkey and Rice Quiche

3 cups cooked rice, cooled to room
   temperature
1½ cups chopped cooked turkey
1 medium tomato, seeded and finely
   diced
¼ cup sliced green onions
¼ cup finely diced green bell pepper
1 tablespoon chopped fresh basil *or*
   1 teaspoon dried basil leaves
½ teaspoon seasoned salt
⅛ to ¼ teaspoon ground red pepper
½ cup skim milk
3 eggs, beaten
   Vegetable cooking spray
½ cup (2 ounces) shredded Cheddar
   cheese
½ cup (2 ounces) shredded mozzarella
   cheese

Combine rice, turkey, tomato, onions, bell pepper, basil, salt, red pepper, milk and eggs in 13×9×2-inch pan coated with cooking spray. Top with cheeses. Bake at 375°F for 20 minutes or until knife inserted near center comes out clean. To serve, cut quiche into 8 squares; cut each square diagonally into 2 triangles.

Makes 8 servings (2 triangles each)

Favorite recipe from **USA Rice Federation**

Turkey and Rice Quiche

20-Minute White Bean Chili

1 cup chopped onions
1 clove garlic, minced
1 tablespoon vegetable oil
1 pound ground turkey
1 cup COLLEGE INN® Chicken Broth or Lower Sodium Chicken Broth
1 (14½-ounce) can stewed tomatoes
⅓ cup GREY POUPON® Dijon Mustard
1 tablespoon chili powder
⅛ to ¼ teaspoon ground red pepper
1 (15-ounce) can cannellini beans, drained and rinsed
1 (8-ounce) can corn, drained
Tortilla chips, shredded Cheddar cheese and cilantro, optional

In 3-quart saucepan, over medium-high heat, sauté onions and garlic in oil until tender. Add turkey; cook until done, stirring occasionally to break up meat. Drain. Stir in chicken broth, tomatoes, mustard, chili powder and pepper. Heat to a boil; reduce heat. Simmer for 10 minutes. Stir in beans and corn; cook for 5 minutes. Top with tortilla chips, shredded cheese and cilantro, if desired.   *Makes 6 servings*

Turkey with Mustard Sauce

1 tablespoon butter or margarine
1 pound turkey cutlets
1 cup BIRDS EYE® frozen Mixed Vegetables
1 box (10 ounces) BIRDS EYE® frozen Pearl Onions in Cream Sauce
1 teaspoon spicy brown mustard

• In large nonstick skillet, melt butter over medium-high heat. Add turkey; cook until browned on both sides.

• Add mixed vegetables, onions with cream sauce and mustard; bring to boil. Reduce heat to medium-low; cover and simmer 6 to 8 minutes or until vegetables are tender and turkey is no longer pink in center.
Makes 4 servings

Serving Suggestion: Serve with a fresh garden salad.

Prep Time: 5 minutes

Cook Time: 15 minutes

One-Dish Meal

2 bags SUCCESS® Rice
Vegetable cooking spray
1 cup cubed cooked turkey-ham*
1 cup (4 ounces) shredded low-fat Cheddar cheese
1 cup peas

*Or, use cooked turkey, ham or turkey franks. Prepare rice according to package directions.

Spray 1-quart microwave-safe dish with cooking spray; set aside. Place rice in medium bowl. Add ham, cheese and peas; mix lightly. Spoon into prepared dish; smooth into even layer with spoon. Microwave on HIGH 1 minute; stir. Microwave 30 seconds or until thoroughly heated.   *Makes 4 servings*

Conventional: Assemble casserole as directed. Spoon into ovenproof 1-quart baking dish sprayed with vegetable cooking spray. Bake at 350°F until thoroughly heated, about 15 to 20 minutes.

20-Minute White Bean Chili

Turkey-Spinach Manicotti

1 package (1.5 ounces) LAWRY'S®
    Original Style Spaghetti Sauce
    Spices & Seasoning
1 can (28 ounces) whole tomatoes,
    cut up
1 can (8 ounces) tomato sauce
¼ cup chopped green onions
1 cup ricotta cheese
2 cups chopped fresh spinach
2 cups cooked, minced turkey or
    chicken
2 tablespoons milk
1 teaspoon LAWRY'S® Seasoned Pepper
½ teaspoon LAWRY'S® Garlic Powder
    with Parsley
8 manicotti shells, cooked and drained
⅓ cup grated Parmesan cheese

In medium saucepan, combine Spaghetti
Sauce Spices & Seasoning, tomatoes,
tomato sauce and onions. Bring to a boil
over medium-high heat; reduce heat to low
and cook, covered, 20 minutes, stirring
occasionally. In medium bowl, combine
ricotta cheese, spinach, turkey, milk,
Seasoned Pepper and Garlic Powder with
Parsley; mix well. Carefully spoon mixture
into manicotti shells. Pour ½ of sauce in
bottom of 12×8×2-inch baking dish. Place
stuffed shells on top of sauce; pour
remaining sauce over shells. Cover and bake
in 375°F oven 30 minutes or until heated
through. Sprinkle with Parmesan cheese.
Makes 4 to 8 servings

Serving Suggestion: Sprinkle with chopped
parsley. Garnish with fresh basil leaves. Serve
with garlic bread.

Hint: 1 package (10 ounces) frozen
chopped spinach, thawed and drained,
can be substituted for the fresh spinach.

Homespun Turkey 'n' Vegetables

1 package (9 ounces) frozen cut green
    beans, thawed and drained
1 can (14 ounces) sliced carrots,
    drained
1⅓ cups FRENCH'S® French Fried Onions,
    divided
1 can (16 ounces) whole potatoes,
    drained
1 can (10¾ ounces) condensed cream
    of celery soup
¼ cup milk
1 tablespoon FRENCH'S® Classic
    Yellow® Mustard
¼ teaspoon garlic powder
1 pound uncooked turkey breast slices

Preheat oven to 375°F. In 12×8-inch baking
dish, combine green beans, carrots and
⅔ cup French Fried Onions. Slice potatoes
into halves; arrange as many halves as will
fit, cut side down, around edges of baking
dish. Combine any remaining potatoes with
vegetables in dish. In medium bowl,
combine soup, milk, mustard and garlic
powder; pour half the soup mixture over
vegetables. Overlap turkey slices on
vegetables. Pour remaining soup mixture
over turkey and potatoes. Bake, covered, at
375° for 40 minutes or until turkey is done.
Top turkey with remaining ⅔ cup onions;
bake, uncovered, 3 minutes or until onions
are golden brown.   *Makes 4 servings*

Turkey-Spinach Manicotti

Rice Lasagna

1 bag SUCCESS® Rice
    Vegetable cooking spray
2 tablespoons reduced-calorie
    margarine
1 pound ground turkey
1 cup chopped onion
1 cup sliced fresh mushrooms
1 clove garlic, minced
2 cans (8 ounces each) no-salt-added
    tomato sauce
1 can (6 ounces) no-salt-added tomato
    paste
1 teaspoon dried oregano leaves,
    crushed
1 carton (15 ounces) lowfat cottage
    cheese
½ cup (2 ounces) grated Parmesan
    cheese
2 cups (8 ounces) shredded mozzarella
    cheese
1 tablespoon dried parsley flakes

Prepare rice according to package directions.

Preheat oven to 350°F.

Spray 13×9-inch baking dish with cooking spray; set aside. Melt margarine in large skillet over medium heat. Add ground turkey, onion, mushrooms and garlic; cook until turkey is no longer pink and vegetables are tender, stirring occasionally to separate turkey. Drain. Stir in tomato sauce, tomato paste and oregano; simmer 15 minutes, stirring occasionally. Layer half each of rice, turkey mixture, cottage cheese, Parmesan cheese and mozzarella cheese in prepared baking dish; repeat layers. Sprinkle with parsley; cover. Bake 30 minutes. Uncover; continue baking 15 minutes.

Makes 8 servings

Garden Patch Turkey Stew with Dumplings

3 cups cubed cooked BUTTERBALL®
    Turkey (1 pound)
1 medium onion, sliced
2 ribs celery, sliced
2 tablespoons butter or margarine
2 cups coarsely chopped cabbage
1 can (14½ ounces) tomatoes,
    undrained, cut up
1 can (15 ounces) kidney beans,
    undrained
2 cans (13¾ ounces each) chicken
    broth
1 cup water
2 tablespoons sugar
1½ teaspoons dried marjoram leaves,
    crushed
1 teaspoon salt
2 cups buttermilk baking mix
⅔ cup milk

Cook and stir onion and celery in butter in Dutch oven or large saucepan over medium heat until crisp-tender. Add turkey, cabbage, tomatoes, beans, broth, water, sugar, marjoram and salt. Cover; reduce heat to low and simmer 25 minutes or until cabbage is tender. Place baking mix in medium bowl. Stir in milk with fork until soft dough forms. Bring stew to a boil over high heat. Drop dough by spoonfuls into boiling stew to make 12 dumplings. Reduce heat to low. Cover and simmer 15 minutes. Serve in bowls.   *Makes 6 to 8 servings (12 cups)*

Rice Lasagna

Turkey 'n Stuffing Pie

1¼ cups water
¼ cup butter or margarine
3½ cups seasoned stuffing crumbs*
1⅓ cups FRENCH'S® French Fried Onions
1 can (10¾ ounces) condensed cream of celery soup
¾ cup milk
1½ cups (7 ounces) cubed cooked turkey
1 package (10 ounces) frozen peas, thawed and drained

*3 cups leftover stuffing may be substituted for water, butter and stuffing crumbs. If stuffing is dry, stir in water, 1 tablespoon at a time, until moist but not wet.

Preheat oven to 350°F. In medium saucepan, heat water and butter; stir until butter melts. Remove from heat. Stir in seasoned stuffing crumbs and ⅔ cup French Fried Onions. Spoon stuffing mixture into 9-inch round or fluted baking dish. Press stuffing evenly across bottom and up sides of dish to form a shell. In medium bowl, combine soup, milk, turkey and peas; pour into stuffing shell. Bake, covered, at 350°F for 30 minutes or until heated through. Top with remaining ⅔ cup onions; bake, uncovered, 5 minutes or until onions are golden brown.

Makes 4 to 6 servings

Microwave Directions: In 9-inch round or fluted microwave-safe dish, place water and butter. Cook, covered, on HIGH 3 minutes or until butter melts. Stir in stuffing crumbs and ⅔ cup onions. Press stuffing mixture into dish as above. Reduce milk to ½ cup. In large microwave-safe bowl, combine soup, milk, turkey and peas; cook, covered, 8 minutes. Stir turkey mixture halfway through cooking time. Pour turkey mixture into stuffing shell. Cook, uncovered, 4 to 6 minutes or until heated through. Rotate dish halfway through cooking time. Top with remaining ⅔ cup onions; cook, uncovered, 1 minute. Let stand 5 minutes.

Easy Tex-Mex Bake

8 ounces uncooked thin mostaccioli
1 pound ground turkey breast
⅔ cup bottled medium or mild salsa
1 package (10 ounces) frozen corn, thawed, drained
1 container (16 ounces) low-fat cottage cheese
1 egg
1 tablespoon minced fresh cilantro
½ teaspoon ground white pepper
¼ teaspoon ground cumin
½ cup (2 ounces) shredded Monterey Jack cheese

1. Cook pasta according to package directions. Drain and rinse well; set aside.

2. Spray large nonstick skillet with nonstick cooking spray. Add turkey; cook until no longer pink, about 5 minutes. Stir in salsa and corn. Remove from heat.

3. Preheat oven to 350°F. Combine cottage cheese, egg, cilantro, white pepper and cumin in small bowl.

4. Spoon ½ turkey mixture in bottom of 11×7-inch baking dish. Top with pasta. Spoon cottage cheese mixture over pasta. Top with remaining turkey mixture. Sprinkle Monterey Jack cheese over casserole.

5. Bake 25 to 30 minutes or until heated through. *Makes 6 servings*

Easy Tex-Mex Bake

Turkey Parmesan

⅔ cup milk
2 tablespoons margarine or butter
2 cups zucchini slices, halved
1 package (5.1 ounces) PASTA RONI® Angel Hair Pasta with Parmesan Cheese
2 cups cooked turkey strips
1 jar (2 ounces) chopped pimentos, drained
2 tablespoons grated Parmesan cheese

1. In round 3-quart microwavable glass casserole, combine 1½ cups water, milk, margarine and zucchini. Microwave, uncovered, on HIGH 6 minutes.

2. Stir in pasta, contents of seasoning packet and turkey. Separate pasta with a fork, if needed.

3. Microwave, uncovered, on HIGH 7 to 8 minutes, stirring after 2 minutes. Separate pasta with a fork, if needed.

4. Sauce will be very thin, but will thicken upon standing. Stir in pimentos and cheese.

5. Let stand 3 to 4 minutes or until desired consistency. Stir before serving.

Makes 4 servings

Tomato and Turkey Soup with Pesto

1 cup uncooked rotini pasta
1 can (10¾ ounces) reduced-sodium tomato soup
1 cup fat-free (skim) milk
2 cups (8 ounces) frozen Italian-style vegetables
2 tablespoons prepared pesto
1 cup coarsely chopped skinless cooked turkey
2 tablespoons grated Parmesan cheese

1. Cook pasta according to package directions. Drain and rinse well under cold water until pasta is cool; drain well.

2. Meanwhile, combine soup, milk, vegetables and pesto in medium saucepan. Bring to a boil over medium heat; reduce heat to low. Simmer, covered, 10 minutes or until vegetables are tender. Add pasta and turkey. Cook 3 minutes or until heated through. Sprinkle with cheese just before serving.

Makes 4 servings

Country Wild Rice Casserole

1 cup chopped onion
¼ cup butter or margarine
1¼ pounds ground turkey
¼ teaspoon black pepper
4 cups frozen potatoes O'Brien with onions and peppers, thawed
3 cups cooked wild rice
2 cups shredded mild Cheddar cheese, divided
1 can (10¾ ounces) condensed cream of chicken soup
1 cup sour cream
⅓ cup bread crumbs

Preheat oven to 350°F. In large skillet, sauté onion in butter; remove from skillet. In same skillet, brown turkey. Sprinkle with pepper. Spread potatoes in greased 13×9-inch baking pan. Combine onion, turkey, wild rice, 1½ cups cheese, soup and sour cream in large bowl. Spread onion mixture over potatoes. Sprinkle remaining ½ cup cheese and bread crumbs on top. Bake 40 minutes.

Makes 8 servings

*Favorite recipe from **Minnesota Cultivated Wild Rice Council***

Turkey Parmesan

SEAFOOD SUPPERS

Fish Creole

1 pound fresh or thawed frozen snapper or sole fillets
1 bag (16 ounces) BIRDS EYE® frozen Farm Fresh Mixtures Broccoli, Green Beans, Pearl Onions & Red Peppers
1 can (16 ounces) tomato sauce
1 tablespoon dried oregano or Italian seasoning
1 tablespoon vegetable oil
1½ teaspoons salt

• Preheat oven to 350°F.

• Place fish in 13×9-inch baking pan.

• In large bowl, combine vegetables, tomato sauce, oregano, oil and salt.

• Pour vegetable mixture over fish.

• Bake 20 minutes or until fish flakes easily when tested with fork.   *Makes 4 servings*

Birds Eye Idea: To remove fish odor from your hands after handling fish, rub your hands with salt and then wash them with cold water.

Prep Time: 5 minutes
Cook Time: 20 minutes

Sole Almondine

1 package (6.5 ounces) RICE-A-RONI® Broccoli Au Gratin
1 medium zucchini
4 sole, scrod or orange roughy fillets
1 tablespoon lemon juice
¼ cup grated Parmesan cheese
   Salt and pepper (optional)
¼ cup sliced almonds
2 tablespoons margarine or butter, melted

1. Prepare Rice-A-Roni® Mix as package directs.

2. While Rice-A-Roni® is simmering, cut zucchini lengthwise into 12 thin slices. Heat oven to 350°F.

3. In 11×7-inch glass baking dish, spread prepared rice evenly. Set aside. Sprinkle fish with lemon juice, 2 tablespoons cheese, salt and pepper, if desired. Place zucchini strips over fish; roll up. Place fish seam-side down on rice.

4. Combine almonds and margarine; sprinkle evenly over fish. Top with remaining 2 tablespoons cheese. Bake 20 to 25 minutes or until fish flakes easily with fork.
Makes 4 servings

Fish Creole

Pescado Viejo (Fish Stew)

1 tablespoon vegetable oil
2 medium onions, chopped
1 green bell pepper, finely chopped
2 cans (14½ ounces each) whole
     peeled tomatoes, undrained and
     cut up
1 large red potato, cubed
1 can (13¾ ounces) beef broth
⅓ cup red wine
1 bay leaf
1 package (1.5 ounces) LAWRY'S®
     Original Style Spaghetti Sauce
     Spices & Seasonings
¾ teaspoon LAWRY'S® Garlic Powder
     with Parsley
½ teaspoon LAWRY'S® Seasoned Salt
½ teaspoon celery seed
1 pound halibut or swordfish steaks,
     rinsed and cubed

In Dutch oven, heat oil. Cook onions and bell pepper over medium-high heat until tender. Stir in remaining ingredients except fish. Bring to a boil over medium-high heat; reduce heat to low and cook, covered, 20 minutes. Add fish. Cook over low heat 10 to 15 minutes longer or until fish flakes easily with fork. Remove bay leaf before serving.

Makes 10 servings

Serving Suggestion: Serve with thick, crusty bread sticks.

Tuna and Broccoli Bake

1 package (16 ounces) frozen broccoli
     cuts, thawed and well drained
2 slices bread, cut in ½-inch cubes
1 can (12 ounces) STARKIST® Solid
     White or Chunk Light Tuna,
     drained and chunked
3 eggs
2 cups cottage cheese
1 cup shredded Cheddar cheese
¼ teaspoon ground black pepper

Place broccoli on bottom of 2-quart baking dish. Top with bread cubes and tuna. In medium bowl, combine eggs, cottage cheese, Cheddar cheese and pepper. Spread evenly over tuna mixture. Bake in 400°F oven 30 minutes or until golden brown and puffed. *Makes 4 servings*

Prep Time: 35 minutes

New England Fisherman's Skillet

4 small red potatoes, diced
1 medium onion, chopped
1 tablespoon olive oil
2 stalks celery, chopped
2 cloves garlic, minced
½ teaspoon dried thyme, crushed
1 can (14½ ounces) DEL MONTE®
     Original Recipe Stewed Tomatoes
1 pound firm white fish (such as
     halibut, snapper or cod)

1. Brown potatoes and onion in oil over medium-high heat in large skillet, stirring occasionally. Season with herb seasoning mix, if desired.

2. Stir in celery, garlic and thyme; cook 4 minutes. Add tomatoes; bring to boil. Cook 4 minutes or until thickened.

3. Add fish; cover and cook over medium heat 5 to 8 minutes or until fish flakes easily with fork. Garnish with lemon wedges and chopped parsley, if desired.

Makes 4 servings

Prep Time: 10 minutes
Cook Time: 25 minutes

Pescado Viejo (Fish Stew)

Creamy Salmon with Green Beans

1 large red salmon steak
    (about ¾ pound)
1 large ripe tomato
1 small onion
2 tablespoons butter or margarine
2 tablespoons all-purpose flour
1 cup vegetable or chicken broth
1 package (9 ounces) frozen green
    bean cuts, partially thawed
1 cup half-and-half
¼ teaspoon salt
¼ teaspoon ground white pepper
5 tablespoons grated Parmesan
    cheese, divided
Hot cooked angel hair pasta

• Rinse salmon and pat dry with paper towels. Remove skin and bones; discard. Cut salmon into ¾-inch pieces. Cut tomato into ½-inch pieces. Coarsely chop onion.

• Heat wok over medium-high heat 1 minute or until hot. Add butter; swirl to coat bottom and heat 30 seconds. Add salmon; stir-fry gently 3 to 4 minutes or until fish flakes easily when tested with fork. Remove to large bowl; cover and keep warm.

• Add tomato and onion to wok; stir-fry about 5 minutes or until onion is tender. Stir in flour until well mixed. Increase heat to high. Stir in broth and beans; cook until sauce boils and thickens. Add salmon, half-and-half, salt and pepper; cook until heated through. Add half of cheese; toss until well mixed. Spoon salmon mixture over angel hair pasta. Sprinkle with remaining cheese. Garnish, if desired.   *Makes 4 servings*

Flounder Fillets over Zesty Lemon Rice

¼ cup margarine or butter
3 tablespoons fresh lemon juice
2 teaspoons chicken bouillon granules
½ teaspoon black pepper
1 cup cooked rice
1 package (10 ounces) frozen chopped
    broccoli, thawed
1 cup (4 ounces) shredded sharp
    Cheddar cheese
1 pound flounder fillets
½ teaspoon paprika

Preheat oven to 375°F. Spray 2-quart square casserole with nonstick cooking spray.

Melt margarine in small saucepan over medium heat. Add lemon juice, bouillon and pepper; cook and stir 2 minutes or until bouillon dissolves.

Combine rice, broccoli, cheese and ¼ cup lemon sauce in medium bowl; spread on bottom of prepared dish. Place fillets over rice mixture. Pour remaining lemon sauce over fillets.

Bake, uncovered, 20 minutes or until fish flakes easily when tested with fork. Sprinkle evenly with paprika.   *Makes 6 servings*

*Flounder Fillets over
Zesty Lemon Rice*

Herb-Baked Fish & Rice

1½ cups hot chicken bouillon
½ cup uncooked regular rice
¼ teaspoon Italian seasoning
¼ teaspoon garlic powder
1 package (10 ounces) frozen chopped broccoli, thawed and drained
1⅓ cups FRENCH'S® French Fried Onions, divided
1 tablespoon grated Parmesan cheese
1 pound unbreaded fish fillets, thawed if frozen
Paprika (optional)
½ cup (2 ounces) shredded Cheddar cheese

Preheat oven to 375°F. In 12×8-inch baking dish, combine hot bouillon, uncooked rice and seasonings. Bake, covered, at 375°F for 10 minutes. Top with broccoli, ⅔ cup French Fried Onions and the Parmesan cheese. Place fish fillets diagonally down center of dish; sprinkle fish lightly with paprika. Bake, covered, at 375°F for 20 to 25 minutes or until fish flakes easily with fork. Stir rice. Top fish with Cheddar cheese and remaining ⅔ cup onions; bake, uncovered, 3 minutes or until onions are golden brown.

Makes 3 to 4 servings

Microwave Directions: In 12×8-inch microwave-safe dish, prepare rice mixture as above, except reduce bouillon to 1¼ cups. Cook, covered, on HIGH 5 minutes, stirring halfway through cooking time. Stir in broccoli, ⅔ cup onions and the Parmesan cheese. Arrange fish fillets in single layer on top of rice mixture; sprinkle fish lightly with paprika. Cook, covered, on MEDIUM (50-60%) 18 to 20 minutes or until fish flakes easily with fork and rice is done. Rotate dish halfway through cooking time. Top fish with Cheddar cheese and remaining ⅔ cup onions; cook, uncovered, on HIGH 1 minute or until cheese melts. Let stand 5 minutes.

Spicy Tuna and Linguine with Garlic and Pine Nuts

2 tablespoons olive oil
4 cloves garlic, minced
2 cups sliced mushrooms
½ cup chopped onion
½ teaspoon crushed red pepper
2½ cups chopped plum tomatoes
1 can (14½ ounces) chicken broth plus water to equal 2 cups
½ teaspoon salt
¼ teaspoon coarsely ground black pepper
1 package (9 ounces) uncooked fresh linguine
1 can (12 ounces) STARKIST® Solid White Tuna, drained and chunked
⅓ cup chopped fresh cilantro
⅓ cup toasted pine nuts or almonds

In 12-inch skillet, heat olive oil over medium-high heat; sauté garlic, mushrooms, onion and red pepper until golden brown. Add tomatoes, chicken broth mixture, salt and black pepper; bring to a boil.

Separate uncooked linguine into strands; place in skillet and spoon sauce over. Reduce heat to simmer; cook, covered, 4 more minutes or until cooked through. Toss gently; add tuna and cilantro and toss again. Sprinkle with pine nuts.

Makes 4 to 6 servings

Spicy Tuna and Linguine with Garlic and Pine Nuts

Mediterranean Cod

1 bag (16 ounces) BIRDS EYE® frozen Farm Fresh Mixtures Broccoli, Green Beans, Pearl Onions and Red Peppers
1 can (14½ ounces) stewed tomatoes
½ teaspoon dried basil leaves
1 pound cod fillets, cut into serving pieces
½ cup orange juice
2 tablespoons all-purpose flour
¼ cup sliced black olives (optional)

• Combine vegetables, tomatoes and basil in large skillet. Bring to boil over medium-high heat.

• Place cod on vegetables. Pour ¼ cup orange juice over fish. Cover and cook 5 to 7 minutes or until fish is tender and flakes with fork.

• Remove cod and keep warm. Blend flour with remaining ¼ cup orange juice; stir into skillet. Cook until liquid is thickened and vegetables are coated.

• Serve fish with vegetables; sprinkle with olives. *Makes about 4 servings*

Serving Suggestion: Serve with rice or couscous.

Prep Time: 5 minutes
Cook Time: 15 minutes

Seafood Gumbo

1 bag SUCCESS® Rice
1 tablespoon reduced-calorie margarine
¼ cup chopped onion
¼ cup chopped green bell pepper
2 cloves garlic, minced
1 can (28 ounces) whole tomatoes, cut up, undrained
2 cups chicken broth
½ teaspoon ground red pepper
½ teaspoon dried thyme leaves, crushed
½ teaspoon dried basil leaves, crushed
¾ pound white fish, cut into 1-inch pieces
1 package (10 ounces) frozen cut okra, thawed and drained
½ pound shrimp, peeled and deveined

Prepare rice according to package directions.

Melt margarine in large saucepan over medium-high heat. Add onion, green pepper and garlic; cook and stir until crisp-tender. Stir in tomatoes, broth, red pepper, thyme and basil. Bring to a boil. Reduce heat to low; simmer, uncovered, until thoroughly heated, 10 to 15 minutes. Stir in fish, okra and shrimp; simmer until fish flakes easily with fork and shrimp curl and turn pink. Add rice; heat thoroughly, stirring occasionally, 5 to 8 minutes.

Makes 4 servings

Mediterranean Cod

Biscuit-Topped Tuna Bake

2 tablespoons vegetable oil
½ cup chopped onion
½ cup chopped celery
1 can (12 ounces) STARKIST® Solid White or Chunk Light Tuna, drained and chunked
1 can (10¾ ounces) condensed cream of potato soup
1 package (10 ounces) frozen peas and carrots, thawed
¾ cup milk
¼ teaspoon ground black pepper
¼ teaspoon garlic powder
1 can (7½ ounces) refrigerator flaky biscuits

In large skillet, heat oil over medium-high heat; sauté onion and celery until onion is soft. Add remaining ingredients except biscuits; heat thoroughly. Transfer mixture to 1½-quart casserole. Arrange biscuits around top edge of dish; bake in 400°F oven 10 to 15 minutes or until biscuits are golden brown. *Makes 4 to 6 servings*

Prep and Cook Time: 25 minutes

Quick and Easy Tuna Rice with Peas

1 can (12½ ounces) tuna, drained and flaked
1 can (10¾ ounces) condensed Cheddar cheese soup
1 package (10 ounces) green peas
1¼ cups water
1 chicken bouillon cube
¼ teaspoon pepper
1½ cups MINUTE® Original Rice, uncooked

BRING tuna, soup, peas, water, bouillon cube and pepper to a full boil in medium saucepan on medium-high heat.

STIR in rice; cover. Remove from heat. Let stand 5 minutes. *Makes 4 servings*

Prep Time: 5 minutes

Cook Time: 10 minutes plus standing

Mediterranean Catch

2 medium onions, sliced
1 each small green and red bell pepper, cut into thin strips
2 tablespoons olive oil
2 large tomatoes, cut into thin wedges
3 cloves garlic, minced
2 pounds firm-textured fish fillets (such as codfish, grouper or red snapper)
1 (8-ounce) package ATHENOS® Feta Natural Cheese, crumbled
1 tablespoon chopped fresh parsley

• Heat oven to 375°F.

• Cook and stir onions and peppers in oil in large skillet over medium-high heat 5 minutes or until tender-crisp. Add tomatoes and garlic; mix lightly.

• Arrange fish in single layer in 13×9-inch baking dish. Spoon vegetable mixture over fish; sprinkle with cheese.

• Bake 25 minutes or until fish flakes easily with fork. Sprinkle with parsley. Season to taste with salt and pepper.
Makes 4 to 6 servings

Variation: Substitute 1 (8-ounce) package ATHENOS® Feta Natural Cheese with Peppercorn for regular Feta Cheese.

Biscuit-Topped Tuna Bake

Louisiana Seafood Bake

⅔ cup uncooked regular rice
1 cup sliced celery
1 cup water
1 can (14½ ounces) whole tomatoes, undrained and cut up
1 can (8 ounces) tomato sauce
1⅓ cups FRENCH'S® French Fried Onions, divided
1 teaspoon FRANK'S® Original REDHOT® Cayenne Pepper Sauce
½ teaspoon garlic powder
¼ teaspoon dried oregano, crumbled
¼ teaspoon dried thyme, crumbled
½ pound white fish, thawed if frozen and cut into 1-inch chunks
1 can (4 ounces) shrimp, drained
⅓ cup sliced pitted ripe olives
¼ cup (1 ounce) grated Parmesan cheese

Preheat oven to 375°F. In 1½-quart casserole, combine uncooked rice, celery, water, tomatoes, tomato sauce, ⅔ cup French Fried Onions and the seasonings. Bake, covered, at 375°F for 20 minutes. Stir in fish, shrimp and olives. Bake, covered, 20 minutes or until heated through. Top with cheese and remaining ⅔ cup onions; bake, uncovered, 3 minutes or until onions are golden brown. *Makes 4 servings*

Microwave Directions: In 2-quart microwave-safe casserole, prepare rice mixture as above. Cook, covered, on HIGH 15 minutes, stirring rice halfway through cooking time. Add fish, shrimp and olives. Cook, covered, 12 to 14 minutes or until rice is cooked. Stir casserole halfway through cooking time. Top with cheese and remaining onions; cook, uncovered, 1 minute. Let stand 5 minutes.

Tuna Quesadilla Stack

4 (10-inch) flour tortillas, divided
¼ cup plus 2 tablespoons pinto or black bean dip
1 can (9 ounces) tuna packed in water, drained and flaked
2 cups (8 ounces) shredded Cheddar cheese
1 can (14½ ounces) diced tomatoes, drained
½ cup thinly sliced green onions
½ tablespoon butter or margarine, melted

1. Preheat oven to 400°F.

2. Place 1 tortilla on 12-inch pizza pan. Spread with 2 tablespoons bean dip, leaving ½-inch border. Top with one third each of tuna, cheese, tomatoes and green onions. Repeat layers twice beginning with tortilla and ending with onions.

3. Top with remaining tortilla, pressing gently. Brush with melted butter.

4. Bake 15 minutes or until cheese melts and top is lightly browned. Cool and cut into 8 wedges. *Makes 4 servings*

Tip: For a special touch, serve with assorted toppings, such as commercial avocado dip, sour cream and salsa.

Prep and Cook Time: 25 minutes

Tuna Quesadilla Stack

Homestyle Tuna Pot Pie

1 package (15 ounces) refrigerated pie
  crusts
1 can (12 ounces) STARKIST® Solid
  White or Chunk Light Tuna,
  drained and chunked
1 package (10 ounces) frozen peas and
  carrots, thawed and drained
½ cup chopped onion
1 can (10¾ ounces) cream of potato or
  cream of mushroom soup
⅓ cup milk
½ teaspoon poultry seasoning or dried
  thyme
  Salt and pepper to taste

Line 9-inch pie pan with one crust; set aside.
Reserve second crust. In medium bowl,
combine remaining ingredients; mix well.
Pour tuna mixture into pie shell; top with
second crust. Crimp edges to seal. Cut slits
in top crust to vent. Bake in 375°F oven 45
to 50 minutes or until golden brown.

Makes 6 servings

Prep and Cook Time: 55 to 60 minutes

Tuna Pesto & Pasta

1 box (10 ounces) BIRDS EYE® frozen
  Peas and Pearl Onions
3 cups cooked rotini or other shaped
  pasta
1 can (6⅛ ounces) tuna packed in
  water, drained
¼ cup mayonnaise
2 to 4 tablespoons prepared pesto
  Grated Parmesan cheese

• Prepare vegetables in medium saucepan
according to package directions.

• Stir in pasta, tuna, mayonnaise and pesto;
heat through.

• Serve with cheese.

Makes about 2 servings

Serving Suggestion: Chill Tuna Pesto &
Pasta and serve as a cold pasta salad.

Prep Time: 5 minutes

Cook Time: 12 minutes

Baked Fish with Potatoes and Onions

1 pound baking potatoes, very thinly
  sliced
1 large onion, very thinly sliced
1 small red or green bell pepper, thinly
  sliced
  Salt
  Black pepper
½ teaspoon dried oregano leaves,
  divided
1 pound lean fish fillets, cut 1 inch
  thick
¼ cup butter or margarine
¼ cup all-purpose flour
2 cups milk
¾ cup (3 ounces) shredded Cheddar
  cheese

Preheat oven to 375°F.

Arrange ½ of potatoes in buttered 3-quart
casserole. Top with ½ of onion and ½ of bell
pepper. Season with salt and black pepper.
Sprinkle with ¼ teaspoon oregano. Arrange
fish in one layer over vegetables. Arrange
remaining potatoes, onion and bell pepper
over fish. Season with salt, black pepper and
remaining ¼ teaspoon oregano.

Melt butter in medium saucepan over
medium heat. Stir in flour; cook until
bubbly, stirring constantly. Gradually stir in
milk. Cook until thickened, stirring
constantly. Pour white sauce over casserole.
Cover and bake at 375°F 40 minutes or until
potatoes are tender. Sprinkle with cheese.
Bake, uncovered, about 5 minutes more or
until cheese is melted. *Makes 4 servings*

*Baked Fish with Potatoes
and Onions*

Superb Fillet of Sole & Vegetables

- 1 can (10¾ ounces) condensed cream of celery soup
- ½ cup milk
- 1 cup (4 ounces) shredded Swiss cheese
- ½ teaspoon dried basil, crumbled
- ¼ teaspoon seasoned salt
- ¼ teaspoon pepper
- 1 package (10 ounces) frozen baby carrots, thawed and drained
- 1 package (10 ounces) frozen asparagus cuts, thawed and drained
- 1⅓ cups FRENCH'S® French Fried Onions, divided
- 1 pound unbreaded sole fillets, thawed if frozen

Preheat oven to 375°F. In small bowl, combine soup, milk, ½ cup cheese and the seasonings; set aside. In 12×8-inch baking dish, combine carrots, asparagus and ⅔ cup French Fried Onions. Roll up fish fillets. (If fillets are wide, fold in half lengthwise before rolling.) Place fish rolls upright along center of vegetable mixture. Pour soup mixture over fish and vegetables. Bake, covered, at 375°F for 30 minutes or until fish flakes easily with fork. Stir vegetables; top fish with remaining cheese and ⅔ cup onions. Bake, uncovered, 3 minutes or until onions are golden brown. *Makes 3 to 4 servings*

Microwave Directions: Prepare soup mixture as above; set aside. In 12×8-inch microwave-safe dish, combine vegetables as above. Roll up fish fillets as above; place upright around edges of dish. Pour soup mixture over fish and vegetables. Cook, covered, on HIGH 14 to 16 minutes or until fish flakes easily with fork. Stir vegetables and rotate dish halfway through cooking time. Top fish with remaining cheese and onions; cook, uncovered, 1 minute or until cheese melts. Let stand 5 minutes.

By-the-Sea Casserole

- 1 bag (16 ounces) BIRDS EYE® frozen Mixed Vegetables
- 2 cans (6½ ounces each) tuna in water, drained
- 1 cup uncooked instant rice
- 1 can (10¾ ounces) cream of celery soup
- 1 cup 1% milk
- 1 cup cheese-flavored fish-shaped crackers

• In medium bowl, combine vegetables and tuna.

• Stir in rice, soup and milk.

• Place tuna mixture in 1½-quart microwave-safe casserole dish; cover and microwave on HIGH 6 minutes. Stir; microwave, covered, 6 to 8 minutes more or until rice is tender.

• Stir casserole and sprinkle with crackers.
Makes 6 servings

Prep Time: 10 minutes
Cook Time: 15 minutes

By-the-Sea Casserole

Thai-Style Tuna Fried Rice

4 to 5 tablespoons vegetable oil, divided
2 eggs, lightly beaten
⅔ cup uncooked, peeled medium shrimp, chopped into ¾-inch pieces
3 cloves garlic
1 to 2 tablespoons minced fresh serrano chiles
4 to 6 cups cooked rice, chilled overnight
1 tablespoon sugar
1 tablespoon nam pla (fish sauce) (optional)
1 tablespoon soy sauce
1 can (6 ounces) STARKIST® Solid White or Chunk Light Tuna, drained and chunked
½ cup chopped dry-roasted peanuts
¼ cup chopped fresh basil
2 tablespoons chopped fresh cilantro
Lime wedges for garnish

In wok, heat 1 tablespoon oil over medium-high heat; add eggs and cook, stirring, until partially cooked but still runny. Return eggs to bowl. Wipe out wok with paper towels. Add 2 tablespoons oil to wok; heat.

Add shrimp, garlic and chiles. Stir-fry until shrimp turn pink, about 3 minutes. Remove shrimp mixture; set aside. Add 1 or 2 tablespoons oil to wok; stir-fry rice, sugar, nam pla, if desired, and soy sauce until rice is heated through. Add tuna and peanuts; heat.

Return shrimp mixture and eggs to pan, chopping eggs into pieces with stir-fry spatula. Add basil and cilantro; toss gently to mix. Serve with lime wedges for garnish; squeeze juice on fried rice, if desired.

Makes 4 to 6 servings

Prep and Cook Time: 15 minutes

Impossibly Easy Salmon Pie

1 can (7½ ounces) salmon packed in water, drained and deboned
½ cup grated Parmesan cheese
¼ cup sliced green onions
1 jar (2 ounces) chopped pimiento, drained
½ cup 1% low-fat cottage cheese
1 tablespoon lemon juice
1½ cups 1% low-fat milk
¾ cup reduced-fat baking and pancake mix
2 whole eggs
2 egg whites *or* ¼ cup egg substitute
¼ teaspoon dried dill weed
¼ teaspoon salt
¼ teaspoon paprika (optional)

1. Preheat oven to 375°F. Spray 9-inch pie plate with nonstick cooking spray. Combine salmon, Parmesan cheese, onions and pimiento in prepared pie plate; set aside.

2. Combine cottage cheese and lemon juice in blender or food processor; blend until smooth. Add milk, baking mix, whole eggs, egg whites, dill and salt. Blend 15 seconds. Pour over salmon mixture. Sprinkle with paprika, if desired.

3. Bake 35 to 40 minutes or until lightly golden and knife inserted halfway between center and edge comes out clean. Cool 5 minutes before serving. Garnish as desired.

Makes 8 servings

Thai-Style Tuna Fried Rice

158

No-Fuss Tuna Quiche

1 unbaked 9-inch deep-dish pastry
    shell
1½ cups low-fat milk
3 extra large eggs
⅓ cup chopped green onions
1 tablespoon chopped drained
    pimiento
1 teaspoon dried basil leaves, crushed
½ teaspoon salt
1 can (6 ounces) STARKIST® Tuna,
    drained and broken into chunks
½ cup (2 ounces) shredded low-fat
    Cheddar cheese
8 spears (4 inches each) broccoli

Preheat oven to 450°F. Bake pastry shell for 5 minutes; remove to rack to cool. *Reduce oven temperature to 325°F.* For filling, in large bowl whisk together milk and eggs. Stir in onions, pimiento, basil and salt. Fold in tuna and cheese. Pour into prebaked pastry shell. Bake at 325°F for 30 minutes.

Meanwhile, in a saucepan steam broccoli spears over simmering water for 5 minutes. Drain; set aside. After 30 minutes baking time, arrange broccoli spears, spoke-fashion, over quiche. Bake 25 to 35 minutes more or until a knife inserted 2 inches from center comes out clean. Let stand for 5 minutes. Cut into 8 wedges, centering a broccoli spear in each wedge. *Makes 8 servings*

Note: If desired, 1 cup chopped broccoli may be added to the filling before baking.

Mediterranean Fish Soup

4 ounces uncooked pastina or other
    small pasta
  Nonstick cooking spray
¾ cup chopped onion
2 cloves garlic, minced
1 teaspoon fennel seeds
1 can (about 14 ounces) no-salt-added
    stewed tomatoes
1 can (about 14 ounces) fat-free
    reduced-sodium chicken broth
1 tablespoon minced fresh parsley
½ teaspoon ground black pepper
¼ teaspoon ground turmeric
8 ounces firm, white-fleshed fish, cut
    into 1-inch pieces
3 ounces small shrimp, peeled and
    deveined

1. Cook pasta according to package directions. Drain and set aside.

2. Spray large nonstick saucepan with cooking spray. Add onion, garlic and fennel seeds; cook over medium heat 3 minutes or until onion is tender.

3. Stir in tomatoes, chicken broth, parsley, pepper and turmeric. Bring to a boil; reduce heat and simmer 10 minutes. Add fish and cook 1 minute. Add shrimp and cook until shrimp just begins to turn pink and opaque.

4. Divide pasta among bowls; ladle soup over pasta. *Makes 4 (1½-cup) servings*

No-Fuss Tuna Quiche

Tuna Tortilla Roll-Ups

1 can (10¾ ounces) condensed cream of celery soup
1 cup milk
1 can (9 ounces) tuna, drained and flaked
1 package (10 ounces) frozen broccoli spears, thawed, drained and cut into 1-inch pieces
1 cup (4 ounces) shredded Cheddar cheese
1⅓ cups FRENCH'S® French Fried Onions, divided
6 (7-inch) flour or corn tortillas
1 medium tomato, chopped

Preheat oven to 350°F. In small bowl, combine soup and milk; set aside. In medium bowl, combine tuna, broccoli, ½ cup cheese and ⅔ cup French Fried Onions; stir in ¾ cup soup mixture. Divide tuna mixture evenly among tortillas; roll up tortillas. Place, seam-side down, in lightly greased 13×9-inch baking dish. Stir tomato into remaining soup mixture; pour down center of roll-ups. Bake, covered, at 350°F for 35 minutes or until heated through. Top center of roll-ups with remaining cheese and ⅔ cup onions; bake, uncovered, 5 minutes or until onions are golden brown.

Makes 6 servings

Microwave Directions: Use corn tortillas only. Prepare soup mixture and roll-ups as above; place roll-ups, seam side down, in 12×8-inch microwave-safe dish. Stir tomato into remaining soup mixture; pour down center of roll-ups. Cook, covered, on HIGH 15 to 18 minutes or until heated through. Rotate dish halfway through cooking time. Top center of roll-ups with remaining cheese and ⅔ cup onions; cook, uncovered, 1 minute or until cheese melts. Let stand 5 minutes.

Fish Broccoli Casserole

1 package (10 ounces) frozen broccoli spears, thawed, drained
1 cup cooked, flaked whitefish
1 can (10¾ ounces) condensed cream of mushroom soup
½ cup milk
¼ teaspoon salt
⅛ teaspoon freshly ground black pepper
½ cup crushed potato chips

Preheat oven to 425°F. Grease 1½-quart casserole. Layer broccoli in prepared casserole. Combine fish, soup, milk, salt and pepper in large bowl.

Spread fish mixture over broccoli. Sprinkle with potato chips. Bake 12 to 15 minutes or until golden brown. *Makes 4 servings*

*Favorite recipe from **Florida Department of Agriculture and Consumer Services, Bureau of Seafood and Aquaculture***

Veggie Tuna Pasta

1 package (16 ounces) medium pasta shells
1 bag (16 ounces) BIRDS EYE® frozen Farm Fresh Mixtures Broccoli, Corn & Red Peppers
1 can (10 ounces) chunky light tuna, packed in water
1 can (10¾ ounces) reduced-fat cream of mushroom soup

• In large saucepan, cook pasta according to package directions. Add vegetables during last 10 minutes; drain and return to saucepan.

• Stir in tuna and soup. Add salt and pepper to taste. Cook over medium heat until heated through. *Makes 4 servings*

Variation: Stir in 1 can (4 to 6 ounces) chopped ripe olives with tuna.

Serving Suggestion: For a creamier dish, add a few tablespoons water; blend well.

Prep Time: 2 minutes

Cook Time: 12 to 15 minutes

Shrimp with Strawberries and Snow Peas

1 tablespoon vegetable oil
½ pound peeled medium shrimp
¼ pound snow peas
2 ounces fresh bean sprouts, rinsed
2 cloves garlic, minced
½ teaspoon minced fresh ginger
2 tablespoons brown sugar
2 tablespoons soy sauce
1 tablespoon dark sesame oil
2 teaspoons balsamic vinegar
2 teaspoons oyster sauce
1 cup strawberries, washed, hulled and quartered
2 cups hot cooked rice

1. Heat large skillet over medium-high heat until hot. Add vegetable oil. Cook and stir shrimp, snow peas, bean sprouts, garlic and ginger 2 to 3 minutes or until shrimp is opaque and bean sprouts are crisp-tender.

2. Combine brown sugar, soy sauce, sesame oil, vinegar and oyster sauce in small bowl; add to skillet. Cook and stir 1 minute or until brown sugar is dissolved.

3. Remove from heat and stir in strawberries. Serve over rice. *Makes 4 servings*

Prep and Cook Time: 20 minutes

Jambalaya

1 teaspoon vegetable oil
½ pound smoked deli ham, cubed
½ pound smoked sausage, cut into ¼-inch-thick slices
1 large onion, chopped
1 large green bell pepper, chopped (about 1½ cups)
3 ribs celery, chopped (about 1 cup)
3 cloves garlic, minced
1 can (28 ounces) diced tomatoes, undrained
1 can (10½ ounces) chicken broth
1 cup uncooked rice
1 tablespoon Worcestershire sauce
1 teaspoon salt
1 teaspoon dried thyme leaves
½ teaspoon black pepper
¼ teaspoon ground red pepper
1 package (12 ounces) frozen ready-to-cook shrimp, thawed
Fresh chives (optional)

Preheat oven to 350°F. Spray 13×9-inch baking dish with nonstick cooking spray.

Heat oil in large skillet over medium-high heat until hot. Add ham and sausage. Cook and stir 5 minutes or until sausage is lightly browned on both sides. Remove from skillet and place in prepared dish. Place onion, bell pepper, celery and garlic in same skillet; cook and stir 3 minutes. Add to sausage mixture.

Combine tomatoes with juice, broth, rice, Worcestershire sauce, salt, thyme and black and red peppers in same skillet; bring to a boil over high heat. Reduce heat to low and simmer 3 minutes. Pour over sausage mixture and stir until combined.

Cover tightly with foil and bake 45 minutes or until rice is almost tender. Remove from oven; place shrimp on top of rice mixture. Bake, uncovered, 10 minutes or until shrimp are pink and opaque. Garnish with chives, if desired. *Makes 8 servings*

Skillet Shrimp with Rotelle

3 tablespoons **FILIPPO BERIO®** Olive Oil
1 medium onion, chopped
2 cloves garlic, minced
2 cups uncooked rotelle or other curly pasta
3 cups chicken broth
1 cup asparagus tips
¾ pound raw medium shrimp, shelled and deveined
¾ cup halved cherry tomatoes
¼ cup pitted ripe olives
1 teaspoon dried oregano leaves
1 teaspoon dried basil leaves
Salt and freshly ground black pepper

In large skillet, heat olive oil over medium heat until hot. Add onion and garlic; cook and stir 4 to 6 minutes or until onion is softened, but not brown. Add pasta; stir to coat pasta with oil. Increase heat to high; pour in chicken broth. Bring to a boil. Reduce heat to medium-high; cook, stirring occasionally, 12 to 14 minutes or until pasta is al dente (tender but still firm). Add asparagus. Cook, stirring frequently, 2 to 3 minutes or until asparagus is tender-crisp. Add shrimp, tomatoes, olives, oregano and basil. Cook, stirring frequently, 3 minutes or until liquid is almost completely absorbed and shrimp are opaque (do not overcook shrimp). Season to taste with salt and pepper. *Makes 4 to 6 servings*

Scallops & Snow Peas

¾ pound fresh or thawed bay scallops
¾ cup water
2 tablespoons **KIKKOMAN®** Soy Sauce
2 tablespoons dry white wine
4 teaspoons cornstarch
½ teaspoon sugar
3 small dried whole red chili peppers
1 tablespoon vegetable oil
1 medium onion, cut into 1-inch pieces
2 teaspoons slivered fresh ginger root
½ pound fresh snow peas, trimmed and cut diagonally into halves
1½ teaspoons Oriental sesame oil

Cook scallops in small amount of boiling water 30 seconds; drain. Combine ¾ cup water, soy sauce, wine, cornstarch and sugar in small bowl; set aside. Cut each chili pepper open lengthwise, being careful not to cut all the way through; set aside. Heat vegetable oil in hot wok or large skillet over medium heat; add chilies and stir-fry 30 seconds. Remove chilies; increase heat to high. Add onion and ginger; stir-fry 1 minute. Add snow peas; stir-fry 2 minutes longer. Add scallops, chilies and soy sauce mixture; cook and stir until sauce boils and thickens. Remove from heat and stir in sesame oil. Serve immediately. *Makes 4 servings*

Skillet Shrimp with Rotelle

Stir-Fried Scallops with Vegetables

1 pound sea scallops
¼ teaspoon salt
⅛ teaspoon black pepper
½ cup vegetable broth
1 tablespoon cornstarch
3 tablespoons butter or margarine, divided
1 package (6 ounces) red radishes, quartered
¼ cup dry white wine
1 package (6 ounces) frozen snow peas, partially thawed
½ cup sliced bamboo shoots
Hot cooked couscous

• Rinse scallops and pat dry with paper towels. Sprinkle with salt and black pepper.

• Stir broth into cornstarch in cup until smooth; set aside.

• Heat wok over high heat about 1 minute or until hot. Add 1½ tablespoons butter; swirl to coat bottom and heat 30 seconds. Arrange half the scallops in single layer in wok, leaving ½ inch between. (Scallops should not touch.) Cook scallops until browned on both sides. Remove scallops to large bowl. Repeat with remaining 1½ tablespoons butter and scallops. Reduce heat to medium-high.

• Add radishes to wok; stir-fry about 1 minute or until crisp-tender. Remove radishes to bowl with scallops.

• Add wine to wok. Stir broth mixture; add to wok. Add snow peas and bamboo shoots; stir-fry until heated through.

• Return scallops and radishes to wok; stir-fry until heated through. Serve over couscous. Garnish, if desired.

Makes 4 servings

Shrimp Noodle Supreme

1 package (8 ounces) spinach noodles, cooked and drained
1 package (3 ounces) cream cheese, cubed and softened
1½ pounds medium shrimp, peeled and deveined
½ cup butter, softened
Salt and pepper to taste
1 can (10¾ ounces) condensed cream of mushroom soup
1 cup dairy sour cream
½ cup half-and-half
½ cup mayonnaise
1 tablespoon chopped chives
1 tablespoon chopped parsley
½ teaspoon Dijon mustard
¾ cup (6 ounces) shredded sharp Cheddar cheese

Preheat oven to 325°F. Combine noodles and cream cheese in medium bowl. Spread noodle mixture into bottom of greased 13×9-inch glass casserole. Cook shrimp in butter in large skillet over medium-high heat until pink and tender, about 5 minutes. Season with salt and pepper. Spread shrimp over noodles.

Combine soup, sour cream, half-and-half, mayonnaise, chives, parsley and mustard in another medium bowl. Spread over shrimp. Sprinkle Cheddar cheese over top. Bake 25 minutes or until hot and cheese is melted. Garnish, if desired. *Makes 6 servings*

Stir-Fried Scallops with Vegetables

Elegant Crabmeat Frittata

3 tablespoons butter or margarine, divided
¼ pound fresh mushrooms, sliced
2 green onions, cut into thin slices
8 eggs, separated
¼ cup milk
¼ teaspoon salt
½ teaspoon hot pepper sauce
½ pound lump crabmeat or imitation crabmeat, flaked and picked over to remove any shells
½ cup (2 ounces) shredded Swiss cheese

1. Melt 2 tablespoons butter in large ovenproof skillet over medium-high heat. Add mushrooms and onions; cook and stir 3 to 5 minutes or until vegetables are tender. Remove from skillet; set aside.

2. Beat egg yolks with electric mixer at high speed until slightly thickened and lemon color. Stir in milk, salt and hot pepper sauce.

3. Beat egg whites in clean large bowl with electric mixer at high speed until foamy. Gradually add to egg yolk mixture, whisking just until blended.

4. Melt remaining 1 tablespoon butter in skillet. Pour egg mixture into skillet. Cook until egg is almost set. Remove from heat.

5. Preheat broiler. Broil frittata 4 to 6 inches from heat until top is set.

6. Top with crabmeat, mushroom mixture and cheese. Return frittata to broiler; broil until cheese is melted. Garnish, if desired. Serve immediately. *Makes 4 servings*

Tex-Mex Stir-Fry

1 package (1.27 ounces) LAWRY'S® Spices & Seasonings for Fajitas
⅓ cup water
2 tablespoons vegetable oil, divided
1½ cups broccoli flowerettes
2 carrots, thinly sliced diagonally
1 red or green bell pepper, thinly sliced
½ cup thinly sliced celery
1 pound medium shrimp, peeled and deveined
1½ tablespoons brown sugar
1 teaspoon ground ginger
1 teaspoon dry mustard

In small bowl, combine Spices & Seasonings for Fajitas and water; set aside. In hot large skillet or wok, add 1 tablespoon oil, broccoli, carrots, bell pepper and celery. Stir-fry 3 minutes. Remove; set aside. Add remaining 1 tablespoon oil and shrimp to same hot skillet; stir-fry 3 minutes. Add vegetables back to skillet. Pour in Spices & Seasonings for Fajitas mixture, brown sugar, ginger and mustard. Cook 2 minutes longer, tossing gently to blend. *Makes 6 servings*

Serving Suggestion: Serve seafood-vegetable mixture over hot rice.

Hint: One pound thinly sliced boneless chicken or pork can be used in place of shrimp. For pork, increase cooking time an additional 1 to 2 minutes.

Elegant Crabmeat Frittata

New England Clam Chowder

24 medium fresh clams
   Salt
 1 bottle (8 ounces) clam juice
 3 medium potatoes, cut into
   ½-inch-thick slices
¼ teaspoon dried thyme leaves
¼ teaspoon white pepper
 4 slices bacon, cut crosswise into
   ¼-inch strips
 1 medium onion, chopped
⅓ cup all-purpose flour
 2 cups milk
 1 cup half-and-half
   Oyster crackers
   Fresh thyme for garnish

1. Scrub clams with stiff brush. Soak in mixture of ⅓ cup salt to 1 gallon water 20 minutes. Drain water; repeat 2 more times. Refrigerate clams 1 hour.

2. To shuck clams, take pointed clam knife in one hand and thick towel or glove in the other. With towel, grip shell in palm of hand. Keeping clam level with knife, insert tip of knife between the shell next to hinge; twist to pry shell until you hear a snap. Twist to open shell, keeping clam level at all times to save juice. Cut muscle from shell and discard top shell.

3. Tip shell over strainer in bowl to catch clams; discard bottom shell. Repeat with remaining clams. Strain clam juice from bowl through triple thickness of dampened cheesecloth into small bowl; pour clam juice into 2-cup glass measure. Refrigerate until needed. Coarsely chop clams; set aside.

4. Add bottled clam juice and enough water to clam juice in glass measure to total 2 cups liquid; place liquid in Dutch oven. Add potatoes, thyme and pepper; bring to a boil. Reduce heat; simmer 15 minutes or until potatoes are tender, stirring occasionally.

5. Cook bacon in medium skillet over medium heat until almost crisp. Add onion; cook until tender but not brown. Stir flour into bacon mixture. Whisk in milk; cook until mixture boils and thickens.

6. Add bacon mixture and half-and-half to potato mixture. Add clams and continue to heat until clams are firm. Serve with oyster crackers. Garnish, if desired.

Makes 6 main-dish servings

Chesapeake Crab Strata

 4 tablespoons butter or margarine
 4 cups unseasoned croutons
 2 cups shredded Cheddar cheese
 2 cups milk
 8 eggs, beaten
½ teaspoon dry mustard
½ teaspoon seafood seasoning
   Salt and black pepper to taste
 1 pound crabmeat, picked over to
   remove any shells

Preheat oven to 325°F. Place butter in 11×7-inch baking dish. Heat in oven until melted, tilting to coat dish. Remove dish from oven; spread croutons over melted butter. Top with cheese; set aside.

Combine milk, eggs, dry mustard, seafood seasoning, salt and black pepper; mix well. Pour egg mixture over cheese in dish; sprinkle with crabmeat. Bake 50 minutes or until mixture is set. Remove from oven and let stand about 10 minutes. Garnish, if desired.

Makes 6 to 8 servings

New England Clam Chowder

Seafood Risotto

1 package (5.2 ounces) rice in creamy
    sauce (Risotto Milanese flavor)
1 package (14 to 16 ounces) frozen
    fully cooked shrimp
1 box (10 ounces) BIRDS EYE® frozen
    Mixed Vegetables
2 teaspoons grated Parmesan cheese

• In 4-quart saucepan, prepare rice
according to package directions. Add frozen
shrimp and vegetables during last 10
minutes.

• Sprinkle with cheese.   *Makes 4 servings*

Serving Suggestion: Serve with garlic bread
and a tossed green salad.

Prep Time: 5 minutes

Cook Time: 15 minutes

Easy Crab-Asparagus Pie

 4 ounces crabmeat, shredded
12 ounces fresh asparagus, cooked
 ½ cup chopped onion, cooked
 1 cup (4 ounces) shredded Monterey
    Jack cheese
 ¼ cup (1 ounce) grated Parmesan
    cheese
    Freshly ground pepper
 ¾ cup all-purpose flour
 ¾ teaspoon baking powder
 ½ teaspoon salt
 2 tablespoons butter or margarine,
    chilled
1½ cups milk
 4 eggs, slightly beaten

1. Preheat oven to 350°F. Lightly grease
10-inch quiche dish or pie plate.

2. Layer crabmeat, asparagus and onion in
prepared pie plate; top with cheeses. Season
with pepper.

3. Combine flour, baking powder and salt in
large bowl. With pastry blender or 2 knives,
cut in butter until mixture forms coarse
crumbs. Stir in milk and eggs; pour over
vegetables and cheeses.

4. Bake 30 minutes or until filling is puffed
and knife inserted near center comes out
clean. Serve hot.   *Makes 6 servings*

Shrimp in Tomatillo Sauce over Rice

 1 teaspoon olive oil
 ¼ cup chopped onion
 1 cup GUILTLESS GOURMET® Green
    Tomatillo Salsa
 ¾ cup white wine
    Juice of ½ lemon
12 ounces medium-size raw shrimp,
    peeled and deveined
 4 cups hot cooked white rice
    Lemon peel strip (optional)

Heat oil in large nonstick skillet over
medium-high heat until hot. Add onion;
cook and stir until onion is translucent. Add
salsa, wine and lemon juice, stirring just until
mixture begins to boil. Reduce heat to
medium-low; simmer 10 minutes. Add
shrimp; cook about 2 minutes or until
shrimp turn pink and opaque, stirring
occasionally. To serve, place 1 cup rice in
each of 4 individual serving bowls. Pour
shrimp mixture evenly over rice. Garnish
with lemon peel, if desired.

Makes 4 servings

Seafood Risotto

West Coast Bouillabaisse

1 cup sliced onion
2 stalks celery, cut diagonally into slices
2 cloves garlic, minced
1 tablespoon vegetable oil
4 cups chicken broth
1 can (28 ounces) tomatoes with juice, cut up
1 can (6½ ounces) minced clams with juice
½ cup dry white wine
1 teaspoon Worcestershire sauce
½ teaspoon dried thyme, crushed
¼ teaspoon bottled hot pepper sauce
1 bay leaf
1 cup frozen cooked bay shrimp, thawed
1 can (12 ounces) STARKIST® Tuna, drained and broken into chunks
  Salt and pepper to taste
6 slices lemon
6 slices French bread

In Dutch oven sauté onion, celery and garlic in oil for 3 minutes. Stir in broth, tomatoes with juice, clams with juice, wine, Worcestershire, thyme, hot pepper sauce and bay leaf. Bring to a boil; reduce heat. Simmer for 15 minutes. Stir in shrimp and tuna; cook for 2 minutes to heat. Remove bay leaf. Season with salt and pepper. Garnish with lemon slices and serve with bread. *Makes 6 servings*

Oriental Shrimp Burritos

1 tablespoon vegetable oil
8 ounces (4 cups packed) shredded cole slaw mix with cabbage and carrots
1 teaspoon bottled minced ginger *or* ½ teaspoon dried ginger
1 teaspoon bottled minced garlic
1 cup bean sprouts
½ cup sliced green onions with tops
8 flour tortillas (6 or 7 inches)
10 to 12 ounces peeled cooked medium shrimp
¼ cup stir-fry sauce
¼ teaspoon dried red pepper flakes
  Plum sauce or sweet and sour sauce

1. Heat oil in large, deep skillet over medium-high heat until hot. Add cole slaw mix, ginger and garlic; stir-fry 2 minutes. Add sprouts and onions; stir-fry 3 minutes.

2. While vegetable mixture is cooking, stack tortillas and wrap in wax paper. Microwave on HIGH 1½ minutes or until warm.

3. Add shrimp, stir-fry sauce and red pepper flakes to skillet; stir-fry 2 minutes or until heated through. Spoon about ⅓ cup shrimp mixture evenly down center of each tortilla. Fold 1 end of tortilla over filling and roll up. Serve with plum sauce. *Makes 4 servings*

Prep and Cook Time: 10 minutes

Oriental Shrimp Burritos

Zesty Seafood Lasagna

2 packages (1.8 ounces each) white
  sauce mix
4½ cups milk
1 teaspoon dried basil leaves
½ teaspoon dried thyme leaves
½ teaspoon garlic powder
¾ cup grated Parmesan cheese, divided
3 tablespoons FRANK'S® Original
  REDHOT® Cayenne Pepper Sauce
9 oven-ready lasagna pasta sheets
2 packages (10 ounces each) frozen
  chopped spinach, thawed and
  squeezed
½ pound cooked shrimp
½ pound raw bay scallops or flaked
  imitation crabmeat
2 cups (8 ounces) shredded mozzarella
  cheese, divided

1. Preheat oven to 400°F. Prepare white sauce according to package directions using milk and adding basil, thyme and garlic powder in large saucepan. Stir in ½ cup Parmesan cheese and RedHot® sauce.

2. Spread 1 cup sauce in bottom of greased 13×9×2-inch casserole. Layer 3 pasta sheets crosswise over sauce. (Do not let edges touch.) Layer half of the spinach and seafood over pasta. Spoon 1 cup sauce over seafood; sprinkle with ¾ cup mozzarella cheese. Repeat layers a second time. Top with final layer of pasta sheets, remaining sauce and cheeses.

3. Cover pan with greased foil. Bake 40 minutes. Remove foil; bake 10 minutes or until top is browned and pasta is fully cooked. Let stand 15 minutes before serving. *Makes 8 servings*

Tip: Splash RedHot® sauce on foods after cooking instead of salt and black pepper. RedHot® sauce perks up the flavor of all foods!

Prep Time: 30 minutes

Cook Time: 50 minutes

Shrimp Primavera Pot Pie

1 can (10¾ ounces) condensed cream
  of shrimp soup, undiluted
1 package (12 ounces) frozen peeled
  uncooked medium shrimp
2 packages (1 pound each) frozen
  mixed vegetables, such as green
  beans, potatoes, onions and red
  peppers, thawed and drained
1 teaspoon dried dill weed
¼ teaspoon salt
¼ teaspoon black pepper
1 package (11 ounces) refrigerated
  soft breadstick dough

1. Preheat oven to 400°F. Heat soup in medium ovenproof skillet over medium-high heat 1 minute. Add shrimp; cook and stir 3 minutes or until shrimp begin to thaw. Stir in vegetables, dill, salt and pepper; mix well. Reduce heat to medium-low; cook and stir 3 minutes.

2. Unwrap breadstick dough; separate into 8 strips. Twist strips, cutting to fit skillet. Arrange attractively over shrimp mixture. Press ends of dough lightly to edges of skillet to secure. Bake 18 minutes or until crust is golden brown and shrimp mixture is bubbly. *Makes 4 to 6 servings*

Prep and Cook Time: 30 minutes

Zesty Seafood Lasagna

Quick Cajun Jambalaya

3 tablespoons butter
1 onion, diced
1 *each* red and green bell pepper, diced
12 slices HILLSHIRE FARM® Ham, cut into ½-inch strips
12 large raw shrimp, peeled and deveined
1 can (28 ounces) crushed tomatoes, undrained
2 teaspoons salt
¼ teaspoon garlic powder
¼ teaspoon red pepper flakes
¼ teaspoon black pepper
¼ teaspoon hot pepper sauce
6 cups cooked white rice
Cajun Garlic Bread (recipe follows)

Heat butter in large saucepan over medium-high heat; cook onion and bell peppers until soft, about 5 minutes. Add Ham and shrimp; cook until shrimp turn pink, about 3 minutes. Add tomatoes with liquid, seasonings and rice; cook 5 minutes or until heated through. Serve with Cajun Garlic Bread.   *Makes 6 servings*

Cajun Garlic Bread

¼ teaspoon garlic powder
⅛ teaspoon ground red pepper
⅛ teaspoon dried oregano or basil leaves
2 tablespoons butter, melted
1 loaf French bread, cut lengthwise into halves

Preheat oven to 350°F. Stir garlic powder, pepper and oregano into butter in small bowl. Drizzle butter mixture over cut sides of bread. Reassemble loaf; wrap in foil. Bake 10 minutes.   *Makes 6 servings*

Louisiana Stir-Fry

2 tablespoons vegetable oil
1 pound raw medium shrimp, shelled and deveined, *or* ½ pound sea scallops
1 bag (16 ounces) BIRDS EYE® frozen Farm Fresh Mixtures Broccoli, Corn & Red Peppers
½ green bell pepper, chopped
2 teaspoons water
1 can (14½ ounces) stewed tomatoes, drained

• In wok or large skillet; heat oil over medium-high heat.

• Add shrimp; stir-fry 2 to 3 minutes or until shrimp turn pink and opaque. Remove to serving plate.

• Add vegetables, pepper and water to wok; cover and cook 4 to 6 minutes.

• Uncover; stir in tomatoes. Cook 3 to 4 minutes or until heated through and slightly thickened.

• Return shrimp to wok; cook and stir about 1 minute or until heated through.
          Makes 4 servings

Variation: Substitute 1 package (16 ounces) frozen fully cooked shrimp or 1 pound imitation crab legs. Add to cooked vegetables and cook until heated through.

Serving Suggestion: Stir ¼ teaspoon hot pepper sauce into stir-fry and serve over hot cooked rice.

Prep Time: 15 minutes
Cook Time: 12 to 15 minutes

Quick Cajun Jambalaya

Smucker's® Mandarin Shrimp and Vegetable Stir-Fry

1 cup SMUCKER'S® Orange Marmalade
3 tablespoons soy sauce
2 tablespoons white vinegar
2 teaspoons hot pepper sauce
1½ tablespoons cornstarch
2 tablespoons vegetable oil
1 tablespoon fresh ginger, chopped
1 tablespoon garlic, chopped
24 fresh jumbo shrimp, peeled and deveined
1 red bell pepper, chopped
1 yellow or green bell pepper, chopped
3 cups broccoli florets
½ cup water
1 cup chopped green onions

Combine Smucker's® Orange Marmalade, soy sauce, vinegar, hot pepper sauce and cornstarch in small bowl. Stir to dissolve cornstarch and set aside.

Place large skillet or wok over high heat. Heat skillet for 1 minute, then add oil. Heat oil for 30 seconds, then add ginger, garlic and shrimp. Stir-fry for 2 to 3 minutes until shrimp begin to turn rosy pink in color. Remove shrimp; set aside.

Add peppers and broccoli to skillet and cook over high heat for 1 minute. Add water; cover and reduce heat to medium. Cook vegetables 4 to 5 minutes or until tender.

Uncover skillet and increase heat to high. Add shrimp and Smucker's® Orange Marmalade mixture. Cook shrimp for 2 minutes until sauce is thickened and shrimp are completely cooked. Correct seasoning with salt and fresh ground black pepper as needed.

Stir in onions and serve with boiled rice.

Makes 4 to 6 servings

Crab and Scallop Creole

1 tablespoon vegetable oil
1 large onion, chopped
1 large green bell pepper, chopped
2 cloves garlic, minced
1 can (15 ounces) crushed tomatoes, undrained
3 to 5 tablespoons FRANK'S® Original REDHOT® Cayenne Pepper Sauce, divided
½ teaspoon dried basil leaves
½ teaspoon dried thyme leaves
1 package (9 ounces) frozen corn
½ pound raw bay scallops
½ pound crabmeat or imitation crabmeat, flaked (2 cups)
Cooked white rice (optional)

1. Heat oil in large nonstick skillet over medium-high heat. Add onion, bell pepper and garlic; cook until tender. Add tomatoes with liquid, 2 to 3 tablespoons RedHot® sauce, basil and thyme. Cover; cook over medium-low heat 10 minutes, stirring occasionally.

2. Add corn and scallops. Bring to a boil. Reduce heat to low. Cover; cook 5 minutes or until scallops are translucent. Stir in crabmeat; heat through.

3. Stir in 1 to 2 tablespoons RedHot® sauce. Serve over rice, if desired.

Makes 4 servings

Prep Time: 20 minutes
Cook Time: 20 minutes

Smucker's® Mandarin Shrimp and Vegetable Stir-Fry

Seafood Stew

2 tablespoons butter or margarine
1 cup chopped onion
1 cup green bell pepper strips
1 teaspoon dried dill weed
  Dash ground red pepper
1 can (14½ ounces) diced tomatoes,
  undrained
½ cup white wine
2 tablespoons lime juice
8 ounces swordfish steak, cut into
  1-inch cubes
8 ounces bay or sea scallops, cut into
  quarters
1 bottle (8 ounces) clam juice
2 tablespoons cornstarch
2 cups frozen diced potatoes, thawed
  and drained
8 ounces frozen cooked medium
  shrimp, thawed and drained
½ cup whipping cream

1. Melt butter in Dutch oven over medium-high heat. Add onion, bell pepper, dill weed and red pepper; cook and stir 5 minutes or until vegetables are tender.

2. Reduce heat to medium. Add tomatoes with juice, wine and lime juice; bring to a boil. Add swordfish and scallops; cook and stir 2 minutes.

3. Combine clam juice and cornstarch in small bowl; stir until smooth.

4. Increase heat to high. Add potatoes, shrimp, whipping cream and clam juice mixture; bring to a boil. Season to taste with salt and black pepper. *Makes 6 servings*

Serving Suggestion: For a special touch, garnish stew with fresh lemon wedges and basil leaves.

Prep and Cook Time: 20 minutes

Shrimp Classico

⅔ cup milk
2 tablespoons margarine or butter
1 package (4.8 ounces) PASTA RONI®
  Angel Hair Pasta with Herbs
1 clove garlic, minced
1 package (10 ounces) frozen chopped
  spinach, thawed and well drained
1 package (10 ounces) frozen
  precooked shrimp, thawed and
  well drained
1 jar (2 ounces) chopped pimentos,
  drained

1. Microwave Directions: In 3-quart round microwavable glass casserole, combine 1⅔ cups water, milk and margarine. Microwave, uncovered, at HIGH 4 to 5 minutes or until boiling.

2. Gradually add pasta while stirring. Separate pasta with a fork, if needed. Stir in contents of seasoning packet and garlic.

3. Microwave, uncovered, at HIGH 4 minutes, stirring gently after 2 minutes. Separate pasta with a fork, if needed. Stir in spinach, shrimp and pimentos. Microwave at HIGH 1 to 2 minutes. Sauce will be very thin, but will thicken upon standing.

4. Let stand, uncovered, 2 minutes or until desired consistency. Stir before serving.
Makes 4 servings

Seafood Stew

Pink Shrimp and Pineapple

¼ cup KIKKOMAN® Stir-Fry Sauce
2 tablespoons water
2 medium zucchini
3 tablespoons vegetable oil, divided
½ pound medium-size raw shrimp, peeled and deveined
1 medium onion, chunked
1 teaspoon minced fresh ginger root
1 can (20 ounces) pineapple chunks in syrup, drained

Blend stir-fry sauce and water; set aside. Cut zucchini lengthwise in half, then crosswise into ¼-inch-thick slices. Heat 1 tablespoon oil in hot wok or large skillet over high heat. Add shrimp and stir-fry 1 minute; remove. Heat remaining 2 tablespoons oil in same pan. Add zucchini, onion and ginger; stir-fry 3 minutes. Add shrimp, pineapple and stir-fry sauce mixture; cook and stir until shrimp and vegetables are coated and heated through. *Makes 4 servings*

Shrimp Creole Stew

1½ cups raw small shrimp, shelled
1 bag (16 ounces) BIRDS EYE® frozen Farm Fresh Mixtures Broccoli, Cauliflower & Red Peppers
1 can (14½ ounces) diced tomatoes
1½ teaspoons salt
1 teaspoon hot pepper sauce
1 teaspoon vegetable oil

• In large saucepan, combine all ingredients.

• Cover; bring to boil. Reduce heat to medium-low; simmer 20 minutes or until shrimp turn opaque. *Makes 4 servings*

Serving Suggestion: Serve over Spanish or white rice and with additional hot pepper sauce for added zip.

Prep Time: 5 minutes

Cook Time: 20 minutes

Creamy "Crab" Fettuccine

1 pound imitation crabmeat sticks
6 ounces uncooked fettuccine
3 tablespoons margarine or butter, divided
1 small onion, chopped
2 ribs celery, chopped
½ medium red bell pepper, chopped
2 cloves garlic, minced
1 cup reduced-fat sour cream
1 cup reduced-fat mayonnaise
1 cup (4 ounces) shredded sharp Cheddar cheese
2 tablespoons chopped fresh parsley
¼ teaspoon salt
⅛ teaspoon black pepper
½ cup cornflake crumbs
Fresh chives (optional)

Preheat oven to 350°F. Spray 2-quart square baking dish with nonstick cooking spray.

Cut crabmeat into bite-size pieces. Cook pasta according to package directions until al dente. Drain and set aside.

Meanwhile, melt 1 tablespoon margarine in large skillet over medium-high heat. Add onion, celery, bell pepper and garlic; cook and stir 2 minutes or until vegetables are tender.

Combine sour cream, mayonnaise, cheese, parsley, salt and black pepper in large bowl. Add crabmeat, pasta and vegetable mixture, stirring gently to combine. Pour into prepared dish.

Melt remaining 2 tablespoons margarine. Combine cornflake crumbs and margarine in small bowl; sprinkle evenly over casserole.

Bake, uncovered, 30 minutes or until hot and bubbly. Garnish with chives, if desired. *Makes 6 servings*

Creamy "Crab" Fettuccine

EASY MEATLESS
MEALS

Vegetable & Cheese Platter

1 cup water
2 cups DOLE® Broccoli or Cauliflower
  Florets
1½ cups DOLE® Peeled Mini Carrots
1 cup DOLE® Sugar Peas or green
  beans
2 medium DOLE® Red, Yellow or Green
  Bell Peppers, cut into 2-inch pieces
1 package (8 ounces) mushrooms,
  stems trimmed
3 cups hot cooked brown or white rice
1 cup (4 ounces) shredded low-fat
  Cheddar cheese
⅓ cup crumbled feta cheese

• Pour water into large pot; bring to boil.
Add broccoli and carrots. Reduce heat to
low; cover and cook 5 minutes. Add sugar
peas, bell peppers and mushrooms; cook
5 minutes more or until vegetables are
tender-crisp. Drain vegetables.

• Spoon hot rice onto large serving platter;
top with vegetables. Sprinkle with cheeses.

• Cover with aluminum foil; let stand
3 minutes or until cheeses melt.

Makes 4 servings

Prep Time: 15 minutes

Cook Time: 15 minutes

Singapore Spicy Noodles

1¼ cups water
2 tablespoons ketchup
2½ teaspoons packed brown sugar
1½ teaspoons chopped cilantro
1 teaspoon cornstarch
¾ teaspoon LAWRY'S® Seasoned Salt
¾ teaspoon LAWRY'S® Garlic Powder
  with Parsley
¼ teaspoon crushed red pepper
¼ cup sliced green onions
2½ tablespoons chunky peanut butter
8 ounces linguine, cooked and drained
1 cup shredded red cabbage

In medium saucepan, combine water,
ketchup, sugar, cilantro, cornstarch and
seasonings. Bring to a boil. Reduce heat;
simmer, uncovered, 5 minutes. Cool 10
minutes; add green onions and peanut
butter; mix well. Toss sauce with hot
linguine and red cabbage.

Makes 4 servings

Serving Suggestion: Garnish with green
onion curls. Serve with a marinated
cucumber salad.

Vegetable & Cheese Platter

186

Greek Spinach and Feta Pie

⅓ cup butter, melted
2 eggs
1 package (10 ounces) frozen chopped
    spinach, thawed and squeezed dry
1 container (15 ounces) ricotta cheese
1 package (4 ounces) crumbled feta
    cheese
¾ teaspoon finely grated lemon peel
¼ teaspoon black pepper
⅛ teaspoon ground nutmeg
1 package (16 ounces) frozen phyllo
    dough, thawed

Preheat oven to 350°F. Brush 13×9-inch baking dish lightly with butter.

Beat eggs in medium bowl. Stir in spinach, ricotta, feta, lemon peel, pepper and nutmeg. Set aside.

Unwrap phyllo dough; remove 8 sheets. Cut dough in half crosswise forming 16 rectangles about 13×8½ inches. Cover dough with damp cloth or plastic wrap to keep moist while assembling pie. Reserve remaining dough for another use.

Place 1 piece of dough in prepared dish; brush top lightly with butter. Top with another piece of dough and brush lightly with butter. Continue layering with 6 pieces of dough, brushing each lightly with butter. Spoon spinach mixture evenly over dough.

Top spinach mixture with piece of dough; brush lightly with butter. Repeat layering with remaining 7 pieces of dough, brushing each piece lightly with butter.

Bake, uncovered, 35 to 40 minutes or until golden brown.   *Makes 6 servings*

Tip: Serve with a Greek vegetable salad made of cucumbers, tomatoes and red onions on a bed of romaine lettuce drizzled with red wine vinegar salad dressing.

Eggplant Pasta Bake

4 ounces bow-tie pasta
1 pound eggplant, diced
1 clove garlic, minced
¼ cup olive oil
1½ cups shredded Monterey Jack cheese
1 cup sliced green onions
½ cup grated Parmesan cheese
1 can (14½ ounces) DEL MONTE®
    FreshCut™ Brand Diced Tomatoes
    with Basil, Garlic & Oregano

1. Preheat oven to 350°F. Cook pasta according to package directions; drain.

2. Cook eggplant and garlic in oil in large skillet over medium-high heat until tender.

3. Toss eggplant with cooked pasta, 1 cup Jack cheese, green onions and Parmesan cheese.

4. Place in greased 9-inch square baking dish. Top with tomatoes and remaining ½ cup Jack cheese. Bake 15 minutes or until heated through.   *Makes 6 servings*

Prep and Cook Time: 30 minutes

Greek Spinach and Feta Pie

Celebration Pasta

2 cups fresh tortellini
1 bag (16 ounces) BIRDS EYE® frozen
    Farm Fresh Mixtures Broccoli, Corn
    & Red Peppers
1 tablespoon olive oil
1 teaspoon salt
1 teaspoon lemon juice
½ cup fresh or canned diced tomatoes

• In large saucepan, cook tortellini according to package directions; drain and return to saucepan.

• Cook vegetables according to package directions; drain and add to tortellini.

• In small bowl, combine oil, salt and lemon juice. Stir in tomatoes.

• Stir tomato mixture into pasta and vegetables; cook over medium heat 5 minutes or until heated through.

Makes 4 servings

Prep Time: 10 minutes

Cook Time: 10 minutes

Harvest Casserole

2 cups USA lentils, rinsed and cooked
2 cups fresh or frozen broccoli,
    chopped
1½ cups cooked rice
1¼ cups (6 ounces) shredded Cheddar
    cheese
1 tablespoon soy sauce
½ teaspoon salt (optional)
¼ teaspoon dried thyme
¼ teaspoon dried marjoram
¼ teaspoon dried rosemary
4 eggs
1 cup milk

Preheat oven to 350°F.

Mix lentils, broccoli, rice, cheese, soy sauce, salt, thyme, marjoram and rosemary in large bowl. Place mixture in greased 9-inch casserole dish.

Stir together eggs and milk in medium bowl. Pour egg mixture over lentil mixture. Bake 45 minutes or until lightly browned. Top with additional shredded Cheddar cheese, if desired.

Makes 8 servings

Favorite recipe from **USA Dry Pea & Lentil Council**

Vegetarian Tofu Stir-Fry

1 block tofu
2 tablespoons vegetable oil
1 teaspoon minced fresh gingerroot
1 medium onion, chunked
⅛ teaspoon salt
6 ounces fresh snow peas, trimmed
    and cut diagonally in half
⅓ cup KIKKOMAN® Stir-Fry Sauce
2 medium-size fresh tomatoes,
    chunked
¼ cup slivered blanched almonds,
    toasted

Cut tofu into ½-inch cubes; drain well on several layers of paper towels. Heat oil in hot wok or large skillet over high heat. Add ginger; stir-fry 30 seconds, or until fragrant. Add onion and salt; stir-fry 2 minutes. Add snow peas; stir-fry 1 minute. Add stir-fry sauce, tomatoes and tofu. Gently stir to coat tofu and vegetables with sauce. Reduce heat and cook only until tomatoes and tofu are heated through. Sprinkle with almonds; serve immediately.

Makes 4 servings

Celebration Pasta

Vegetable-Bean Chowder

½ cup chopped onion
½ cup chopped celery
2 cups water
½ teaspoon salt
2 cups cubed, peeled potatoes
1 cup carrot slices
1 can (15 ounces) cream-style corn
1 can (15 ounces) cannellini beans or
   navy beans, drained and rinsed
¼ teaspoon dried tarragon leaves
¼ teaspoon ground black pepper
2 cups 1% low-fat milk
2 tablespoons cornstarch

1. Spray 4-quart Dutch oven or large saucepan with nonstick cooking spray; heat over medium heat until hot. Add onion and celery. Cook and stir 3 minutes or crisp-tender.

2. Add water and salt; bring to a boil over high heat. Add potatoes and carrot. Reduce heat to medium. Simmer, covered, 10 minutes or until potatoes and carrot are tender.

3. Stir in corn, beans, tarragon and pepper. Simmer, covered, 10 minutes or until heated through.

4. Stir milk into cornstarch in medium bowl until smooth. Stir into vegetable mixture. Simmer, uncovered, until thickened.

Makes 5 (1½ cup) servings

Valley Eggplant Parmigiano

2 eggplants (about 1 pound each)
⅓ cup olive or vegetable oil
1 container (15 ounces) ricotta cheese
2 packages (1 ounce each) HIDDEN
   VALLEY® Milk Recipe Original
   Ranch® Salad Dressing Mix
2 eggs
2 teaspoons dry bread crumbs
1 cup tomato sauce
½ cup shredded mozzarella cheese
1 tablespoon grated Parmesan cheese
   Chopped parsley

Preheat oven to 350°F. Cut eggplants into ½-inch slices. Brush some of the oil onto two large baking sheets. Arrange eggplant slices in single layer on sheets and brush tops with additional oil. Bake until eggplant is fork-tender, about 20 minutes.

In large bowl, whisk together ricotta cheese and salad dressing mix; whisk in eggs. In 13×9×2-inch baking dish, layer half the eggplant. Sprinkle 1 teaspoon of the bread crumbs over eggplant; spread all the ricotta mixture on top. Arrange remaining eggplant in another layer. Sprinkle with remaining 1 teaspoon bread crumbs; top with tomato sauce. Sprinkle cheeses on top. Bake until cheeses begin to brown, about 30 minutes. Sprinkle with parsley.

Makes 6 to 8 servings

Vegetable-Bean Chowder

Bean Ragoût with Cilantro-Cornmeal Dumplings

1 tablespoon vegetable oil
2 large onions, chopped
1 poblano chili, seeded and chopped
3 cloves garlic, minced
3 tablespoons chili powder
2 teaspoons ground cumin
1 teaspoon dried oregano leaves
1 can (28 ounces) tomatoes,
 undrained, chopped
2 small zucchini, cut into ½-inch pieces
2 cups chopped red bell peppers
1 can (15 ounces) pinto beans, drained
1 can (15 ounces) black beans, drained
¾ teaspoon salt, divided
 Ground black pepper
½ cup all-purpose flour
½ cup cornmeal
1 teaspoon baking powder
2 tablespoons vegetable shortening
¼ cup shredded Cheddar cheese
1 tablespoon minced fresh cilantro
½ cup milk

1. Heat oil in Dutch oven over medium heat until hot. Add onions; cook and stir 5 minutes or until tender. Add chili, garlic, chili powder, cumin and oregano; cook and stir 1 to 2 minutes.

2. Add tomatoes, zucchini, bell peppers, beans and ¼ teaspoon salt; bring to a boil. Reduce heat to medium-low. Simmer, uncovered, 5 to 10 minutes or until zucchini is tender. Season to taste with salt and black pepper.

3. To prepare dumplings, combine flour, cornmeal, baking powder and remaining ½ teaspoon salt in medium bowl; cut in shortening with pastry blender or two knives until mixture resembles coarse crumbs.

4. Stir in cheese and cilantro. Pour milk into flour mixture; blend just until dry ingredients are moistened.

5. Drop dumpling dough into 6 mounds on top of simmering ragoût. Cook, uncovered, 5 minutes. Cover and cook 5 to 10 minutes more or until wooden toothpick inserted in dumplings comes out clean.

Makes 6 servings

Mushroom & Onion Egg Bake

1 tablespoon vegetable oil
4 green onions, chopped
4 ounces mushrooms, sliced
1 cup low-fat cottage cheese
1 cup sour cream
6 eggs
2 tablespoons all-purpose flour
¼ teaspoon salt
⅛ teaspoon freshly ground pepper
 Dash hot pepper sauce

1. Preheat oven to 350°F. Grease shallow 1-quart baking dish.

2. Heat oil in medium skillet over medium heat. Add onions and mushrooms; cook until tender. Set aside.

3. In blender or food processor, blend cottage cheese until almost smooth. Add sour cream, eggs, flour, salt, pepper and hot pepper sauce; process until combined. Stir in onions and mushrooms. Pour into greased dish. Bake about 40 minutes or until knife inserted near center comes out clean.

Makes about 6 servings

*Bean Ragoût with
Cilantro-Cornmeal Dumplings*

Sesame Peanut Spaghetti Squash

1 spaghetti squash (3 pounds)
⅓ cup sesame seeds
⅓ cup vegetable broth
2 tablespoons reduced-sodium soy sauce
1 tablespoon sugar
2 teaspoons sesame oil
1 teaspoon cornstarch
1 teaspoon red pepper flakes
1 teaspoon Worcestershire sauce
1 tablespoon vegetable oil
2 medium carrots, julienned
1 large red bell pepper, seeded and thinly sliced
¼ pound fresh snow peas, cut diagonally in half
½ cup coarsely chopped unsalted peanuts
⅓ cup minced fresh cilantro

1. Preheat oven to 350°F. Spray 13×9-inch baking dish with cooking spray. Wash squash; cut in half lengthwise. Remove and discard seeds. Place squash, cut-side down, in prepared dish. Bake 45 minutes to 1 hour or until just tender.

2. Using fork, remove spaghettilike strands from hot squash and place strands in large bowl. Cover and keep warm.

3. To toast sesame seeds, heat wok over medium-high heat until hot. Add sesame seeds; cook and stir 45 seconds or until golden brown. Remove to blender. Add broth, soy sauce, sugar, sesame oil, cornstarch, red pepper flakes and Worcestershire sauce. Process until mixture is coarsely puréed.

4. Heat wok or large skillet over medium-high heat 1 minute or until hot. Drizzle vegetable oil into wok; heat 30 seconds. Add carrots; stir-fry 1 minute. Add bell pepper; stir-fry 2 minutes or until vegetables are crisp-tender. Add snow peas; stir-fry 1 minute. Stir sesame seed mixture; add to wok. Cook and stir 1 minute or until sauce is thickened.

5. Pour vegetable mixture over spaghetti squash. Add peanuts and cilantro; toss well.

Makes 4 servings

Green Bean Casserole

1 can (10¾ ounces) condensed cream of mushroom soup
¾ cup milk
⅛ teaspoon ground black pepper
2 packages (9 ounces each) frozen cut green beans, thawed and drained *or* 2 cans (14½ ounces each) cut green beans, drained
1⅓ cups FRENCH'S® French Fried Onions, divided

Preheat oven to 350°F. Combine soup, milk and ground pepper in 1½-quart casserole; stir until well blended. Stir in beans and ⅔ cup French Fried Onions.

Bake, uncovered, 30 minutes or until hot. Stir; sprinkle with remaining ⅔ cup onions. Bake 5 minutes or until onions are golden.

Makes 6 servings

Microwave Directions: Prepare green bean mixture as above. Pour into 1½-quart microwavable casserole. Cover loosely with plastic wrap. Microwave on HIGH 8 to 10 minutes or until heated through, stirring halfway through cooking time. Uncover; sprinkle with remaining onions. Cook 1 minute or until onions are golden. Let stand 5 minutes.

Prep Time: 5 minutes

Cook Time: 35 minutes

Sesame Peanut Spaghetti Squash

Cheesy Polenta with Zucchini Stew

2¼ cups water, divided
  1 cup stone-ground or regular yellow
    cornmeal
  2 eggs
  2 egg whites
  ¾ cup reduced-fat sharp Cheddar
    cheese
  1 jalapeño pepper, minced*
  1 teaspoon margarine
  ½ teaspoon salt, divided
  1 tablespoon olive oil
  1 cup chopped onion
  2 cups coarsely chopped peeled
    eggplant
  3 cloves minced garlic
  3 cups chopped zucchini
  1 cup chopped tomato
  ½ cup chopped yellow bell pepper
  2 tablespoons minced fresh parsley
  1 tablespoon minced fresh oregano
  ¼ teaspoon minced fresh rosemary
  ¼ teaspoon red pepper flakes
  ¼ teaspoon freshly ground pepper
    blend

*Jalapeño peppers can sting and irritate the skin; wear rubber gloves when handling peppers and do not touch your eyes. Wash hands after handling jalapeño peppers.

1. Bring 2 cups water to a boil. Slowly add cornmeal, stirring constantly. Bring to a boil, stirring constantly, until mixture thickens. Lightly beat eggs and egg whites with remaining ¼ cup water. Add to cornmeal; cook and stir until bubbly. Remove from heat; stir in cheese, jalapeño pepper, margarine and ¼ teaspoon salt. Pour into 9-inch square baking pan. Cover and refrigerate several hours or until firm.

2. Heat olive oil in medium saucepan over medium heat until hot. Cook and stir onion, eggplant and garlic 5 minutes or until onion is transparent. Add zucchini, tomato, bell pepper, parsley, oregano, rosemary, remaining ¼ teaspoon salt, red pepper flakes and pepper blend. Simmer, uncovered, 1 hour.

3. Spray large nonstick skillet with nonstick vegetable cooking spray. Heat skillet over medium heat until hot. Cut polenta in 6 rectangles. Cook over medium heat 8 minutes on each side or until crusty and lightly browned. Serve zucchini stew over polenta. *Makes 6 servings*

Baked Tomato Risotto

1 jar (28 ounces) spaghetti sauce
  1 can (14 ounces) vegetable broth
  2 cups halved sliced zucchini
  1 can (4 ounces) sliced mushrooms
  1 cup arborio rice
  2 cups (8 ounces) shredded mozzarella
    cheese

Preheat oven to 350°F. Spray 3-quart casserole with nonstick cooking spray.

Combine spaghetti sauce, broth, zucchini, mushrooms and rice in prepared dish.

Bake, covered, 30 minutes. Remove from oven and stir casserole. Cover and bake 15 to 20 minutes more or until rice is tender. Remove from oven; sprinkle evenly with cheese. Bake, uncovered, 5 minutes or until cheese is melted. *Makes 6 servings*

Baked Tomato Risotto

Stuffed Manicotti

MANICOTTI

12 ounces manicotti (about 12 noodles)
2 cups (8 ounces) shredded ALPINE LACE® Reduced Fat Mozzarella Cheese
2 cups part-skim ricotta cheese
⅓ cup slivered fresh basil leaves or 2 tablespoons dried basil
¼ cup Italian seasoned dry bread crumbs

PARMESAN SAUCE

1½ cups 2% low fat milk
2 tablespoons all-purpose flour
1 teaspoon Worcestershire sauce
¼ teaspoon crushed red pepper flakes
1 cup (4 ounces) shredded ALPINE LACE® Fat Free Pasteurized Process Skim Milk Cheese Product—For Parmesan Lovers, divided

1. Preheat the oven to 375°F. Spray a 13×9×2-inch baking dish with nonstick cooking spray. Prepare the manicotti according to package directions, transfer to paper towels and keep warm.

2. To stuff the Manicotti: In a small bowl, stir together the mozzarella cheese, ricotta cheese, basil and bread crumbs. Using a small spoon, stuff the manicotti with the cheese mixture. Arrange in a single layer in the baking dish.

3. To make the Parmesan Sauce: In a medium-size saucepan, combine the milk, flour, Worcestershire and red pepper flakes. Bring to a boil, stirring constantly, over medium-high heat until the sauce thickens. Stir in ½ cup of the Parmesan.

4. Pour the sauce over the manicotti, completely covering the top. Sprinkle with the remaining ½ cup of the Parmesan. Cover with foil and bake for 20 minutes or until bubbly.

5. Uncover, turn the oven to broil and broil 4 inches from the heat for 2 minutes or until golden brown.

Makes 6 main-dish servings

Hearty Minestrone Soup

2 cans (10¾ ounces each) condensed Italian tomato soup
3 cups water
3 cups cooked vegetables, such as zucchini, peas, corn or beans
2 cups cooked ditalini pasta
1⅓ cups FRENCH'S® French Fried Onions

Combine soup and water in large saucepan. Add vegetables and pasta. Bring to a boil. Reduce heat. Cook until heated through, stirring often.

Place French Fried Onions in microwavable dish. Microwave on HIGH 1 minute or until onions are golden.

Ladle soup into individual bowls. Sprinkle with onions.

Makes 6 servings

Prep Time: 10 minutes

Cook Time: 5 minutes

Hearty Minestrone Soup

Chilies Rellenos Casserole

3 eggs, separated
¾ cup milk
¾ cup all-purpose flour
½ teaspoon salt
1 tablespoon butter or margarine
½ cup chopped onion
2 cans (7 ounces each) whole green
   chilies, drained
8 slices (1 ounce each) Monterey Jack
   cheese, cut into halves
   Garnishes: sour cream, sliced green
    onions, pitted ripe olive slices,
    guacamole and salsa

1. Preheat oven to 350°F.

2. Combine egg yolks, milk, flour and salt in blender or food processor container; blend until smooth. Pour into bowl; let stand until ready to use.

3. Melt butter in small skillet over medium heat. Add onion; cook and stir until tender.

4. Pat chilies dry with paper towels. Slit each chili lengthwise and carefully remove seeds. Place 2 slices of cheese and 1 tablespoon onion in each chili; reshape chilies to cover cheese. Place in single layer in greased 13×9-inch baking dish.

5. In small clean bowl, beat egg whites until soft peaks form; fold into yolk mixture. Pour over chilies.

6. Bake 20 to 25 minutes or until topping is puffed and knife inserted in center comes out clean. Broil 4 inches from heat source 30 seconds or until topping is golden brown. Serve with desired garnishes.

Makes 4 servings

Wild Rice, Mushroom and Spinach Skillet

⅓ cup uncooked wild rice
⅓ cup uncooked brown rice
⅓ cup uncooked long-grain white rice
1½ cups water
1 can (10½ ounces) reduced-sodium
   vegetable broth
2 tablespoons margarine
2 cups sliced shiitake mushrooms
2 cups quartered brown mushrooms
2 cups sliced bok choy
2 cups shredded spinach
¼ cup crumbled feta cheese

1. Combine wild rice, brown rice, long-grain white rice, water and vegetable broth in medium saucepan. Bring to a boil over high heat; reduce heat to low. Simmer, covered, 45 minutes or until rice is tender.

2. Melt margarine in large saucepan over medium heat. Add mushrooms; cook and stir 3 minutes. Add bok choy and spinach; cook and stir 3 minutes or until greens are wilted.

3. Add rice to greens in saucepan; stir until blended. Sprinkle with cheese just before serving. Garnish, if desired.

Makes 8 servings

*Wild Rice, Mushroom
and Spinach Skillet*

202

Vegetable Soup with Delicious Dumplings

SOUP

2 tablespoons WESSON® Vegetable Oil
1 cup diced onion
¾ cup sliced celery
7 cups homemade chicken broth *or*
    4 (14½-ounce) cans chicken broth
2 (14.5-ounce) cans HUNT'S® Stewed
    Tomatoes
½ teaspoon garlic powder
½ teaspoon salt
½ teaspoon fines herbs seasoning
⅛ teaspoon pepper
1 (16-ounce) bag frozen mixed
    vegetables
1 (15½-ounce) can HUNT'S® Red
    Kidney Beans, drained
⅓ cup uncooked long-grain rice

DUMPLINGS

2 cups all-purpose flour
3 tablespoons baking powder
1 teaspoon salt
⅔ cup milk
⅓ cup WESSON® Vegetable Oil
1½ teaspoons chopped fresh parsley

Soup: In a large Dutch oven, heat Wesson® Oil. Add onion and celery; sauté until crisp-tender. Stir in *next 6* ingredients, ending with pepper; bring to a boil. Add vegetables, beans and rice. Reduce heat; cover and simmer 15 to 20 minutes or until rice is cooked and vegetables are tender.

Dumplings: Meanwhile, in a medium bowl, combine flour, baking powder and salt; blend well. Add milk, Wesson® Oil and parsley; mix until batter forms a ball in the bowl. Drop dough by rounded tablespoons into simmering soup. Cook, covered, 10 minutes; remove lid and cook an additional 10 minutes. *Makes 10 servings*

Ratatouille Pot Pie

¼ cup olive oil
1 medium eggplant (about 1 pound),
    peeled and cut into ½-inch pieces
1 large onion, chopped
1 green or yellow bell pepper,
    chopped
1½ teaspoons minced garlic
1 can (14½ ounces) pasta-ready diced
    tomatoes with garlic and herbs or
    Italian stewed tomatoes,
    undrained
1 teaspoon dried basil leaves
½ teaspoon red pepper flakes
¼ teaspoon salt
1 tablespoon balsamic vinegar
2 cups (8 ounces) shredded mozzarella
    cheese, divided
1 package (10 ounces) refrigerated
    pizza dough

1. Preheat oven to 425°F. Heat oil in large skillet over medium heat until hot. Add eggplant, onion, bell pepper and garlic. Cook 10 minutes or until eggplant begins to brown, stirring occasionally. Stir in tomatoes with juice, basil, pepper flakes and salt. Cook, uncovered, over medium-low heat 5 minutes.

2. Remove from heat; stir in vinegar. Let stand 10 minutes; stir in 1 cup cheese. Transfer mixture to ungreased 11×7-inch casserole dish. Sprinkle with remaining cheese.

3. Unroll pizza dough; make decorative cut-outs using small cookie cutter, if desired. Arrange dough over top of casserole. Spray dough with nonstick cooking spray. Bake 15 minutes or until crust is golden brown and vegetable mixture is bubbly. Let stand 5 minutes before serving. *Makes 6 servings*

Vegetable Soup with Delicious Dumplings

Spinach and Mushroom Enchiladas

2 packages (10 ounces each) frozen chopped spinach, thawed
1½ cups sliced mushrooms
1 can (15 ounces) pinto beans, drained and rinsed
3 teaspoons chili powder, divided
¼ teaspoon red pepper flakes
1 can (8 ounces) low-sodium tomato sauce
2 tablespoons water
½ teaspoon hot pepper sauce
8 (8-inch) corn tortillas
1 cup shredded Monterey Jack cheese
Shredded lettuce (optional)
Chopped tomatoes (optional)
Light sour cream (optional)

1. Combine spinach, mushrooms, beans, 2 teaspoons chili powder and red pepper flakes in large skillet over medium heat. Cook and stir 5 minutes; remove from heat.

2. Combine tomato sauce, water, remaining 1 teaspoon chili powder and pepper sauce in medium skillet. Dip tortillas into tomato sauce mixture; stack tortillas on waxed paper.

3. Divide spinach filling into 8 portions. Spoon onto center of tortillas; roll up and place in 11×8- inch microwavable dish. (Secure rolls with wooden picks if desired.) Spread remaining tomato sauce mixture over enchiladas.

4. Cover with vented plastic wrap. Microwave at MEDIUM (50%) 10 minutes or until heated through. Sprinkle with cheese. Microwave at MEDIUM 3 minutes or until cheese is melted. Serve with lettuce, tomatoes and sour cream, if desired.

Makes 4 servings

Noodles Thai Style

¼ cup ketchup
2 tablespoons reduced-sodium soy sauce
1 tablespoon sugar
¼ to ½ teaspoon crushed red pepper
¼ teaspoon ground ginger
2 teaspoons FLEISCHMANN'S® Original Margarine (70% corn oil), divided
1 cup EGG BEATERS® Healthy Real Egg Substitute
8 green onions, cut in 1½-inch pieces
1 clove garlic, minced
¾ pound fresh bean sprouts, rinsed and well drained
8 ounces linguine, cooked and drained
¼ cup PLANTERS® Dry Roasted Unsalted Peanuts, chopped

In small bowl, combine ketchup, soy sauce, sugar, pepper and ginger; set aside.

In large nonstick skillet over medium heat, melt 1 teaspoon margarine. Pour Egg Beaters® into skillet. Cook, stirring occasionally until set. Remove to another small bowl.

In same skillet over medium heat, sauté green onions and garlic in remaining 1 teaspoon margarine for 2 minutes. Stir in bean sprouts; cook for 2 minutes. Stir in ketchup mixture. Cook until heated through. Transfer to large bowl; add eggs and linguine. Toss until combined. Top with peanuts. *Makes 6 (1-cup) servings*

Prep Time: 25 minutes

Cook Time: 5 minutes

Spinach and Mushroom Enchiladas

Zesty Mixed Vegetables

8 ounces green beans
½ small head cauliflower
2 green onions with tops
2 cloves garlic
1 or 2 jalapeño or Thai chili peppers*
2 tablespoons vegetable oil
8 ounces peeled fresh baby carrots
1 cup vegetable broth, divided
1 tablespoon cornstarch
1 teaspoon sugar
¼ teaspoon salt
2 tablespoons oyster sauce
    Red and yellow bell pepper strips for garnish

Chili peppers can sting and irritate the skin; wear rubber gloves when handling and do not touch eyes. Wash hands after handling chili peppers.

• Trim ends from beans; discard. Cut beans diagonally into thirds or quarters. Cut cauliflower into florets. Cut onions into ½-inch pieces; keep white part and green tops of onions in separate piles. Chop garlic. Cut jalapeño lengthwise in half. Remove stem and seeds. Cut jalapeño crosswise into thin slices.

• Heat wok over high heat about 1 minute or until hot. Drizzle oil into wok and heat 30 seconds. Add white part of onions, beans, cauliflower, garlic and jalapeño; stir-fry until tender. Add carrots and ¾ cup broth. Cover and bring to a boil. Reduce heat to low; cook until carrots and beans are crisp-tender.

• Combine cornstarch, sugar and salt in cup; stir in remaining ¼ cup broth and oyster sauce until smooth. Stir into wok. Cook until sauce boils and thickens. Stir in onion tops. Transfer to serving dish. Garnish, if desired.

Makes 4 servings

Double Cheese Strata

10 to 12 slices Italian bread, about ½ inch thick
⅔ cup (about 5 ounces) sharp Cheddar light cold pack cheese food, softened
1⅓ cups FRENCH'S® French Fried Onions
1 package (10 ounces) frozen chopped broccoli, thawed and drained
½ cup (2 ounces) shredded Swiss cheese
5 eggs
3 cups milk
2 tablespoons FRENCH'S® Deli Brown Mustard
½ teaspoon salt
¼ teaspoon ground white pepper

Grease 3-quart baking dish. Spread bread slices with Cheddar cheese. Arrange slices in a single layer in bottom of prepared baking dish, pressing to fit. Layer French Fried Onions, broccoli and Swiss cheese over bread.

Beat together eggs, milk, mustard, salt and pepper in medium bowl until well blended. Pour egg mixture over layers. Let stand 10 minutes. Preheat oven to 350°F. Bake 35 minutes or until knife inserted in center comes out clean. (Cover loosely with foil near end of baking if top becomes too brown.) Cool on wire rack 10 minutes. Cut into squares to serve.   *Makes 8 servings*

Prep Time: 15 minutes

Cook Time: 35 minutes

Stand Time: 10 minutes

Zesty Mixed Vegetables

208

Tuscan Vegetable Stew

2 tablespoons olive oil
2 teaspoons bottled minced garlic
2 packages (4 ounces each) sliced
    mixed exotic mushrooms *or*
    1 package (8 ounces) sliced button
    mushrooms
¼ cup sliced shallots or chopped sweet
    onion
1 jar (7 ounces) roasted red peppers
1 can (14½ ounces) Italian-style stewed
    tomatoes, undrained
1 can (19 ounces) cannellini beans,
    drained
1 bunch fresh basil*
1 tablespoon balsamic vinegar
    Salt
    Black pepper
    Grated Romano, Parmesan or Asiago
    cheese

If fresh basil is not available, add 2 teaspoons dried basil leaves to stew with tomatoes.

1. Heat oil and garlic in large deep skillet over medium heat. Add mushrooms and shallots; cook 5 minutes, stirring occasionally.

2. While mushroom mixture is cooking, drain and rinse peppers; cut into 1-inch pieces. Snip tomatoes in can into small pieces with scissors.

3. Add tomatoes, peppers and beans to skillet; bring to a boil. Reduce heat to medium-low. Cover and simmer 10 minutes, stirring once.

4. While stew is simmering, cut basil leaves into thin strips to measure ¼ cup packed. Stir basil and vinegar into stew; add salt and pepper to taste. Sprinkle each serving with cheese. *Makes 4 servings*

Prep and Cook Time: 18 minutes

Herbed Veggie Cheese and Rice

1 bag (16 ounces) BIRDS EYE® frozen
    Farm Fresh Mixtures Broccoli,
    Green Beans, Pearl Onions & Red
    Peppers
2 cups cooked white rice
2 tablespoons grated Parmesan cheese
1 teaspoon dried basil
1 teaspoon dill weed
½ cup reduced-fat shredded Cheddar
    cheese
½ cup reduced-fat shredded Monterey
    Jack cheese

• In large saucepan, cook vegetables according to package directions; drain and return to saucepan.

• Add rice, using fork to keep rice fluffy.

• Add Parmesan cheese, basil, dill and salt and pepper to taste.

• Add Cheddar and Monterey Jack cheeses; toss together. Cook over medium heat until heated through. *Makes 4 servings*

Prep Time: 6 minutes

Cook Time: 12 to 15 minutes

Minestrone Soup

¾ cup small shell pasta
2 cans (about 14 ounces each)
    vegetable broth
1 can (28 ounces) crushed tomatoes
    in tomato purée
1 can (15 ounces) white beans,
    drained and rinsed
1 package (16 ounces) frozen
    vegetable medley, such as broccoli,
    green beans, carrots and red
    peppers
4 to 6 teaspoons prepared pesto

1. Bring 4 cups water to a boil in large saucepan over high heat. Stir in pasta; cook 8 to 10 minutes or until tender. Drain.

2. While pasta is cooking, combine broth, tomatoes and beans in Dutch oven. Cover and bring to a boil over high heat. Reduce heat to low; simmer 3 to 5 minutes.

3. Add vegetables to broth mixture and return to a boil over high heat. Stir in pasta. Ladle soup into bowls; spoon about 1 teaspoon pesto in center of each serving.

Makes 4 to 6 servings

Prep and Cook Time: 20 minutes

Monterey Spaghetti Casserole

  4 ounces uncooked spaghetti
  1 cup sour cream
  1 egg, beaten
  2 cups (8 ounces) shredded Monterey
      Jack cheese
  ¼ cup grated Parmesan cheese
  1 package (10 ounces) frozen chopped
      spinach, thawed and drained
  1⅓ cups FRENCH'S® French Fried Onions,
      divided

Preheat oven to 350°F. Cook spaghetti according to package directions using shortest cooking time. Drain.

Combine sour cream and egg in 8-inch square baking dish. Stir in spaghetti, cheeses, spinach and ⅔ cup French Fried Onions.

Cover; bake 30 minutes or until heated through. Stir. Top with remaining ⅔ cup onions. Bake, uncovered, 5 minutes or until onions are golden. *Makes 4 servings*

Prep Time: 10 minutes

Cook Time: 35 minutes

Mac & Cheese with Crunchy Herb Crust

  1 pound elbow macaroni
  1 cup chopped yellow onion
  1 cup chopped red bell pepper
  1 cup herb seasoned dry stuffing,
      crumbled, divided
  1½ cups skim milk
  12 ounces (2 cartons) ALPINE LACE®
      Reduced Fat Cream Cheese with
      Garlic & Herbs
  1 teaspoon low sodium Worcestershire
      sauce
  ¼ teaspoon ground nutmeg
      Paprika
  2 tablespoons extra virgin olive oil

• Preheat the oven to 350°F. Spray a 12-inch round or oval ovenproof baking dish with nonstick cooking spray. Cook the macaroni according to package directions until al dente. Drain well, place in the baking dish and keep warm.

• Spray a large nonstick skillet with the nonstick cooking spray and heat over medium-high heat for 1 minute. Add the onion and bell pepper and sauté for 5 minutes or until soft. Toss with the macaroni and ½ cup of the stuffing.

• In a small saucepan, bring the milk to a boil over medium heat. Add the cream cheese and stir until melted. Remove from the heat and stir in the Worcestershire and nutmeg. Pour over the macaroni mixture. (Do not stir.)

• Top with the remaining ½ cup of stuffing, then sprinkle with the paprika and olive oil. Cover tightly with foil and bake for 30 minutes or until bubbly and hot. Serve hot.

Makes 8 servings

Szechuan Vegetable Stir-Fry

8 ounces firm tofu, drained and cut
    into cubes
1 cup canned vegetable broth, divided
½ cup orange juice
⅓ cup soy sauce
1 to 2 teaspoons hot chili oil
½ teaspoon fennel seeds
½ teaspoon ground black pepper
2 tablespoons cornstarch
3 tablespoons vegetable oil
1 cup sliced green onions and tops
3 medium carrots, peeled and
    diagonally sliced
3 cloves garlic, minced
2 teaspoons minced fresh ginger
¼ pound button mushrooms, sliced
1 medium red bell pepper, seeded and
    cut into 1-inch squares
¼ pound fresh snow peas, cut
    diagonally in half
8 ounces broccoli florets, steamed
½ cup peanuts
4 to 6 cups hot cooked rice

1. Place tofu in 8-inch round or square glass baking dish. Combine ½ cup broth, orange juice, soy sauce, chili oil, fennel seeds and black pepper in 2-cup measure; pour over tofu. Let stand 15 to 60 minutes. Drain, reserving marinade.

2. Combine cornstarch and remaining ½ cup broth in medium bowl. Add reserved marinade; set aside.

3. Heat vegetable oil in wok or large skillet over high heat until hot. Add onions, carrots, garlic and ginger; stir-fry 3 minutes. Add tofu, mushrooms, bell pepper and snow peas; stir-fry 2 to 3 minutes or until vegetables are crisp-tender. Add broccoli; stir-fry 1 minute or until heated through.

4. Stir cornstarch mixture. Add to wok; cook 1 to 2 minutes or until bubbly. Stir in peanuts. Serve over rice.

Makes 4 to 6 servings

Eggplant Bulgur Casserole

1 cup bulgur wheat
½ cup chopped green bell pepper
¼ cup chopped onion
¼ cup butter
4 cups cubed peeled eggplant
1 (15-ounce) can tomato sauce
1 (14½-ounce) can tomatoes,
    undrained, cut up
½ cup cold water
½ teaspoon dried oregano leaves,
    crushed
1 (8-ounce) package PHILADELPHIA
    BRAND® Cream Cheese, softened
1 egg
    KRAFT® 100% Grated Parmesan
    Cheese

• Preheat oven to 350°F.

• Sauté bulgur wheat, pepper and onion in butter in large skillet until vegetables are tender.

• Stir in eggplant, tomato sauce, tomatoes, water and oregano. Cover; simmer 15 to 20 minutes or until eggplant is tender, stirring occasionally.

• Beat cream cheese and egg in small mixing bowl at medium speed with electric mixer until well blended.

• Place half of vegetable mixture in 1½-quart baking dish or casserole; top with cream cheese mixture and remaining vegetable mixture. Cover.

• Bake 15 minutes. Remove cover; sprinkle with Parmesan cheese. Continue baking 10 minutes or until thoroughly heated.

Makes 8 to 10 servings

Prep Time: 30 minutes

Cook Time: 25 minutes

Szechuan Vegetable Stir-Fry

Broccoli-Stuffed Shells

1 tablespoon butter or margarine
¼ cup chopped onion
1 cup ricotta cheese
1 egg
2 cups chopped cooked broccoli *or*
  1 package (10 ounces) frozen
  chopped broccoli, thawed and well
  drained
1 cup (4 ounces) shredded Monterey
  Jack cheese
20 jumbo pasta shells
1 can (28 ounces) crushed tomatoes
  with added puree
1 package (1 ounce) HIDDEN VALLEY®
  Milk Recipe Original Ranch® salad
  dressing mix
¼ cup grated Parmesan cheese

Preheat oven to 350°F. In small skillet, melt butter over medium heat. Add onion; cook until onion is tender but not browned. Remove from heat; cool. In large bowl, stir ricotta cheese and egg until well-blended. Add broccoli and Jack cheese; mix well. In large pot of boiling water, cook pasta shells 8 to 10 minutes or just until tender; drain. Rinse under cold running water; drain again. Stuff each shell with about 2 tablespoons broccoli-cheese mixture.

In medium bowl, combine tomatoes, sautéed onion and salad dressing mix; mix well. Pour one-third of the tomato mixture into 13×9-inch baking dish. Arrange filled shells in dish. Spoon remaining tomato mixture over top. Sprinkle with Parmesan cheese. Bake, covered, until hot and bubbly, about 30 minutes. *Makes 4 servings*

Vegetarian Paella

1 tablespoon olive oil
1 medium onion, chopped
1 serrano pepper, finely chopped
1 red bell pepper, diced
1 green bell pepper, diced
3 cloves garlic, minced
½ teaspoon saffron threads, crushed
½ teaspoon paprika
1 cup uncooked long-grain white rice
3 cups water
1 can (15 ounces) chick-peas
  (garbanzo beans), rinsed and
  drained
1 can (14 ounces) artichoke hearts in
  water, drained and cut into halves
1 cup frozen green peas
1½ teaspoons grated lemon peel

1. Preheat oven to 375°F. Heat oil in large paella pan or heavy, ovenproof skillet over medium-high heat. Add onion, serrano pepper and bell peppers; cook and stir about 7 minutes.

2. Add garlic, saffron and paprika; cook 3 minutes. Add rice; cook and stir 1 minute. Add water, chick-peas, artichoke hearts, green peas and lemon peel; mix well.

3. Cover and bake 25 minutes or until rice is tender. Garnish with fresh bay leaves and lemon slices, if desired. *Makes 6 servings*

Broccoli-Stuffed Shells

Indian Vegetable Curry

2 to 3 teaspoons curry powder
1 can (16 ounces) sliced potatoes,
    drained
1 bag (16 ounces) BIRDS EYE® frozen
    Farm Fresh Mixtures Broccoli,
    Cauliflower and Carrots
1 can (15 ounces) chick-peas, drained
1 can (14½ ounces) stewed tomatoes
1 can (13¾ ounces) vegetable broth
2 tablespoons cornstarch

• Stir curry powder in large skillet over high
heat until fragrant, about 30 seconds.

• Stir in potatoes, vegetables, chick-peas and
tomatoes; bring to boil. Reduce heat to
medium-high; cover and cook 8 minutes.

• Blend broth with cornstarch; stir into
vegetables. Cook until thickened.

Makes about 6 servings

Serving Suggestion: Serve with white or
brown rice.

Prep Time: 5 minutes
Cook Time: 15 minutes

Veggie Soup

1 bag (16 ounces) BIRDS EYE® frozen
    Mixed Vegetables
1 can (11 ounces) tomato rice soup
1 can (10 ounces) French onion soup
1 soup can of water

• In large saucepan, cook vegetables
according to package directions; drain.

• Add both cans of soup and water; cook
over medium-high heat until heated
through.

Makes 4 servings

Serving Suggestion: Sprinkle individual
servings evenly with 1 cup shredded
Cheddar cheese.

Prep Time: 2 minutes
Cook Time: 10 to 12 minutes

Southwestern Pasta Sauce

¼ cup olive oil
 2 medium onions, sliced
 1 clove garlic, minced
3½ cups canned tomatoes, crushed or
     coarsely chopped
 ¾ teaspoon TABASCO® Pepper Sauce
 2 tablespoons fresh cilantro, minced
 ¼ teaspoon salt
 ¼ teaspoon granulated sugar
12 ounces angel hair pasta, freshly
     cooked
    Grated Parmesan cheese

Heat oil over medium heat in large, heavy
non-aluminum saucepan. Stir in onions and
garlic; sauté 10 to 12 minutes or until
tender, stirring occasionally. Add tomatoes,
TABASCO® Sauce, cilantro, salt and sugar;
bring to a boil. Reduce heat to low; simmer,
uncovered, 30 minutes or until slightly
thickened.

Place hot cooked pasta on heated serving
platter; top with sauce. Sprinkle with
Parmesan cheese. *Makes 4 servings*

Indian Vegetable Curry

Farmstand Frittata

½ cup chopped onion
1 medium red bell pepper, seeded and cut into thin strips
1 cup broccoli florets, blanched and drained
1 cup cooked, quartered, unpeeled red-skinned potatoes
6 egg whites
1 cup cholesterol-free egg substitute
1 tablespoon chopped fresh parsley
½ teaspoon salt
¼ teaspoon ground black pepper
½ cup (2 ounces) shredded reduced-fat Cheddar cheese

1. Spray large nonstick ovenproof skillet with cooking spray; heat over medium heat until hot. Add onion and bell pepper; cook and stir 3 minutes or until crisp-tender.

2. Add broccoli and potatoes; cook and stir 1 to 2 minutes or until heated through.

3. Whisk together egg whites, egg substitute, parsley, salt and black pepper in medium bowl.

4. Spread vegetables into even layer in skillet. Pour egg white mixture over vegetables; cover and cook over medium heat 10 to 12 minutes or until egg mixture is set.

5. Meanwhile, preheat broiler. Top frittata with cheese. Broil 4 inches from heat 1 minute or until cheese is bubbly and golden brown. Cut into wedges.

Makes 4 servings

Curried Vegetable-Rice Soup

1 package (16 ounces) frozen vegetable medley, such as broccoli, cauliflower, sugar snap peas and red bell peppers
1 can (about 14 ounces) vegetable broth
¾ cup uncooked instant brown rice
2 teaspoons curry powder
½ teaspoon salt
½ teaspoon hot pepper sauce or to taste
1 can (14 ounces) unsweetened coconut milk
1 tablespoon fresh lime juice

1. Combine vegetables and broth in large saucepan. Cover and bring to a boil over high heat. Stir in rice, curry powder, salt and pepper sauce; reduce heat to medium-low. Cover and simmer 8 minutes or until rice is tender, stirring once.

2. Stir in coconut milk; cook 3 minutes or until heated through. Remove from heat. Stir in lime juice. Ladle into shallow bowls and serve immediately.   *Makes 4 servings*

Tip: For a less rich soup with less fat and calories, substitute light unsweetened coconut milk. Most large supermarkets carry this in their international foods section.

Prep and Cook Time: 16 minutes

Farmstand Frittata

Jamaican Black Bean Stew

2 cups brown rice
2 pounds sweet potatoes
3 pounds butternut squash
1 large onion, coarsely chopped
1 can (about 14 ounces) vegetable broth
3 cloves garlic, minced
1 tablespoon curry powder
1½ teaspoons allspice
½ teaspoon ground red pepper
¼ teaspoon salt
2 cans (15 ounces each) black beans, drained and rinsed
½ cup raisins
3 tablespoons fresh lime juice
1 cup diced tomato
1 cup diced, peeled cucumber

1. Prepare rice according to package directions. Peel sweet potatoes; cut into ¾-inch chunks to measure 4 cups. Peel squash; remove seeds. Cut flesh into ¾-inch cubes to measure 5 cups.

2. Combine potatoes, squash, onion, broth, garlic, curry powder, allspice, pepper and salt in Dutch oven. Bring to a boil; reduce heat to low. Simmer, covered, 5 minutes. Add beans and raisins. Simmer 5 minutes or just until sweet potatoes and squash are tender and beans are hot. Remove from heat; stir in lime juice.

3. Serve stew over brown rice and top with tomato and cucumber. *Makes 8 servings*

Spinach and Mushroom Soup

1½ cups 1% milk
3 medium potatoes, peeled and chopped (1 cup)
1 box (10 ounces) BIRDS EYE® frozen Chopped Spinach
1 can (10¾ ounces) cream of mushroom soup

• In large saucepan, heat milk and potatoes over medium-low heat 10 minutes.

• Add spinach and soup.

• Cook about 10 minutes or until soup begins to bubble and potatoes are tender, stirring frequently. *Makes 4 servings*

Prep Time: 5 minutes
Cook Time: 20 minutes

Cheese Enchiladas with Green Chiles

1¼ cups (10-ounce can) ORTEGA® Enchilada Sauce
1 cup ORTEGA® Garden Style Salsa, mild
15 corn tortillas
1 pound Monterey Jack cheese, sliced into 3×1-inch strips, divided
1 can (7 ounces) ORTEGA® Whole Green Chiles, sliced into thirds
1 cup (4 ounces) shredded Monterey Jack Cheese

COMBINE enchilada sauce and salsa in medium bowl; mix well. Pour *1½ cups* sauce mixture onto bottom of ungreased 13×9-inch baking pan.

HEAT tortillas, one at a time, in lightly greased medium skillet over medium-high heat for 20 seconds on each side or until soft. Place 1 strip cheese and 1 strip chile in center of each tortilla; roll up. Place seam-side down in baking pan. Repeat with remaining tortillas, cheese and chiles. Ladle *remaining* sauce mixture over enchiladas; sprinkle with shredded cheese.

BAKE, covered, in preheated 350°F. oven for 20 minutes; remove cover. Bake for additional 5 minutes or until heated through and cheese is melted.

Makes 6 to 8 servings

Jamaican Black Bean Stew

Eggplant Italiano

1¼ pounds eggplant
2 medium onions
2 ribs celery
½ cup pitted ripe olives
2 tablespoons olive oil, divided
1 can (16 ounces) diced tomatoes, drained
1 tablespoon sugar
1 tablespoon capers, drained
2 tablespoons balsamic vinegar
1 teaspoon dried oregano or basil leaves
    Salt and black pepper to taste
    Fresh basil leaves, leaf lettuce and red jalapeño pepper for garnish

• Cut eggplant into 1-inch cubes. Thinly slice onions. Cut celery into 1-inch pieces. Cut olives crosswise in half; set aside.

• Heat wok over medium-high heat 1 minute or until hot. Drizzle 1 tablespoon oil into wok and heat 30 seconds. Add onions and celery; stir-fry about 2 minutes or until tender. Move onions and celery up side of wok. Reduce heat to medium.

• Add remaining 1 tablespoon oil to bottom of wok and heat 30 seconds. Add eggplant; stir-fry about 4 minutes or until tender. Add tomatoes; mix well. Cover and cook 10 minutes.

• Stir olives, sugar, capers, vinegar and oregano into eggplant mixture. Season with salt and black pepper. Transfer to serving dish. Garnish, if desired.   *Makes 6 servings*

Thai Noodles with Peanut Sauce

2 packages (3 ounces each) Oriental flavor instant ramen noodles
2 cups BIRDS EYE® frozen Farm Fresh Mixtures Broccoli, Carrots and Water Chestnuts
⅓ cup hot water
¼ cup creamy peanut butter
1 teaspoon sugar
⅛ to ¼ teaspoon crushed red pepper flakes

• Reserve seasoning packets from noodles.

• Bring 4 cups water to boil in large saucepan. Add noodles and vegetables. Cook 3 minutes, stirring occasionally; drain.

• Meanwhile, whisk together hot water, peanut butter, sugar, red pepper flakes and reserved seasoning packets in large bowl until blended.

• Add noodles and vegetables; toss to coat. Serve warm.   *Makes about 4 servings*

Serving Suggestion: Add shredded carrot, thinly sliced cucumber or green onion for additional flavor and color.

Prep Time: 5 minutes
Cook Time: 10 minutes

Eggplant Italiano

Southwestern Two-Bean Chili & Rice

1 bag (about ½ cup uncooked) boil-in-bag white rice
1 tablespoon vegetable oil
1 cup chopped onion
1 cup chopped green bell pepper
1½ teaspoons minced garlic
1 can (15½ ounces) chili beans in spicy or mild sauce, undrained
1 can (15½ ounces) black or pinto beans, drained
1 can (10 ounces) diced tomatoes with green chilies, undrained
1 tablespoon chili powder
2 teaspoons ground cumin
1 cup (4 ounces) shredded Cheddar or Monterey Jack cheese

1. Cook rice according to package directions.

2. While rice is cooking, heat oil in large saucepan over medium-high heat until hot. Add onion, bell pepper and garlic. Cook 5 minutes, stirring occasionally. Stir in chili beans with sauce, black beans, tomatoes with juice, chili powder and cumin. Cover; bring to a boil over high heat. Reduce heat to medium-low. Simmer, covered, 10 minutes.

3. Transfer rice to 4 shallow bowls. Ladle bean mixture over rice; top with cheese.

Makes 4 servings

Prep and Cook Time: 20 minutes

Roasted Vegetables with Fettuccine

2 pounds assorted fresh vegetables*
1 envelope LIPTON® RECIPE SECRETS® Savory Herb with Garlic Soup Mix
3 tablespoons olive or vegetable oil
½ cup light cream, whipping or heavy cream or half-and-half
¼ cup grated Parmesan cheese
8 ounces fettuccine or linguine, cooked and drained

Preheat oven to 450°F.

In large plastic bag or bowl, combine vegetables, savory herb with garlic soup mix and oil. Close bag and shake, or toss in bowl, until vegetables are evenly coated. In 13×9-inch baking or roasting pan, arrange vegetables; discard bag.

Bake uncovered, stirring once, 20 minutes or until vegetables are tender. Stir in light cream and cheese until evenly coated. Toss with hot fettuccine. Serve, if desired, with additional grated Parmesan cheese and freshly ground black pepper.

*Use any of the following, cut into 1-inch chunks: red, green or yellow bell peppers, zucchini, yellow squash, red onion or eggplant.

Makes about 2 main-dish or 4 side-dish servings

Tip: Also terrific with LIPTON® Recipe Secrets® Golden Onion or Golden Herb with Lemon Soup Mix.

Southwestern Two-Bean Chili & Rice

Meatless Italian Minestrone

1 tablespoon CRISCO® Vegetable Oil
1⅓ cups chopped celery
½ cup chopped onion
2 to 3 cloves garlic, minced
2 cans (14½ ounces *each*) no salt added tomatoes, undrained and chopped
4 cups chopped cabbage
1⅓ cups chopped carrots
1 can (46 ounces) no salt added tomato juice
1 can (19 ounces) white kidney beans (cannellini), drained
1 can (15½ ounces) red kidney beans, drained
1 can (15 ounces) garbanzo beans, drained
¼ cup chopped fresh parsley
1 tablespoon *plus* 1 teaspoon dried oregano leaves
1 tablespoon *plus* 1 teaspoon dried basil leaves
¾ cup (4 ounces) uncooked small elbow macaroni, cooked (without salt or fat) and well drained
¼ cup grated Parmesan cheese
Salt and pepper (optional)

1. Heat Crisco® Oil in large saucepan on medium heat. Add celery, onion and garlic. Cook and stir until crisp-tender. Stir in tomatoes with liquid, cabbage and carrots. Reduce heat to low. Cover. Simmer until vegetables are tender.

2. Stir in tomato juice, beans, parsley, oregano and basil. Simmer until beans are heated. Stir in macaroni just before serving. Serve sprinkled with Parmesan cheese. Season with salt and pepper, if desired.

Makes 16 servings

Sombrero Vegetable Bake

1 tablespoon olive oil
1 clove garlic, minced
¼ teaspoon ground cumin
1 can (14½ ounces) stewed tomatoes
1 package (9 ounces) frozen corn, thawed
2 small zucchini, cut into ¾-inch chunks
2 tablespoons FRANK'S® Original REDHOT® Cayenne Pepper Sauce
¼ teaspoon salt
1⅓ cups FRENCH'S® French Fried Onions

Whisk together oil, garlic and cumin in 2-quart microwavable bowl. Microwave, uncovered, on HIGH 1 minute.

Stir in tomatoes with liquid, corn, zucchini, RedHot® sauce and salt. Cover tightly with plastic wrap. Microwave on HIGH 8 to 10 minutes or until zucchini is crisp-tender, stirring twice. Uncover; sprinkle with French Fried Onions. Microwave on HIGH 1 minute or until onions are golden.

Makes 6 side-dish servings

Prep Time: 10 minutes
Cook Time: 12 minutes

Sombrero Vegetable Bake

Hot Three-Bean Casserole

2 tablespoons olive oil
1 cup coarsely chopped onion
1 cup chopped celery
2 cloves garlic, minced
1 can (15 ounces) chick-peas, drained and rinsed
1 can (15 ounces) kidney beans, drained and rinsed
1 cup coarsely chopped tomato
1 can (8 ounces) tomato sauce
1 cup water
1 to 2 jalapeño peppers, minced*
1 tablespoon chili powder
2 teaspoons sugar
1½ teaspoons ground cumin
1 teaspoon salt
1 teaspoon dried oregano leaves
¼ teaspoon ground black pepper
2½ cups (10 ounces) frozen cut green beans
Fresh oregano for garnish

Jalapeño peppers can sting and irritate the skin; wear rubber gloves when handling peppers and do not touch your eyes. Wash hands after handling jalapeño peppers.

1. Heat olive oil in large skillet over medium heat until hot. Add onion, celery and garlic; cook and stir 5 minutes or until onion is translucent.

2. Add remaining ingredients except green beans. Bring to a boil; reduce heat to low. Simmer, uncovered, 20 minutes. Add green beans. Simmer, uncovered, 10 minutes or until green beans are just tender. Garnish with fresh oregano.

Makes 12 (½-cup) servings

Viking Vegetable Cassoulet

4 cups sliced mushrooms
2 tablespoons olive oil
2 large onions, thickly sliced
1 large clove garlic, minced
2 medium zucchini, cut into 1-inch pieces
1½ cups sliced yellow squash
2 cans (16 ounces each) white beans, drained
1 can (14½ ounces) plum tomatoes, cut up, with juice
⅓ cup chopped parsley
1 teaspoon dried basil, crushed
½ teaspoon dried oregano, crushed
½ cup bread crumbs
1 teaspoon butter, melted
2 cups (8 ounces) shredded JARLSBERG Cheese

In large, deep skillet, brown mushrooms in oil. Add onions and garlic; sauté 5 minutes. Add zucchini and squash; sauté until vegetables are crisp-tender. Blend in beans, tomatoes, parsley, basil and oregano.

Spoon into 2-quart baking dish. Combine bread crumbs and butter in small bowl. Sprinkle bread crumbs around edge. Bake at 350°F 20 minutes. Top with cheese and bake 20 minutes longer.

Makes 6 to 8 servings

Hot Three-Bean Casserole

Broccoli-Tofu Stir-Fry

2 cups uncooked rice
1 can (14½ ounces) vegetable broth, divided
3 tablespoons cornstarch
1 tablespoon reduced-sodium soy sauce
½ teaspoon sugar
¼ teaspoon sesame oil
1 package (16 ounces) extra-firm tofu
1 teaspoon peanut oil
1 tablespoon minced fresh ginger
3 cloves garlic, minced
3 cups broccoli florets
2 cups sliced mushrooms
½ cup chopped green onions
1 large red bell pepper, seeded and cut into strips
Prepared Szechuan sauce (optional)

1. Cook rice according to package directions. Combine ¼ cup vegetable broth, cornstarch, soy sauce, sugar and sesame oil in small bowl. Drain tofu and cut into 1-inch cubes.

2. Heat peanut oil in large nonstick wok or skillet over medium heat until hot. Add ginger and garlic; cook and stir 5 minutes. Add remaining vegetable broth and broccoli, mushrooms, green onions and bell pepper; cook and stir over medium-high heat 5 minutes or until vegetables are crisp-tender. Add tofu; cook 2 minutes, stirring occasionally. Stir cornstarch mixture; add to vegetable mixture. Cook and stir until sauce thickens. Serve over rice with Szechuan sauce, if desired. *Makes 6 servings*

Eggplant and Feta Skillet

¼ cup olive oil
1 medium eggplant, cut into 1-inch pieces
1 medium zucchini, cut into ½-inch slices
1 package (16 ounces) frozen bell peppers and onions blend, thawed and drained
2 teaspoons minced garlic
2 cans (14½ ounces each) Italian-style diced tomatoes, drained
1 can (2¼ ounces) sliced black olives, drained
1½ cups prepared croutons
¾ cup feta cheese with basil and tomato, crumbled

1. Heat oil in large skillet over high heat until hot.

2. Add eggplant, zucchini, bell peppers, onions and garlic; cook and stir 6 minutes. Add tomatoes; simmer 3 minutes. Stir in olives.

3. Sprinkle croutons and feta cheese over top. *Makes 6 servings*

Prep and Cook Time: 20 minutes

Broccoli-Tofu Stir-Fry

Polenta with Vegetable Medley

4 ounces medium Brussels sprouts
   (6 to 8)
1 medium fennel bulb with stalks
   Cheese Polenta (recipe follows)
1 tablespoon butter or margarine
2 teaspoons olive oil
1 cup chopped onions
2 tablespoons snipped chives
½ teaspoon sugar
2 carrots, cut into julienne strips
½ to 1 cup canned vegetable broth,
   divided
   Salt
   Ground black pepper

1. To prepare Brussels sprouts, cut stems and pull off outer discolored leaves. Cut Brussels sprouts in half.

2. To prepare fennel, wash bulb. Trim stalks, reserving feathery leaves for garnish. Trim bottom of bulb leaving ⅛ inch of base. Remove any dry or discolored outer layers. Cut bulb into narrow wedges; trim core from wedges.

3. Prepare Cheese Polenta.

4. Heat butter and oil in large skillet over medium heat until butter melts. Add fennel. Cook 6 to 8 minutes or until lightly browned on both sides. Place in medium bowl.

5. Add onions, chives and sugar to skillet. Cook and stir 5 minutes or until onions are tender. Return fennel to skillet. Add carrots, Brussels sprouts and ½ cup broth. Bring to a boil over high heat. Reduce heat to low. Cover and simmer 15 to 20 minutes or until Brussels sprouts are tender, adding more broth if necessary to keep mixture moist. Season to taste with salt and pepper.

6. Spray large nonstick skillet with cooking spray. Heat over medium heat until hot. Cut Cheese Polenta into wedges. Cook 3 minutes per side or until browned. Place on serving plates; top with vegetable mixture. Garnish, if desired.   *Makes 4 to 6 servings*

Cheese Polenta

1 cup cold water
1 cup yellow cornmeal
1½ cups boiling water
2 to 4 tablespoons crumbled
   Gorgonzola cheese
1 clove garlic, minced
1 teaspoon salt

Stir water into cornmeal in large saucepan. Heat over medium heat until warm. Slowly stir in boiling water. Bring to a boil over medium-high heat. Reduce heat to low. Cook 15 minutes or until mixture is thick, stirring constantly. Stir in cheese, garlic and salt. Pour into greased 8-inch round pan; let stand 10 minutes or until firm.

Makes 4 to 6 servings

Polenta with Vegetable Medley

Vegetable Risotto

2 tablespoons olive oil, divided
1 medium zucchini, cubed
1 medium yellow summer squash, cubed
1 cup shiitake mushroom slices
1 cup chopped onion
1 clove garlic, minced
6 plum tomatoes, quartered and seeded
1 teaspoon dried oregano leaves
3 cups vegetable broth
¾ cup Arborio rice
¼ cup grated Parmesan cheese
Salt
Black pepper
½ cup frozen peas, thawed

1. Heat 1 tablespoon oil in large saucepan over medium heat until hot. Add zucchini and summer squash; cook and stir 5 minutes or until crisp-tender. Place in medium bowl; set aside.

2. Add mushrooms, onion and garlic to saucepan; cook and stir 5 minutes or until tender. Add tomatoes and oregano; cook and stir 2 to 3 minutes or until tomatoes are soft. Place in bowl with zucchini mixture. Wipe saucepan clean with paper towels.

3. Place broth in small saucepan; bring to a boil over medium heat. Reduce heat to medium-low to keep broth hot, but not boiling.

4. Meanwhile, heat remaining 1 tablespoon oil in saucepan over medium heat until hot. Add rice; cook and stir 2 minutes.

5. Using ladle or measuring cup, add ¾ cup broth to rice. Reduce heat to medium-low, maintaining a simmer throughout cooking process. Cook and stir until rice has absorbed broth. Repeat, adding broth 3 more times, cooking and stirring until rice has absorbed broth. (Total cooking time of rice will be 20 to 25 minutes.)

6. Stir cheese into rice mixture. Season to taste with salt and pepper. Stir in reserved vegetables and peas; cook until heated through. Serve immediately. Garnish, if desired. *Makes 4 to 6 servings*

Country Corn Bake

2 cans (11 ounces each) Mexican-style whole kernel corn, drained*
1 can (10¾ ounces) condensed cream of potato soup
½ cup milk
½ cup thinly sliced celery
1⅓ cups FRENCH'S® French Fried Onions, divided
½ cup (2 ounces) shredded Cheddar cheese

Or, substitute 1 bag (16 ounces) frozen whole kernel corn, thawed and drained.

Preheat oven to 375°F. Combine corn, soup, milk, celery, ⅔ cup French Fried Onions, and cheese in large bowl. Spoon mixture into 2-quart square baking dish. Cover; bake 30 minutes or until hot and bubbly. Stir; sprinkle with remaining ⅔ cup onions. Bake, uncovered, 3 minutes or until onions are golden. *Makes 4 to 6 servings*

Prep Time: 10 minutes

Cook Time: 33 minutes

Vegetable Risotto

Vegetable Lasagna

Tomato-Basil Sauce (recipe follows)
2 tablespoons olive oil
4 medium carrots, sliced
3 medium zucchini, sliced
6 ounces spinach leaves, stemmed and chopped
¼ teaspoon salt
¼ teaspoon ground black pepper
1 egg
3 cups ricotta cheese
½ cup plus 2 tablespoons grated Parmesan cheese, divided
12 uncooked lasagna noodles
1½ cups (6 ounces) shredded mozzarella cheese
1½ cups (6 ounces) shredded Monterey Jack cheese
½ cup water
Belgian endive leaves, Bibb lettuce leaves and fresh basil sprigs for garnish

1. Prepare Tomato-Basil Sauce.

2. Heat oil in large skillet over medium heat until hot. Add carrots; cook and stir 4 minutes. Add zucchini; cook and stir 8 minutes or until crisp-tender. Add spinach; cook and stir 1 minute or until spinach is wilted. Stir in salt and pepper.

3. Preheat oven to 350°F. Beat egg in medium bowl. Stir in ricotta cheese and ½ cup Parmesan cheese.

4. Spread 1 cup Tomato-Basil Sauce in bottom of 13×9-inch baking pan; top with 4 uncooked lasagna noodles.

5. Spread ⅓ of ricotta cheese mixture over noodles; top with ⅓ of vegetable mixture and 1 cup Tomato-Basil Sauce. Sprinkle with ½ cup each mozzerella and Monterey Jack cheeses. Repeat layers two times, beginning with noodles and ending with Mozzerella and Monterey Jack cheeses. Sprinkle with remaining 2 tablespoons Parmesan Cheese.

6. Carefully pour water around sides of pan. Cover pan tightly with foil.

7. Bake lasagna 1 hour or until bubbly. Uncover. Let stand 10 to 15 minutes. Cut into squares. Garnish, if desired.

Makes 8 servings

Tomato-Basil Sauce

2 cans (28 ounces each) plum tomatoes
1 teaspoon olive oil
1 medium onion, chopped
3 cloves garlic, minced
1 tablespoon sugar
1 tablespoon dried basil leaves
¼ teaspoon salt
¼ teaspoon ground black pepper

1. Drain tomatoes, reserving ½ cup juice. Seed and chop tomatoes.

2. Heat oil in large skillet over medium heat until hot. Add onion and garlic; cook and stir 5 minutes or until tender. Stir in tomatoes, reserved juice, sugar, basil, salt and pepper.

3. Bring to a boil over high heat. Reduce heat to low. Simmer, uncovered, 25 to 30 minutes or until most of juices have evaporated.

Makes 4 cups

Vegetable Lasagna

Ratatouille-Stuffed Pepper Halves

3 large bell peppers (1 red, 1 yellow and 1 green or any combination)
¼ cup olive oil
1 small eggplant (¾ pound), unpeeled, cut into ½-inch cubes
1 small onion, thinly sliced
1 large tomato, seeded and coarsely chopped
1 cup sliced fresh mushrooms
1 clove garlic, minced
½ teaspoon dried basil leaves
½ teaspoon dried oregano leaves
½ teaspoon salt
   Dash black pepper
   Dash ground red pepper
1 zucchini, quartered and cut into ½-inch chunks

1. Cut peppers (including stems) in half lengthwise. Scrape out seeds and membrane with spoon.

2. To steam pepper halves, place steamer basket in large saucepan or stockpot; add 1 inch of water. (Water should not touch bottom of basket.) Place pepper halves, cut sides up, in steamer basket; cover. Bring to a boil; steam 5 minutes or until peppers are crisp-tender. Add water, as necessary, to prevent pan from boiling dry. Plunge pepper halves into ice water to stop cooking. Place pepper halves in 13×9-inch baking dish.

3. Heat oil in large skillet over medium heat. Cook eggplant and onion in hot oil 10 minutes or until vegetables are soft, stirring occasionally. Add tomato, mushrooms, garlic, basil, oregano, salt, black and red peppers. Bring to a boil over medium-high heat; reduce heat to medium-low. Simmer about 5 minutes, stirring occasionally. Add zucchini; simmer 5 minutes more or until mixture thickens slightly.

4. Preheat oven to 350°F. Spoon mixture evenly into pepper halves. Bake 15 minutes or until heated through. Garnish, if desired. Serve immediately.

Makes 6 side-dish servings

Creamy Cheddar Cheese Soup

2 cans (10¾ ounces each) condensed Cheddar cheese soup
3 cups milk or water
3 cups cooked vegetables, such as cauliflower, carrots and asparagus, cut into bite-size pieces
2 cups cooked medium shell pasta
1⅓ cups FRENCH'S® French Fried Onions

Combine soup and milk in large saucepan. Stir in vegetables and pasta. Bring to a boil. Reduce heat. Cook until heated through, stirring often.

Place French Fried Onions on microwavable dish. Microwave on HIGH 1 minute or until onions are golden.

Ladle soup into individual bowls. Sprinkle with onions.

Makes 6 servings

Prep Time: 10 minutes
Cook Time: 5 minutes

Ratatouille-Stuffed Pepper Halves

Cheese-Sauced Manicotti

8 manicotti shells
1 cup chopped onion
¼ cup water
2 cloves garlic, minced
3 tablespoons all-purpose flour
1⅔ cups skim milk, divided
¾ cup shredded part-skim mozzarella
    cheese
1 teaspoon dried Italian seasoning
¼ teaspoon ground black pepper
1 package (10 ounces) frozen chopped
    spinach, thawed and well drained
1 cup nonfat ricotta cheese
½ cup 1% low-fat cottage cheese
½ teaspoon dried marjoram leaves
1 medium tomato, sliced

Prepare manicotti according to package directions; drain. Rinse under cold water; drain.

Meanwhile, preheat oven to 350°F. Coat 13×9-inch baking dish with nonstick cooking spray.

For sauce, combine onion, water and garlic in medium saucepan. Bring to a boil over high heat. Reduce heat to medium-low. Cover and simmer 3 to 4 minutes or until onion is tender. Blend flour and ⅓ cup milk in small bowl until smooth. Stir into onion mixture. Stir in remaining 1⅓ cups milk. Cook and stir over medium heat until mixture boils and thickens. Cook and stir 1 minute. Add mozzarella cheese, Italian seasoning and pepper. Cook and stir until cheese melts.

Combine spinach, ricotta cheese, cottage cheese, marjoram and ⅓ cup sauce in medium bowl. Spoon ⅓ cup spinach mixture into each manicotti shell. Place in prepared baking dish. Pour remaining sauce over top. Cover and bake 30 to 35 minutes or until heated through. Arrange tomato slices on top. Bake, uncovered, 4 to 5 minutes or until tomato is heated through.
Makes 4 servings

Garden Gazpacho

6 large ripe tomatoes, peeled and
    seeded
½ cup chopped, seeded, peeled
    cucumber
½ cup coarsely chopped green bell
    pepper
½ cup coarsely chopped onion
1 clove garlic, minced
1 cup low-sodium tomato juice
1 teaspoon lemon juice
⅛ teaspoon hot pepper sauce
⅛ teaspoon ground black pepper
    Nonfat yogurt (optional)

1. In food processor or blender, combine tomatoes, cucumber, bell pepper, onion and garlic; process using on/off pulsing action just until mixture is thick and chunky. Pour into medium bowl.

2. Stir in tomato juice, lemon juice, pepper sauce and black pepper. Cover and chill until ready to serve. Garnish with yogurt, if desired. *Makes 4 (1¼-cup) servings*

Garden Gazpacho

Louisiana Red Beans & Rice

1 package (7.2 ounces) RICE-A-RONI®
  Herb & Butter
1 cup chopped green or yellow bell
  pepper
¾ cup chopped onion
2 cloves garlic, minced
2 tablespoons vegetable oil or olive oil
1 can (15 or 16 ounces) red beans or
  kidney beans, rinsed and drained
1 can (14½ or 16 ounces) tomatoes or
  stewed tomatoes, undrained
1 teaspoon dried thyme leaves or dried
  oregano leaves
⅛ teaspoon hot pepper sauce or black
  pepper
2 tablespoons chopped parsley
  (optional)

1. Prepare Rice-A-Roni® Mix as package directs.

2. While Rice-A-Roni® is simmering, in second large skillet, sauté green pepper, onion and garlic in oil 5 minutes.

3. Stir in beans, tomatoes, thyme and hot pepper sauce. Simmer, uncovered, 10 minutes, stirring occasionally. Stir in parsley. Serve over rice. *Makes 5 servings*

Serving Suggestion: Serve with one 8-ounce glass of milk per serving.

Cheesy Vegetarian Stir-Fry

2 teaspoons olive oil
3 cloves garlic, minced
1 cup thinly sliced onion
4 cups small zucchini squash, cut
  lengthwise in quarters then into
  1½-inch pieces
1 to 2 teaspoons dried Italian herbs
1 (9-ounce) package frozen artichoke
  hearts, thawed, cooked and
  drained (optional)
½ cup marinara sauce
½ cup shredded JARLSBERG LITE™
  Cheese

Heat oil in wok over high heat; stir-fry garlic and onion 3 minutes or until lightly browned. Add zucchini and herbs; stir-fry 3 minutes or until crisp-tender. Remove from heat and stir in artichoke hearts, marinara sauce and cheese.

Serve with cannellini beans or over pasta such as orrechiette or linguine.

Makes 4 to 6 servings

Louisiana Red Beans & Rice

Barley, Bean and Corn Frittata

2 cups water
½ cup barley
¾ teaspoon salt, divided
2 teaspoons olive oil
1 can (15 ounces) black beans, drained and rinsed
2 cups (8 ounces) shredded Cheddar cheese, divided
¾ cup fresh cut corn*
½ cup chopped green bell pepper
¼ cup chopped cilantro
7 eggs *or* 1¾ cups egg substitute
1 cup cottage cheese
½ teaspoon ground red pepper
1 cup medium fresh or prepared salsa
Sour cream for garnish

Frozen corn can be substituted for fresh; thaw before using.

Bring water to a boil in medium saucepan over high heat. Add barley and ¼ teaspoon salt. Reduce heat to low. Cover and simmer 40 to 45 minutes or until tender. Let stand, covered, 5 minutes. Drain.

Preheat oven to 400°F. Brush 10-inch cast iron or ovenproof skillet with olive oil. Layer barley, beans, 1 cup Cheddar cheese, corn, bell pepper and cilantro in skillet. Blend eggs, cottage cheese, remaining ½ teaspoon salt and ground red pepper in blender or food processor just until smooth. Carefully pour egg mixture over layers.

Bake 30 minutes or until egg mixture is set. Sprinkle with remaining 1 cup Cheddar cheese. Bake 5 minutes or until cheese is melted. Spoon salsa evenly over top. Let stand 5 minutes before cutting into wedges. Garnish, if desired.   *Makes 6 to 8 servings*

Stir-Fry Rice and Vegetables

3 tablespoons vegetable oil
1 bunch green onions, white and green parts chopped separately
1 medium sweet potato, peeled, halved lengthwise and thinly sliced
1 small green bell pepper, cut into thin strips
2 carrots, thinly sliced
1 zucchini, thinly sliced
2 cups cooked brown rice
1 cup bean sprouts
1 cup fresh mushrooms, sliced
¼ cup honey
¼ cup soy sauce

Heat oil in wok or large, heavy skillet over medium-high heat. Stir-fry white parts of onions, sweet potato, bell pepper, carrots and zucchini until barely tender. Add rice, sprouts, mushrooms and green onion tops. Cook quickly until heated through. If necessary, add more oil. Combine honey and soy sauce in cup. Pour over mixture and stir. Serve immediately.

Makes 6 to 8 servings

Favorite recipe from **National Honey Board**

Barley, Bean and Corn Frittata

Spicy Vegetable Stew

1 tablespoon vegetable oil
2 carrots, chopped
½ onion, chopped
2 cloves garlic, minced
1 teaspoon ground cumin
1 teaspoon paprika
¾ teaspoon ground cinnamon
½ teaspoon salt
½ teaspoon ground ginger
½ teaspoon black pepper
1 can (14½ ounces) diced tomatoes
1 can (about 14 ounces) vegetable broth
1 cup frozen hash brown potatoes
1 cup frozen green beans
2 tablespoons tomato paste
¼ to ½ teaspoon hot pepper sauce
1⅓ cups water
1⅓ cups uncooked couscous
Fresh Italian parsley

1. Heat oil in large saucepan over medium-high heat until hot. Add carrots, onion, garlic, cumin, paprika, cinnamon, salt, ginger and black pepper; cook and stir about 5 minutes or until vegetables are tender.

2. Stir in tomatoes, broth, potatoes, green beans, tomato paste and hot pepper sauce; bring to a boil. Reduce heat to low and simmer, uncovered, 10 minutes.

3. While stew is simmering, prepare couscous. Bring water to a boil in small saucepan over high heat. Stir in couscous. Cover and remove saucepan from heat; let stand 5 minutes.

4. Fluff couscous with fork. Serve vegetable stew over couscous. Garnish with parsley.

Makes 4 servings

Prep and Cook Time: 23 minutes

Middle Eastern Lentil Soup

1 cup dried lentils
2 tablespoons olive oil
1 onion, chopped
1 red bell pepper, chopped
½ teaspoon ground cumin
1 teaspoon fennel seed
¼ teaspoon ground red pepper
½ teaspoon salt
1 tablespoon lemon juice
2 tablespoons chopped parsley
½ cup plain yogurt

1. Rinse lentils, discarding any debris or blemished lentils; drain.

2. Heat oil in large saucepan over medium-high heat until hot. Add onion and bell pepper; cook and stir 5 minutes or until tender. Add cumin, fennel seed and ground red pepper; cook and stir 1 minute.

3. Add 4 cups water and lentils. Bring to a boil. Reduce heat to low; cover and simmer 20 minutes. Stir in salt; simmer 5 to 10 minutes more or until lentils are tender. Stir in lemon juice.

4. Stir parsley into yogurt. Serve soup topped with yogurt mixture.

Makes 4 servings

Tip: For a special touch, top each serving with yellow bell pepper strips.

Middle Eastern Lentil Soup

Eggplant Parmigiana

2 cups plain dry bread crumbs
1 cup (4 ounces) shredded ALPINE
    LACE® Fat Free Pasteurized Process
    Skim Milk Cheese Product—For
    Parmesan Lovers
2 tablespoons Italian seasoning
2 teaspoons minced garlic, divided
2 medium-size unpeeled eggplants
    (2 pounds), cut crosswise into
    ½-inch-thick slices
2 egg whites, lightly beaten
2 tablespoons olive oil, divided
1½ cups thin strips red onion
1 can (28 ounces) crushed tomatoes in
    purée, undrained
⅓ cup water
½ cup slivered fresh basil leaves
1 teaspoon sugar
¼ teaspoon red pepper flakes
¼ teaspoon salt
2 cups (8 ounces) shredded ALPINE
    LACE® Fat Free Pasteurized Process
    Skim Milk Cheese Product—For
    Mozzarella Lovers
¼ cup minced fresh parsley

1. Preheat the oven to 375°F. Spray 2 baking sheets and a 13×9×3-inch baking dish with nonstick cooking spray. In a food processor or blender, process the bread crumbs, Parmesan, Italian seasoning and 1 teaspoon of the garlic for 30 seconds. Spread on a plate.

2. Dip the eggplant slices into the egg whites, coat both sides with the crumb mixture, then arrange in a single layer on the baking sheets. Drizzle with 1 tablespoon of the oil. Bake the eggplant for 40 minutes or until crisp, turning the slices over once. Remove the eggplant from the oven and reduce the temperature to 350°F.

3. While the eggplant bakes, make the sauce: In a large skillet, heat the remaining tablespoon of the oil over medium-high heat. Add the onion and the remaining teaspoon of garlic and sauté for 5 minutes or until soft. Stir in the tomatoes and their purée, the water, basil, sugar, red pepper flakes and salt. Simmer, uncovered, for 5 minutes.

4. In the baking dish, layer a third of the eggplant slices, a third of the sauce and a third of the mozzarella cheese; repeat 2 times. Bake for 30 minutes or until bubbly; sprinkle with the parsley.   *Makes 8 servings*

Cheesy Rice Casserole

2 cups hot cooked rice
1⅓ cups FRENCH'S® French Fried Onions,
    divided
1 cup sour cream
1 jar (16 ounces) medium salsa,
    divided
1 cup (4 ounces) shredded Cheddar
    or taco blend cheese, divided

Combine rice and ⅔ cup French Fried Onions in large bowl. Spoon half of the rice mixture into microwavable 2-quart shallow casserole. Spread sour cream over rice mixture.

Layer half of the salsa and half of the cheese over sour cream. Sprinkle with remaining rice mixture, salsa and cheese. Cover loosely with plastic wrap. Microwave on HIGH 8 minutes or until heated through. Sprinkle with remaining ⅔ cup onions. Microwave 1 minute or until onions are golden.

Makes 6 servings

Prep Time: 15 minutes
Cook Time: 9 minutes

Cheesy Rice Casserole

PASTA
PIZZAZZ

Broccoli and Beef Pasta

1 pound lean ground beef
2 cloves garlic, minced
1 can (about 14 ounces) beef broth
1 medium onion, thinly sliced
1 cup uncooked rotini pasta
½ teaspoon dried basil leaves
½ teaspoon dried oregano leaves
½ teaspoon dried thyme leaves
1 can (15 ounces) Italian-style
  tomatoes, undrained
2 cups broccoli florets *or* 1 package
  (10 ounces) frozen broccoli,
  thawed
3 ounces shredded Cheddar cheese or
  grated Parmesan cheese

1. Combine meat and garlic in large nonstick skillet; cook over high heat until meat is no longer pink, breaking meat apart with wooden spoon. Pour off drippings. Place meat in large bowl; set aside.

2. Add broth, onion, pasta, basil, oregano and thyme to skillet. Bring to a boil. Reduce heat to medium-high and boil 10 minutes (if using frozen broccoli, boil 15 minutes); add tomatoes and juice. Increase heat to high and bring to a boil; stir in broccoli. Cook, uncovered, 6 to 8 minutes, stirring occasionally, until broccoli is crisp-tender and pasta is tender. Return meat to skillet and stir 3 to 4 minutes or until heated through.

3. With slotted spoon, transfer to serving platter. Sprinkle with cheese. Cover with lid or tent with foil several minutes, until cheese melts. Meanwhile, bring liquid left in skillet to a boil over high heat. Boil until thick and reduced to 3 to 4 tablespoons. Spoon over pasta. *Makes 4 servings*

Serving Suggestion: Serve with garlic bread.

Prep and Cook Time: 30 minutes

Broccoli and Beef Pasta

Chicken Primavera Buffet

12 ounces uncooked thin spaghetti
¼ cup prepared pesto
¼ cup prepared fat-free Italian salad
　　dressing
½ teaspoon red pepper flakes
2 cups water
1 cup thinly sliced carrots
1 cup broccoli florets
1 cup snow peas
1 can (4 ounces) sliced water
　　chestnuts, drained
8 boneless skinless chicken breast
　　halves

1. Preheat oven to 350°F. Cook pasta according to package directions. Drain and rinse well under cold water until pasta is cool; drain well. Place in large bowl; set aside.

2. Combine pesto, Italian dressing and red pepper flakes in small bowl. Reserve 1 tablespoon pesto mixture. Add remaining pesto mixture to pasta; toss to coat well.

3. In large saucepan, bring water to a boil over high heat. Add carrots, broccoli and snow peas; cook 3 minutes. Drain vegetables. Add water chestnuts and vegetables to pasta; toss to blend well. Spray 13×9-inch baking pan with nonstick cooking spray. Transfer pasta and vegetables to baking pan.

4. Spray large nonstick skillet with cooking spray; heat over medium heat until hot. Add chicken; cook until browned on both sides. Cover; cook 10 minutes or until no longer pink in center and juices run clear. Place chicken on pasta and vegetables. Pour juices from skillet over chicken. Spread reserved pesto mixture over chicken. Bake 45 minutes or until heated through.　　*Makes 8 servings*

Skillet Pasta Roma

½ pound Italian sausage, sliced or
　　crumbled
1 large onion, coarsely chopped
1 large clove garlic, minced
2 cans (14½ ounces each) DEL
　　MONTE® Pasta Style Chunky
　　Tomatoes, undrained
1 can (8 ounces) DEL MONTE® Tomato
　　Sauce
1 cup water
8 ounces uncooked rotini or other
　　spiral pasta
8 sliced mushrooms, optional
　　Grated Parmesan cheese and fresh
　　parsley sprigs, optional

1. Brown sausage in large skillet. Add onion and garlic. Cook until onion is soft; drain. Stir in tomatoes with juice, tomato sauce, water and pasta.

2. Cover and bring to a boil; reduce heat. Simmer, covered, 25 to 30 minutes or until pasta is tender, stirring occasionally.

3. Stir in mushrooms; simmer 5 minutes. Serve in skillet garnished with cheese and parsley, if desired.　　*Makes 4 servings*

Chicken Primavera Buffet

Curly Macaroni Pie

1 pound uncooked rotini
1 cup seasoned dry bread crumbs
½ cup (2 ounces) grated ALPINE LACE®
   Fat Free Pasteurized Process Skim
   Milk Cheese Product—For
   Parmesan Lovers
½ cup packed fresh parsley
2 tablespoons unsalted butter
   substitute, melted
1½ cups chopped red onions
1½ cups coarsely chopped red bell
   peppers
2 cups (8 ounces) shredded ALPINE
   LACE® Reduced Fat Swiss Cheese
2 cups (8 ounces) shredded ALPINE
   LACE® American Flavor Pasteurized
   Process Cheese Product with
   Jalapeño Peppers
2½ cups 2% low fat milk
2 tablespoons Dijon mustard

1. Preheat the oven to 350°F. Spray a
14-inch oval or round ovenproof baking
dish and a large nonstick skillet with
nonstick cooking spray. Cook the rotini
according to package directions just until
al dente. Drain well, place in the baking
dish and keep warm.

2. In a food processor, place the bread
crumbs, Parmesan, parsley and butter.
Process 1 minute or until finely chopped;
set aside.

3. Heat the skillet over medium-high heat for
1 minute. Add the onions and bell peppers
and sauté for 5 minutes or until soft.
Sprinkle over the rotini in the baking dish.
Sprinkle with 1½ cups of the bread crumb
mixture and the Swiss and pepper cheeses;
toss to mix well.

4. In a measuring cup, whisk together the
milk and mustard; fold into the rotini
mixture until well coated. Top with the
remaining bread crumb mixture. Sprinkle
with paprika, if you wish. Cover tightly with

foil and bake for 50 minutes or until bubbly.
Remove the foil and bake 5 minutes more.
Transfer to a rack and let stand for 15
minutes. Garnish the pie with fresh parsley
leaves, if you wish. Serve hot or warm.
Makes 14 servings

Chili Wagon Wheel Casserole

8 ounces uncooked wagon wheel or
   other pasta
1 pound lean ground sirloin or ground
   turkey breast
¾ cup chopped green bell pepper
¾ cup chopped onion
1 can (14½ ounces) no-salt-added
   stewed tomatoes
1 can (8 ounces) no-salt-added tomato
   sauce
½ teaspoon black pepper
¼ teaspoon ground allspice
½ cup (2 ounces) shredded reduced-fat
   Cheddar cheese

1. Preheat oven to 350°F. Cook pasta
according to package directions. Drain and
rinse; set aside.

2. Spray large nonstick skillet with nonstick
cooking spray. Add ground sirloin, bell
pepper and onion; cook 5 minutes or until
meat is no longer pink, stirring frequently.
(Drain mixture if using ground sirloin.)

3. Stir in tomatoes, tomato sauce, black
pepper and allspice; cook 2 minutes. Stir in
pasta. Spoon mixture into 2½-quart
casserole. Sprinkle with cheese.

4. Bake 20 to 25 minutes or until heated
through. *Makes 6 servings*

Curly Macaroni Pie

Beef Stroganoff Casserole

1 pound lean ground beef
¼ teaspoon salt
⅛ teaspoon black pepper
1 teaspoon vegetable oil
8 ounces sliced mushrooms
1 large onion, chopped
3 cloves garlic, minced
¼ cup dry white wine
1 can (10¾ ounces) condensed cream
 of mushroom soup, undiluted
½ cup sour cream
1 tablespoon Dijon mustard
4 cups cooked egg noodles
 Chopped fresh parsley (optional)

Preheat oven to 350°F. Spray 13×9-inch baking dish with nonstick cooking spray.

Place beef in large skillet; season with salt and pepper. Brown beef over medium-high heat until no longer pink, stirring to separate beef. Drain fat from skillet; set beef aside.

Heat oil in same skillet over medium-high heat until hot. Add mushrooms, onion and garlic; cook and stir 2 minutes or until onion is tender. Add wine. Reduce heat to medium-low and simmer 3 minutes. Remove from heat; stir in soup, sour cream and mustard until well combined. Return beef to skillet.

Place noodles in prepared dish. Pour beef mixture over noodles; stir until noodles are well coated.

Bake, uncovered, 30 minutes or until heated through. Sprinkle with parsley, if desired.

Makes 6 servings

Fettucine à la Tuna

½ cup broccoli florets
½ cup chopped red bell pepper
1 tablespoon sliced green onion
1 clove garlic, minced
1 tablespoon butter or margarine
¼ cup low-fat milk
¼ cup low-fat ricotta cheese
 Salt and pepper to taste
1 can (6 ounces) STARKIST® Tuna,
 drained and broken into small
 chunks
2 ounces fettucine or linguine, cooked
 and drained
1 tablespoon grated Parmesan or
 Romano cheese (optional)

In small saucepan, steam broccoli and bell pepper over simmering water 5 minutes. Drain liquid from vegetables and remove steamer. In same pan sauté onion and garlic in butter 2 minutes. Add milk and ricotta cheese, stirring well with wire whisk. Season to taste with salt and pepper. Add tuna and vegetables; cook over low heat 2 minutes. Toss fettucine with tuna mixture. Spoon onto plate; sprinkle with Parmesan cheese, if desired.

Makes 1 serving

Preparation Time: 15 minutes

Beef Stroganoff Casserole

Pasta Primavera with Roasted Garlic Sauce

3 large heads garlic
2 tablespoons FLEISCHMANN'S® Original Margarine, melted
3 tablespoons GREY POUPON® COUNTRY DIJON® Mustard
3 tablespoons lemon juice
¼ teaspoon coarsely ground black pepper
1 cup sliced fresh mushrooms
½ cup julienned zucchini
½ cup julienned carrot
1 cup chopped tomato
½ cup COLLEGE INN® Lower Sodium Chicken Broth or water
1 tablespoon chopped fresh basil leaves or 1 teaspoon dried basil leaves
8 ounces angel hair pasta, cooked and drained

Brush each head of garlic lightly with 1 teaspoon melted margarine; wrap each head separately in foil. Place in small baking pan; bake at 400°F for 45 minutes or until tender. Cool 10 minutes. Separate cloves; squeeze cloves to extract pulp (discard skins).

In electric blender or food processor, purée garlic pulp, mustard, lemon juice and pepper; set aside.

In skillet, over medium-high heat, sauté mushrooms, zucchini and carrot in remaining margarine until tender-crisp, about 3 minutes; add garlic mixture, tomato, broth or water and basil. Reduce heat to low; cook and stir until sauce is heated through. Toss with hot cooked pasta. Serve immediately.   *Makes 4 servings*

Soba Stir-Fry

8 ounces uncooked soba noodles (Japanese buckwheat pasta)
1 tablespoon light olive oil
2 cups sliced fresh shiitake mushrooms
1 medium red bell pepper, cut into thin strips
2 whole dried red peppers or ¼ teaspoon red pepper flakes
1 clove garlic, minced
2 cups shredded napa cabbage
½ cup fat-free reduced-sodium chicken broth
2 tablespoons reduced-sodium tamari or soy sauce
1 tablespoon rice wine or dry sherry
2 teaspoons cornstarch
1 package (14 ounces) firm tofu, drained and cut into 1-inch cubes
2 green onions, thinly sliced

1. Cook noodles according to package directions. Drain and set aside.

2. Heat oil in large nonstick skillet or wok over medium heat. Add mushrooms, bell pepper, dried peppers and garlic. Cook 3 minutes or until mushrooms are tender.

3. Add cabbage. Cover. Cook 2 minutes or until cabbage is wilted.

4. Combine chicken broth, tamari, rice wine and cornstarch in small bowl. Stir sauce into vegetable mixture. Cook 2 minutes or until sauce is bubbly.

5. Stir in tofu and noodles; toss gently until heated through. Sprinkle with green onions. Serve immediately.

Makes 4 (2-cup) servings

Soba Stir-Fry

Baked Cheesey Rotini

¾ pound lean ground beef
½ cup chopped onion
2 cups cooked rotini, drained
1 (15-ounce) can HUNT'S® Ready
    Tomato Sauces Chunky Italian
¼ cup chopped green bell pepper
¾ teaspoon garlic salt
¼ teaspoon pepper
1½ cups cubed processed American
    cheese

Preheat oven to 350°F. In large skillet, brown beef with onion; drain. Stir in rotini, tomato sauce, bell pepper, garlic salt and pepper. Pour beef mixture into 1½-quart casserole. Top with cheese. Bake, covered, 20 minutes or until sauce is bubbly. *Makes 6 servings*

Shrimp and Vegetables with Lo Mein Noodles

2 tablespoons vegetable oil
1 pound medium shrimp, peeled
2 packages (21 ounces each) frozen
    lo mein stir-fry mix with sauce
¼ cup peanuts
    Fresh cilantro
1 small wedge cabbage

1. Heat oil in wok or large skillet over medium-high heat. Add shrimp; stir-fry 3 minutes or until shrimp are pink and opaque. Remove shrimp from wok to medium bowl. Set aside.

2. Remove sauce packet from stir-fry mix. Add frozen vegetables and noodles to wok; stir in sauce. Cover and cook 7 to 8 minutes, stirring frequently.

3. While vegetable mixture is cooking, chop peanuts and enough cilantro to measure 2 tablespoons. Shred cabbage.

4. Stir shrimp, peanuts and cilantro into vegetable mixture; heat through. Serve immediately with cabbage.

Makes 6 servings

Prep and Cook Time: 19 minutes

Chili Spaghetti Casserole

8 ounces uncooked spaghetti
1 pound lean ground beef
1 medium onion, chopped
¼ teaspoon salt
⅛ teaspoon black pepper
1 can (15 ounces) vegetarian chili with
    beans
1 can (14½ ounces) Italian-style stewed
    tomatoes, undrained
1½ cups (6 ounces) shredded sharp
    Cheddar cheese, divided
½ cup reduced-fat sour cream
1½ teaspoons chili powder
¼ teaspoon garlic powder

Preheat oven to 350°F. Spray 13 X 9-inch baking dish with nonstick cooking spray.

Cook pasta according to package directions until al dente. Drain and place in prepared dish.

Meanwhile, place beef and onion in large skillet; season with salt and pepper. Brown beef over medium-high heat until beef is no longer pink, stirring to separate meat. Drain fat. Stir in chili, tomatoes with juice, 1 cup cheese, sour cream, chili powder and garlic powder.

Add chili mixture to pasta; stir until pasta is well coated. Sprinkle with remaining ½ cup cheese.

Cover tightly with foil and bake 30 minutes or until hot and bubbly. Let stand 5 minutes before serving. *Makes 8 servings*

Shrimp and Vegetables with Lo Mein Noodles

Broccoli Lasagna Bianca

1 (15- to 16-ounce) container fat-free ricotta cheese
1 cup EGG BEATERS® Healthy Real Egg Substitute
1 tablespoon minced basil (or 1 teaspoon dried basil leaves)
½ cup chopped onion
1 clove garlic, minced
2 tablespoons FLEISCHMANN'S® Original Margarine
¼ cup all-purpose flour
2 cups skim milk
2 (10-ounce) packages frozen chopped broccoli, thawed and well drained
1 cup (4 ounces) shredded part-skim mozzarella cheese
9 lasagna noodles, cooked and drained
1 small tomato, chopped
2 tablespoons grated Parmesan cheese
Fresh basil leaves, for garnish

In medium bowl, combine ricotta cheese, Egg Beaters® and minced basil; set aside.

In large saucepan over medium heat, sauté onion and garlic in margarine until tender-crisp. Stir in flour; cook for 1 minute. Gradually stir in milk; cook, stirring until mixture thickens and begins to boil. Remove from heat; stir in broccoli and mozzarella cheese.

In lightly greased 13×9×2-inch baking dish, place 3 lasagna noodles; top with ⅓ each ricotta and broccoli mixtures. Repeat layers 2 more times. Top with tomato; sprinkle with Parmesan cheese. Bake at 350°F for 1 hour or until set. Let stand 10 minutes before serving. Garnish with basil leaves.

Makes 8 servings

Prep Time: 20 minutes
Cook Time: 90 minutes

Alfredo Pasta Swirls

4 ounces uncooked fettuccini pasta
1 package (10 ounces) frozen peas and carrots, thawed and drained
1 package (10 ounces) frozen cauliflower florets, thawed and drained
1 cup (4 ounces) shredded mozzarella cheese
1⅓ cups FRENCH'S® French Fried Onions, divided
1 container (10 ounces) refrigerated Alfredo sauce
½ cup milk
⅓ cup grated Parmesan cheese

Preheat oven to 375°F. Prepare pasta according to package directions using shortest cooking time. Drain; keep warm.

Combine vegetables, mozzarella cheese and ⅔ cup French Fried Onions in 2-quart oblong baking dish. Twirl few strands of warm fettuccini around long-tined fork to form pasta swirl. Remove pasta swirl from fork; stand upright on top of vegetable layer. Repeat to form 5 more swirls.

Combine Alfredo sauce and milk in medium bowl. Pour over pasta and vegetables. Cover loosely with foil; bake 35 minutes or until heated through. Gently stir sauce and vegetables around pasta. Top with Parmesan cheese. Sprinkle remaining ⅔ cup onions around pasta. Bake, uncovered, 3 minutes or until onions are golden. *Makes 6 servings*

Prep Time: 15 minutes
Cook Time: 38 minutes

Broccoli Lasagna Bianca

Penne, Sausage & Ham Casserole

1 pound HILLSHIRE FARM® Smoked Sausage, cut into ½-inch slices
4 ounces HILLSHIRE FARM® Ham, cubed
2 cups milk
2 tablespoons all-purpose flour
8 ounces uncooked penne pasta, cooked and drained
2½ cups (10 ounces) shredded mozzarella cheese
⅓ cup grated Parmesan cheese
1 jar (16 ounces) prepared pasta sauce
⅓ cup bread crumbs

Preheat oven to 350°F.

Lightly brown Smoked Sausage and Ham in large skillet over medium heat. Stir in milk and flour; bring to a boil, stirring constantly. Stir in pasta and cheeses. Pour sausage mixture into small casserole; pour pasta sauce over top. Bake, covered, 25 minutes. Uncover and sprinkle with bread crumbs; place under broiler to brown topping.

Makes 4 servings

Crazy Lasagna Casserole

1½ pounds ground beef
1 teaspoon LAWRY'S® Seasoned Salt
1 package (1.5 ounces) LAWRY'S® Original-Style Spaghetti Sauce Spices & Seasonings
1 can (8 ounces) tomato sauce
1 can (6 ounces) tomato paste
1½ cups water
1 package (10 ounces) medium-size shell macaroni, cooked and drained
1 carton (16 ounces) small curd cottage cheese
1½ cups (6 ounces) grated cheddar cheese

In large skillet, brown ground beef until crumbly; drain fat. Add Seasoned Salt, Original-Style Spaghetti Sauce Spices & Seasonings, tomato sauce, tomato paste and water; mix well. Bring to a boil over medium-high heat; reduce heat to low and cook, uncovered, 10 minutes, stirring occasionally. In shallow 2-quart casserole, layer half of macaroni, cottage cheese and meat sauce. Sprinkle ½ cup cheese over meat sauce. Repeat layers, ending with meat sauce. Top with remaining 1 cup cheese. Bake, uncovered, in 350°F oven 30 to 40 minutes or until bubbly and cheese is melted. *Makes 8 servings*

Serving Suggestion: Serve with garlic bread.

Pizza Hot Dish

1½ to 2 pounds ground beef
¼ cup chopped onion
1 package (10 ounces) egg noodles
2 jars (15½ ounces each) pizza sauce
1 can (10¾ ounces) condensed Cheddar cheese soup
2 cups (8 ounces) shredded mozzarella cheese

1. In large skillet brown ground beef with onion. Drain.

2. Prepare egg noodles according to package directions.

3. Add sauce, soup and cooked noodles to ground beef; mix well. Spoon into 13×9-inch baking pan or large casserole. Bake at 350°F for 30 minutes. Sprinkle with mozzarella cheese and bake an additional 15 minutes. *Makes 8 to 12 servings*

Favorite recipe from **North Dakota Beef Commission**

Penne, Sausage & Ham Casserole

Rigatoni with Four Cheeses

3 cups milk
1 tablespoon chopped carrot
1 tablespoon chopped celery
1 tablespoon chopped onion
1 tablespoon fresh parsley sprigs
¼ teaspoon black peppercorns
¼ teaspoon hot pepper sauce
½ bay leaf
　Dash nutmeg
¼ cup Wisconsin butter
¼ cup flour
½ cup (2 ounces) grated Wisconsin
　Parmesan cheese
¼ cup (1 ounce) grated Wisconsin
　Romano cheese
12 ounces rigatoni, cooked, drained
1½ cups (6 ounces) shredded Wisconsin
　Cheddar cheese
1½ cups (6 ounces) shredded Wisconsin
　Mozzarella cheese
¼ teaspoon chili powder

In a 2-quart saucepan, combine milk, carrot, celery, onion, parsley, peppercorns, hot pepper sauce, bay leaf and nutmeg. Bring to boil. Reduce heat to low; simmer 10 minutes. Strain, reserving liquid. Melt butter in 2-quart saucepan over low heat. Blend in flour. Gradually add reserved liquid; cook, stirring constantly, until thickened. Remove from heat. Add Parmesan and Romano cheeses; stir until blended. Pour over pasta; toss well. Combine Cheddar and Mozzarella cheeses. In buttered 2-quart casserole, layer ½ of pasta mixture, Cheddar cheese mixture and remaining pasta mixture. Sprinkle with chili powder. Bake at 350°F for 25 minutes or until hot. *Makes 6 servings*

Favorite recipe from **Wisconsin Milk Marketing Board**

Stir-Fry Chicken & Sesame Noodle Salad

8 ounces uncooked vermicelli
10 cherry tomatoes, cut into halves
2 carrots, cut into julienne strips
½ cup chopped green onions and tops
1 tablespoon sesame seed, toasted
5 tablespoons KIKKOMAN® Stir-Fry
　Sauce, divided
3 tablespoons vinegar
2 tablespoons water
1 tablespoon sugar
1 clove garlic, minced
1 teaspoon minced fresh ginger root
½ pound boneless, skinless chicken, cut
　into thin strips
3 tablespoons vegetable oil, divided
2 ounces fresh snow peas, trimmed
　and cut into julienne strips

Cook vermicelli according to package directions, omitting salt; drain. Cool under cold water; drain thoroughly. Combine vermicelli, tomatoes, carrots, green onions and sesame seed in large bowl. Blend 4 tablespoons stir-fry sauce, vinegar, water, sugar, garlic and ginger in small bowl; set aside. Coat chicken with remaining 1 tablespoon stir-fry sauce in small bowl. Heat 1 tablespoon oil in hot wok or large skillet over high heat. Add chicken and stir-fry 2 minutes; remove. Reduce heat to medium; heat remaining 2 tablespoons oil in same pan. Add snow peas; stir-fry 1 minute. Add chicken and stir-fry sauce mixture; cook and stir only until chicken and snow peas are coated with sauce and heated through. Pour over noodles and toss to coat all pieces well. *Makes 4 servings*

Rigatoni with Four Cheeses

15-Minute Pasta Combo

8 ounces uncooked spaghetti, broken in half
½ cup KRAFT® House Italian with Olive Oil Blend Dressing
2 large tomatoes, seeded and chopped
2 cups LOUIS RICH® Hickory Smoked Breast of Turkey cubes
1 cup (4 ounces) KRAFT® 100% Grated Parmesan Cheese

PREPARE spaghetti as directed on package; drain.

HEAT dressing on medium heat using same pan used to cook spaghetti. Add spaghetti; toss until well coated.

ADD tomatoes, turkey and Parmesan cheese; toss lightly. *Makes 6 servings*

Angel Hair Mornay

1 package (16 ounces) angel hair pasta (capellini)
1 teaspoon olive oil
1 box (10 ounces) BIRDS EYE® frozen Deluxe Broccoli Florets
1 box (10 ounces) BIRDS EYE® frozen Cauliflower with Cheese Sauce

• Preheat oven to 350°F.

• In large saucepan, cook pasta according to package directions; drain.

• Combine pasta, oil and broccoli in 13×9-inch baking pan.

• Cover with cauliflower/cheese sauce mixture. Bake 20 minutes or until heated through. *Makes 4 servings*

Prep Time: 10 minutes

Cook Time: 20 minutes

Johnnie Marzetti

1 tablespoon CRISCO® Vegetable Oil
1 cup chopped celery
1 cup chopped onion
1 medium green bell pepper, chopped
1 pound ground beef round
1 can (14½ ounces) Italian-style stewed tomatoes
1 can (8 ounces) tomato sauce
1 can (6 ounces) tomato paste
1 cup water
1 bay leaf
1½ teaspoons dried basil leaves
1¼ teaspoons salt
¼ teaspoon black pepper
1 package (12 ounces) egg noodles, cooked and well drained
½ cup plain dry bread crumbs
1 cup (4 ounces) shredded sharp Cheddar cheese

1. Heat oven to 375°F. Oil 12½×8½×2-inch baking dish lightly.

2. Heat Crisco® Oil in large skillet on medium heat. Add celery, onion and green pepper. Cook and stir until tender. Remove vegetables from skillet. Set aside. Add meat to skillet. Cook until browned, stirring occasionally. Return vegetables to skillet. Add tomatoes, tomato sauce, tomato paste, water, bay leaf, basil, salt and black pepper. Reduce heat to low. Simmer 5 minutes, stirring occasionally. Remove bay leaf.

3. Place noodles in baking dish. Spoon meat mixture over noodles. Sprinkle with bread crumbs and cheese.

4. Bake at 375°F for 15 to 20 minutes or until cheese melts. Garnish, if desired. *Makes 8 servings*

Johnnie Marzetti

Bacon-Tuna Parmesano

½ cup milk
2 tablespoons margarine or butter
1 package (4.8 ounces) PASTA RONI®
    Parmesano
1 package (10 ounces) frozen peas
1 can (6⅛ ounces) white tuna in water,
    drained, flaked
4 slices crisply cooked bacon, crumbled
½ cup sliced green onions

1. In round 3-quart microwaveable glass casserole, combine 1⅔ cups water, milk and margarine. Microwave, uncovered, on HIGH 4 to 5 minutes or until boiling.

2. Stir in pasta, contents of seasoning packet, frozen peas, tuna, bacon and onions.

3. Microwave, uncovered, on HIGH 9 to 10 minutes or until peas are tender, stirring after 3 minutes.

4. Cover; let stand 3 to 4 minutes. Sauce will thicken upon standing. Stir before serving.
Makes 4 servings

Chicken and Veggie Lasagna

Tomato-Herb Sauce (recipe follows)
1½ cups thinly sliced zucchini
1 cup thinly sliced carrots
3 cups torn fresh spinach leaves
½ teaspoon salt
1 package (15 ounces) fat-free ricotta
    cheese
½ cup grated Parmesan cheese
9 lasagna noodles, cooked and drained
2 cups (8 ounces) reduced-fat
    shredded mozzarella cheese

1. Prepare Tomato-Herb Sauce.

2. Preheat oven to 350°F. Spray large nonstick skillet with cooking spray; heat over medium heat until hot. Add zucchini and carrots; cook and stir about 5 minutes or until almost tender. Remove from heat; stir in spinach and salt.

3. Combine ricotta and Parmesan cheese in small bowl. Spread 1⅔ cups Tomato-Herb Sauce on bottom of 13×9-inch baking pan. Top with 3 noodles. Spoon half of ricotta cheese mixture over noodles; spread lightly with spatula. Spoon half of zucchini mixture over ricotta cheese mixture; sprinkle with 1 cup mozzarella cheese. Repeat layers; place remaining 3 noodles on top.

4. Spread remaining Tomato-Herb Sauce over noodles. Cover with aluminum foil; bake 1 hour or until sauce is bubbly. Let stand 5 to 10 minutes; cut into rectangles. Garnish as desired.   *Makes 12 servings*

Tomato-Herb Sauce

1½ cups chopped onions (about
    2 medium)
4 cloves garlic, minced
1 tablespoon dried basil leaves
1 teaspoon dried oregano leaves
½ teaspoon dried tarragon leaves
¼ teaspoon dried thyme leaves
2½ pounds ripe tomatoes, peeled and
    cut into wedges
1 pound ground chicken, cooked,
    crumbled and drained
¾ cup water
¼ cup no-salt-added tomato paste
½ teaspoon salt
½ teaspoon pepper

1. Spray large nonstick skillet with cooking spray; heat over medium heat until hot. Add onions, garlic, basil, oregano, tarragon and thyme; cook and stir about 5 minutes or until onions are tender.

2. Add tomatoes, chicken, water and tomato paste; heat to a boil. Reduce heat to low and simmer, uncovered, about 20 minutes or until sauce is reduced to 5 cups. Stir in salt and pepper.   *Makes 5 cups*

Chicken and Veggie Lasagna

Sesame Noodles

    1 pound spaghetti
    1 cup chunky peanut butter
    1 cup orange juice
    ¼ cup soy sauce
    ¼ cup sesame oil
    ¼ cup vegetable oil
    2 tablespoons cider vinegar
    1 tablespoon TABASCO® Pepper Sauce
    1 teaspoon salt
    2 large green onions, sliced
    1 medium cucumber, sliced

Prepare spaghetti as package directs. Drain.

Meanwhile, in a large bowl, whisk peanut butter, orange juice, soy sauce, sesame oil, vegetable oil, cider vinegar, TABASCO® Sauce and salt until smooth. Add cooked spaghetti and green onions; toss well. Serve warm or cover and refrigerate to serve cold later. Just before serving, toss with additional orange juice, if necessary. Garnish with cucumber slices. *Makes 6 servings*

Macaroni and Cheese Dijon

    1¼ cups milk
    12 ounces pasteurized process Cheddar
        cheese spread, cubed
    ½ cup GREY POUPON® Dijon Mustard
    ⅓ cup sliced green onions
    6 slices bacon, cooked and crumbled
    ⅛ teaspoon ground red pepper
    12 ounces tri-color rotelle or spiral-
        shaped pasta, cooked
    1 (2.8-ounce) can French fried onion
        rings

In medium saucepan over low heat, heat milk, cheese and mustard until cheese melts and mixture is smooth. Stir in green onions, bacon and pepper; remove from heat.

In large bowl, combine hot pasta and cheese mixture, tossing until well coated; spoon into greased 2-quart casserole. Cover; bake at 350°F for 15 to 20 minutes. Uncover and stir; top with onion rings. Bake, uncovered, for 5 minutes more. Let stand 10 minutes before serving. Garnish as desired. *Makes 6 servings*

Zucchini Pasta Bake

    1½ cups uncooked pasta tubes
    ½ pound ground beef
    ½ cup chopped onion
    1 clove garlic, minced
        Salt and pepper
    1 teaspoon dried basil, crushed
    1 can (14½ ounces) DEL MONTE®
        Zucchini with Italian-Style Tomato
        Sauce
    1 cup (4 ounces) shredded Monterey
        Jack cheese

1. Cook pasta according to package directions; drain.

2. Cook beef with onion and garlic in large skillet; drain. Season with salt and pepper.

3. Stir in basil and zucchini with tomato sauce. Place pasta in 8-inch square baking dish. Top with meat mixture.

4. Bake at 350°F for 15 minutes. Top with cheese. Bake 3 minutes or until cheese is melted. *Makes 4 servings*

Prep and Cook Time: 33 minutes

Macaroni and Cheese Dijon

Shrimp in Angel Hair Pasta Casserole

2 eggs
1 cup half-and-half
1 cup plain yogurt
½ cup (2 ounces) shredded Swiss cheese
⅓ cup crumbled feta cheese
⅓ cup chopped fresh parsley
¼ cup chopped fresh basil *or* 1 teaspoon dried basil leaves, crushed
1 teaspoon dried oregano leaves, crushed
1 package (9 ounces) fresh angel hair pasta, uncooked
1 jar (16 ounces) mild, thick and chunky salsa
1 pound medium shrimp, peeled and deveined
½ cup (2 ounces) shredded Monterey Jack cheese

Preheat oven to 350°F. Grease 12×8-inch baking pan. Combine eggs, half-and-half, yogurt, Swiss cheese, feta cheese, parsley, basil and oregano in medium bowl; mix well. Place half the pasta in bottom of prepared pan. Cover with salsa. Add half the shrimp. Cover with remaining pasta. Spread egg mixture over pasta and top with remaining shrimp. Sprinkle with Monterey Jack cheese. Bake 30 minutes or until bubbly. Let stand 10 minutes. Garnish as desired.   *Makes 6 servings*

Favorite recipe from **Southeast United Dairy Industry Association, Inc.**

Eggplant & Feta Ziti

1 pound ground beef
1 medium eggplant, peeled, cut into ½-inch cubes (about 6 cups)
½ cup chopped onion
1 clove garlic, minced
1 jar (32 ounces) spaghetti sauce
¼ teaspoon ground cinnamon
1 package (8 ounces) ATHENOS® Feta Cheese with Garlic & Herb, crumbled
2 cups (8 ounces) shredded low-moisture part-skim mozzarella cheese
2 cups ziti, cooked, drained

BROWN meat in large skillet; drain. Remove and set aside. Cook eggplant, onion and garlic on medium heat 10 minutes or until vegetables are tender, stirring occasionally. Stir in spaghetti sauce, cinnamon and reserved meat. Reduce heat to low; simmer 5 minutes. Mix feta and mozzarella cheese.

LAYER ziti, meat sauce and cheese mixture in greased 13×9-inch baking dish.

BAKE at 375°F for 25 to 30 minutes or until thoroughly heated and lightly browned. Let stand 10 minutes before serving.
                    Makes 8 to 10 servings

Prep time: 35 minutes

Baking time: 30 minutes plus standing

Shrimp in Angel Hair Pasta Casserole

Wisconsin Swiss Linguine Tart

½ cup butter, divided
2 garlic cloves, minced
30 thin French bread slices
3 tablespoons flour
1 teaspoon salt
¼ teaspoon white pepper
    Dash nutmeg
2½ cups milk
¼ cup grated Wisconsin Parmesan
    cheese
2 eggs, beaten
2 cups (8 ounces) shredded Wisconsin
    Baby Swiss cheese
8 ounces fresh linguine, cooked and
    drained
⅓ cup green onion slices
2 tablespoons minced fresh basil *or*
    2 teaspoons dried basil, crushed
2 plum tomatoes

Melt ¼ cup butter. Add garlic; cook 1 minute. Brush 10-inch pie plate with butter mixture; line bottom and sides with bread, allowing bread to come 1 inch over sides. Brush bread with remaining butter mixture. Bake at 350°F for 5 minutes or until lightly browned. Set aside.

Melt remaining butter in saucepan over low heat. Blend in flour and seasonings. Gradually add milk; cook, stirring constantly, until thickened. Remove from heat; add Parmesan cheese. Stir small amount of sauce into eggs; mix well. Stir in remaining sauce.

Toss 1¼ cups Swiss cheese with linguine, green onions and basil. Pour sauce over linguine mixture; mix well. Pour into crust. Cut each tomato lengthwise into eight slices; place on tart. Sprinkle with remaining ¾ cup Swiss cheese. Bake at 350°F for 25 minutes or until warm. Let stand 5 minutes.

Makes 8 servings

Favorite recipe from **Wisconsin Milk Marketing Board**

Tortellini Bake Parmesano

1 package (12 ounces) fresh or frozen
    cheese tortellini or ravioli
½ pound lean ground beef
½ medium onion, finely chopped
2 cloves garlic, minced
½ teaspoon dried oregano, crushed
1 can (26 ounces) DEL MONTE®
    Chunky Spaghetti Sauce with
    Garlic & Herb
2 small zucchini, sliced
⅓ cup (about 1½ ounces) grated
    Parmesan cheese

1. Cook pasta according to package directions; rinse and drain.

2. Meanwhile, brown beef with onion, garlic and oregano in large skillet over medium-high heat; drain. Season with salt and pepper, if desired.

3. Add spaghetti sauce and zucchini. Cook 15 minutes or until thickened, stirring occasionally.

4. Arrange half of pasta in oiled 2-quart microwavable dish; top with half each of sauce and cheese. Repeat layers ending with cheese; cover.

5. Microwave on HIGH 8 to 10 minutes or until heated through, rotating dish halfway through cooking time.   *Makes 4 servings*

Hint: For convenience, double recipe and freeze one for later use. The recipe can also be made ahead, refrigerated and heated just before serving (allow extra time in microwave if dish is chilled).

Prep and Cook Time: 35 minutes

Wisconsin Swiss Linguine Tart

Italian Pasta Bake

1 pound ground beef *or* Italian sausage
4 cups cooked mostaccioli *or* penne
    pasta
1 jar (28 to 30 ounces) spaghetti sauce
    (about 2¾ cups)
¾ cup (3 ounces) KRAFT® 100% Grated
    Parmesan Cheese, divided
2 cups KRAFT® Shredded Low-Moisture
    Part-Skim Mozzarella Cheese

BROWN meat in large skillet; drain.

STIR in mostaccioli, spaghetti sauce and
½ cup of the Parmesan cheese. Spoon into
13×9-inch baking dish. Top with mozzarella
cheese and remaining ¼ cup Parmesan
cheese.

BAKE at 375°F for 20 minutes.

Makes 6 servings

Prep Time: 10 minutes
Bake Time: 20 minutes

Cheesy Turkey and Spaghetti

1 pound ground turkey
1 tablespoon vegetable oil
1 can (15 ounces) VEG-ALL® Mixed
    Vegetables, undrained
1 can (10¾ ounces) condensed cream
    of chicken soup
1 can (10¾ ounces) condensed cream
    of mushroom soup
1 cup milk
¼ cup dry sherry
12 ounces spaghetti or linguini, cooked
1 cup sliced mushrooms
¾ cup Parmesan cheese, divided

1. In large skillet cook turkey in oil until no
longer pink.

2. Drain Veg-All® vegetables, reserving liquid.
Combine liquid with soups, milk and sherry.

3. Add soup mixture to spaghetti and mix
with turkey, vegetables, mushrooms and
½ cup Parmesan cheese. Spoon into 2-quart
casserole. Sprinkle with remaining ¼ cup
Parmesan cheese.

4. Bake at 400°F for 30 minutes.

Makes 8 servings

Chicken Paprika

3 tablespoons all-purpose flour
1 tablespoon paprika
¼ teaspoon salt
⅛ teaspoon black pepper
4 chicken breasts, skinned (about
    1½ pounds)
1 teaspoon olive oil
1 medium onion, chopped
1 cup chicken broth
¼ cup sour cream
    Hot cooked spaetzel or noodles
    Fresh parsley (optional)

Combine flour, paprika, salt and pepper on
sheet of waxed paper. Coat chicken breasts
with flour mixture. Reserve remaining flour
mixture.

Heat oil in large skillet over medium heat.
Add chicken; cook about 10 minutes or until
browned on all sides. Remove chicken from
skillet.

Add onion to same skillet; cook 2 minutes.
Stir in remaining flour mixture. Gradually stir
in chicken broth; cook and stir until mixture
comes to a boil. Return chicken to skillet.
Reduce heat to low; cover and simmer 25
minutes or until juices run clear.

Remove chicken to platter. Spoon off fat
from gravy in skillet. Add sour cream to
skillet; stir to combine. Serve with spaetzel.
Garnish with fresh parsley, if desired.

Makes 4 servings

Chicken Paprika

Creamy Shell Soup

4 cups water
3 or 4 chicken pieces
1 cup chopped onion
¼ cup chopped celery
¼ cup minced fresh parsley *or*
    1 tablespoon dried parsley flakes
1 bay leaf
1 teaspoon salt
¼ teaspoon white pepper
2 medium potatoes, diced
4 or 5 green onions, chopped
3 chicken bouillon cubes
½ teaspoon seasoned salt
½ teaspoon poultry seasoning
4 cups milk
2 cups medium shell macaroni,
    cooked and drained
¼ cup butter or margarine
¼ cup all-purpose flour
    Ground nutmeg (optional)
    Chopped fresh parsley (optional)

Combine water, chicken, chopped onion, celery, minced parsley, bay leaf, salt and pepper in Dutch oven. Bring to a boil. Reduce heat to low; simmer until chicken is tender. Remove bay leaf; discard. Remove chicken; cool. Skin, debone and cut into small cubes; set aside.

Add potatoes, green onions, bouillon cubes, seasoned salt and poultry seasoning to broth. Simmer 15 minutes. Add milk, macaroni and chicken; return to simmer.

Melt butter in skillet over medium heat. Add flour, stirring constantly, until mixture begins to brown. Add to soup; blend well. Let soup simmer on very low heat 20 minutes to blend flavors. Season to taste. Sprinkle with ground nutmeg and additional chopped parsley, if desired. *Makes 8 servings*

Favorite recipe from **North Dakota Wheat Commission**

Cavatelli and Broccoli

4 cloves garlic, minced
3 tablespoons olive oil
2 (14½-ounce) cans COLLEGE INN®
    Chicken Broth
1 pound frozen cavatelli pasta
4 cups chopped broccoli
1 tablespoon chopped fresh basil
    leaves *or* 1 teaspoon dried basil
    leaves
½ cup chopped roasted red peppers
    Salt and pepper, to taste
    Grated Parmesan cheese

In 4-quart saucepan, sauté garlic in oil until tender. Stir in chicken broth; heat to a boil. Add pasta; heat to a boil. Reduce heat; cover and simmer for 5 minutes. Add broccoli; cook 10 minutes more or until pasta and broccoli are tender. Remove from heat; stir in basil and roasted red peppers. Season with salt and pepper. Serve with Parmesan cheese. *Makes 4 servings*

Smoked Sausage and Noodle Skillet

1 tablespoon vegetable oil
1 pound HILLSHIRE FARM® Smoked
    Sausage, cut into ¼-inch slices
1 onion, chopped
3 cups frozen broccoli, cauliflower
    and carrots mixture
4 ounces uncooked medium-size
    noodles or curly noodles
1 can (10¾ ounces) reduced-sodium
    condensed cream of celery soup,
    undiluted
1 cup reduced-sodium chicken broth
½ teaspoon dried marjoram leaves
¼ teaspoon black pepper

Heat oil in medium skillet over medium heat. Cook and stir Smoked Sausage and onion 3 to 4 minutes. Stir in frozen vegetables, noodles, soup, chicken broth, ¾ cup water, marjoram and pepper. Bring to a boil; reduce heat. Simmer, covered, 12 to 15 minutes or until noodles are tender, stirring occasionally. *Makes 4 servings*

Elaine's Tuna Tetrazzini

8 ounces fresh mushrooms, sliced
1 cup chopped onion
2 tablespoons vegetable oil
3 tablespoons all-purpose flour
1 cup chicken broth
½ cup low-fat milk
½ teaspoon paprika
½ teaspoon salt
¼ teaspoon pepper
1 can (6 ounces) STARKIST® Tuna, drained and broken into chunks
¼ cup grated Parmesan or Romano cheese
2 tablespoons minced parsley
8 ounces thin spaghetti or linguine, broken into halves, hot cooked

In large skillet, sauté mushrooms and onion in oil for 3 minutes, or until limp. Sprinkle flour over vegetables; stir until blended. Add chicken broth and milk all at once; cook and stir until mixture thickens and bubbles. Stir in paprika, salt and pepper; cook 2 minutes more. Stir in tuna, cheese and parsley; cook 1 to 2 minutes, or until heated through. Spoon over pasta. *Makes 4 servings*

Preparation time: 20 minutes

Hot & Sour Noodle Stir-Fry

2 teaspoons cornstarch
2 teaspoons KIKKOMAN® Lite Teriyaki Marinade & Sauce
½ pound boneless tender beef steak (sirloin, rib eye or top loin), cut into thin strips
4 ounces uncooked fine egg noodles
¼ cup KIKKOMAN® Lite Teriyaki Marinade & Sauce
2 tablespoons water
1 teaspoon vinegar
2 tablespoons vegetable oil, divided
1 clove garlic, minced
¼ pound fresh snow peas, trimmed and cut into julienne strips
1 red bell pepper, cut into julienne strips
2 tablespoons minced unsalted roasted peanuts
1 tablespoon minced fresh cilantro

Combine cornstarch and 2 teaspoons lite teriyaki sauce in small bowl; stir in beef. Let stand 30 minutes. Meanwhile, cook egg noodles according to package directions, omitting salt; drain. Combine ¼ cup lite teriyaki sauce, water and vinegar; set aside. Heat 1 tablespoon oil in hot wok or large skillet over high heat. Add beef and garlic; stir-fry 1 minute. Remove. Heat remaining 1 tablespoon oil in same pan. Add snow peas and bell pepper; stir-fry 1 minute. Stir in noodles until thoroughly heated. Add beef and lite teriyaki sauce mixture. Cook and stir only until all pieces are coated with sauce. Remove from heat; add peanuts and cilantro, tossing to combine. Serve immediately. *Makes 4 servings*

Baked Ziti with Walnuts

1 cup uncooked ziti pasta
1 box (10 ounces) BIRDS EYE® frozen
    Peas & Pearl Onions
1 cup tomato sauce
½ cup chopped walnuts
1 tablespoon olive oil
2 tablespoons grated Parmesan cheese

• Preheat oven to 350°F.

• Cook ziti according to package directions; drain and set aside.

• In large bowl, combine vegetables, tomato sauce, walnuts and oil. Add ziti; toss well.

• Place mixture in 13×9-inch baking pan. Sprinkle with cheese.

• Bake 20 minutes or until heated through.

Makes 4 servings

Prep Time: 10 minutes
Cook Time: 20 minutes

Creamy Spam™ Broccoli Casserole

Nonstick cooking spray
1 (7-ounce) package elbow macaroni
2 cups frozen cut broccoli, thawed and
    drained
1 (12-ounce) can SPAM® Lite Luncheon
    Meat, cubed
½ cup chopped red bell pepper
2 cups skim milk
2 tablespoons cornstarch
¼ teaspoon black pepper
1 cup (4 ounces) shredded fat-free
    Cheddar cheese
¾ cup soft bread crumbs
2 teaspoons margarine, melted

Heat oven to 350°F. Spray 2-quart casserole with nonstick cooking spray. Cook macaroni according to package directions; drain. In prepared casserole, combine macaroni, broccoli, SPAM® and bell pepper. In small saucepan, stir together milk, cornstarch and black pepper until cornstarch is dissolved. Bring to a boil, stirring constantly, until thickened. Reduce heat to low. Add cheese; stir until melted. Stir sauce into SPAM™ mixture. Combine bread crumbs and margarine; sprinkle on top of casserole. Bake 40 minutes or until thoroughly heated.

Makes 8 servings

Delicious Ground Beef Medley

1 pound ground beef
½ cup chopped onion
¼ cup chopped celery
2 cups uncooked elbow macaroni
1 can (10¾ ounces) condensed cream
    of chicken soup
1 can (10¾ ounces) condensed cream
    of mushroom soup
⅔ cup milk
½ teaspoon salt
    Dash of pepper
½ cup chopped green pepper
1 can (16 ounces) whole kernel corn,
    drained

1. Brown ground beef with onion and celery. Drain.

2. Cook macaroni according to package directions. Drain.

3. In 2½-quart casserole dish, combine soups with milk, salt and pepper. Add ground beef, macaroni, green pepper and corn. Bake at 350°F for 30 minutes.

Makes 8 servings

*Favorite recipe from **North Dakota Beef Commission***

Creamy Spam™ Broccoli Casserole

Spaghetti Pie

    4 ounces uncooked thin spaghetti
    1 egg
    ¼ cup grated Parmesan cheese
    1 teaspoon Italian seasoning
    ⅔ cup reduced-fat ricotta cheese
    ½ pound 93% lean ground turkey
    1 teaspoon chili powder
    ¼ teaspoon crushed fennel seeds
    ¼ teaspoon ground black pepper
    ⅛ teaspoon ground coriander
    1 can (14½ ounces) diced tomatoes,
        undrained
    1½ cups sliced fresh mushrooms
    1 cup chopped onion
    1 can (8 ounces) tomato sauce
    ¼ cup tomato paste
    1 clove garlic, minced
    2 teaspoons dried basil leaves
    1 cup (4 ounces) shredded part-skim
        mozzarella cheese

1. Cook spaghetti according to package directions, omitting salt. Drain and rinse well under cold water until pasta is cool; drain well.

2. Beat egg, Parmesan cheese and Italian seasoning lightly in medium bowl. Add spaghetti; blend well. Spray deep 9-inch pie plate with nonstick cooking spray. Place spaghetti mixture in pie plate. Press onto bottom and up side of pie plate. Spread ricotta cheese on spaghetti layer.

3. Preheat oven to 350°F. Combine turkey, chili powder, fennel seeds, pepper and coriander in medium bowl. Spray large nonstick skillet with nonstick cooking spray; heat over medium heat until hot. Brown turkey mixture until turkey is no longer pink, stirring to break up meat. Add remaining ingredients except mozzarella cheese. Cook and stir until mixture boils. Spoon mixture over ricotta cheese in pie plate.

4. Cover pie plate with foil. Bake 20 minutes. Remove foil. Sprinkle with mozzarella cheese; bake 5 minutes or until cheese is melted. Let stand before cutting and serving. *Makes 6 servings*

Baked Provençal Ziti Provolone

    10 ounces uncooked ziti
    1 cup evaporated skimmed milk
    ½ cup skim milk
    4 egg whites
    1 tablespoon Dijon mustard
    ½ teaspoon salt
    ½ cup finely chopped green onions,
        with tops
    Black pepper
    4 ounces sliced Provolone cheese
    2 tablespoons grated Parmesan cheese

1. Preheat oven to 325°F. Spray 9-inch square baking pan with nonstick cooking spray; set aside. Cook pasta according to package directions; drain. Place in bottom of prepared pan.

2. Meanwhile, combine evaporated milk, skim milk, egg whites, mustard and salt in food processor or blender; process until smooth.

3. Sprinkle green onions over pasta. Pour egg mixture over green onions. Sprinkle with pepper and top with Provolone cheese.

4. Bake 35 minutes or until heated through. Remove from oven. Sprinkle with Parmesan cheese. Let stand 5 minutes before serving. *Makes 4 servings*

Spaghetti Pie

Pastitso

8 ounces uncooked elbow macaroni
½ cup cholesterol-free egg substitute
¼ teaspoon ground nutmeg
¾ pound lean ground lamb, beef or turkey
½ cup chopped onion
1 clove garlic, minced
1 can (8 ounces) tomato sauce
¾ teaspoon dried mint leaves
½ teaspoon dried oregano leaves
½ teaspoon ground black pepper
⅛ teaspoon ground cinnamon
2 teaspoons reduced-calorie margarine
3 tablespoons all-purpose flour
1½ cups skim milk
2 tablespoons grated Parmesan cheese

Cook pasta according to package directions. Drain and transfer to medium bowl; stir in egg substitute and nutmeg.

Lightly spray bottom of 9-inch square baking dish with nonstick cooking spray. Spread pasta mixture in bottom of baking dish. Set aside.

Preheat oven to 350°F. Cook ground lamb, onion and garlic in large nonstick skillet over medium heat until lamb is no longer pink. Stir in tomato sauce, mint, oregano, black pepper and cinnamon. Reduce heat and simmer 10 minutes; spread over pasta.

Melt margarine in small nonstick saucepan. Add flour. Stir constantly for 1 minute. Whisk in milk. Cook, stirring constantly, until thickened, about 6 minutes; spread over meat mixture. Sprinkle with Parmesan cheese. Bake 30 to 40 minutes or until set.

Makes 6 servings

Tex-Mex Lasagna

1 pound ground beef
1 can (16 ounces) whole tomatoes, undrained and cut up
1 package (about 1⅛ ounces) taco seasoning mix
1⅓ cups FRENCH'S® French Fried Onions, divided
1½ cups (12 ounces) cream-style cottage cheese
2 cups (8 ounces) shredded Cheddar cheese
2 eggs, slightly beaten
12 (6-inch) flour or corn tortillas
1 medium tomato, chopped
1 cup shredded lettuce

Preheat oven to 350°. In large skillet, brown ground beef; drain. Stir in canned tomatoes and taco seasoning. Reduce heat and simmer, uncovered, 5 minutes. Remove from heat and stir in ⅔ cup French Fried Onions. In medium bowl, combine cottage cheese, 1 cup Cheddar cheese and the eggs; set aside. Overlap 3 tortillas in bottom of greased 8×12-inch baking dish. Overlap 6 tortillas around sides of dish. Spoon beef mixture over tortillas; top with remaining 3 tortillas. Spoon cheese mixture over beef and tortillas. Bake, covered, at 350° for 45 minutes or until cheese mixture is set. Top with remaining Cheddar cheese. Sprinkle remaining ⅔ cup onions down center of casserole. Bake, uncovered, 5 minutes or until onions are golden brown. Just before serving, arrange tomato and lettuce around edges of casserole. Let stand 5 minutes before serving. *Makes 6 servings*

Pastitso

Turkey Meatball & Olive Casserole

2 cups uncooked rotini
½ pound ground turkey
¼ cup dry bread crumbs
1 egg, slightly beaten
2 teaspoons dried minced onion
2 teaspoons white wine Worcestershire sauce
½ teaspoon dried Italian seasoning
½ teaspoon salt
⅛ teaspoon black pepper
1 tablespoon vegetable oil
1 can (10¾ ounces) condensed cream of celery soup, undiluted
½ cup low-fat plain yogurt
¾ cup pimiento-stuffed green olives, sliced
3 tablespoons Italian-style bread crumbs
1 tablespoon margarine or butter, melted
Paprika (optional)

Preheat oven to 350°F. Spray 2-quart round casserole with nonstick cooking spray.

Cook pasta according to package directions until al dente. Drain and set aside.

Meanwhile, combine turkey, bread crumbs, egg, onion, Worcestershire sauce, Italian seasoning, salt and pepper in medium bowl. Shape mixture into ½-inch meatballs.

Heat oil in medium skillet over high heat until hot. Add meatballs in single layer; cook until lightly browned on all sides and still pink in centers, turning frequently. Do not overcook. Remove from skillet; drain on paper towels.

Mix soup and yogurt in large bowl. Add pasta, meatballs and olives; stir gently to combine. Transfer to prepared dish.

Combine bread crumbs and margarine in small bowl; sprinkle evenly over casserole. Sprinkle lightly with paprika, if desired.

Bake, covered, 30 minutes. Uncover and bake 12 minutes or until meatballs are no longer pink in centers and casserole is hot and bubbly. *Makes 6 to 8 servings*

Chicken Parmesan Noodle Bake

1 package (12 ounces) extra-wide noodles
4 boneless, skinless chicken breast halves
¼ teaspoon rosemary, crushed
2 cans (14½ ounces each) DEL MONTE® *FreshCut*™ Brand Diced Tomatoes with Basil, Garlic & Oregano
½ cup (2 ounces) shredded mozzarella cheese
¼ cup (1 ounce) grated Parmesan cheese

1. Preheat oven to 450°F.

2. Cook noodles according to package directions; drain.

3. Meanwhile, sprinkle chicken with rosemary; season with salt and pepper, if desired. Arrange chicken in 13×9-inch baking dish. Bake, uncovered, 20 minutes or until chicken is no longer pink in center. Drain; remove chicken from dish.

4. Drain tomatoes, reserving liquid. In large bowl, toss reserved liquid with noodles; place in baking dish. Top with chicken and tomatoes; sprinkle with cheeses.

5. Bake 10 minutes or until heated through. Sprinkle with additional Parmesan cheese and garnish, if desired. *Makes 4 servings*

Prep and Cook Time: 35 minutes

Chicken Parmesan Noodle Bake

Mostaccioli with Spinach and Feta

8 ounces mostaccioli or penne
2 tablespoons olive oil
3 cups chopped tomatoes
1 package (10 ounces) frozen chopped spinach, thawed, well drained
½ cup chopped green onions
1 package (8 ounces) ATHENOS® Feta Cheese with Basil & Tomato, crumbled

COOK pasta as directed on package; drain. Return to pan; toss with oil.

ADD tomatoes, spinach and onions; toss lightly. Cook and stir 2 minutes or until thoroughly heated.

ADD cheese; cook 1 minute.

Makes 8 servings

Prep Time: 10 minutes
Cook Time: 15 minutes

Country Sausage Macaroni and Cheese

1 pound BOB EVANS® Special Seasonings Roll Sausage
1½ cups milk
12 ounces pasteurized processed Cheddar cheese, cut into cubes
½ cup Dijon mustard
1 cup diced fresh or drained canned tomatoes
1 cup sliced mushrooms
⅓ cup sliced green onions
⅛ teaspoon cayenne pepper
12 ounces uncooked elbow macaroni
2 tablespoons Parmesan cheese

Preheat oven to 350°F. Crumble and cook sausage in medium skillet until browned. Drain on paper towels. Combine milk, cheese and mustard in medium saucepan; cook and stir over low heat until cheese melts and mixture is smooth. Stir in sausage, tomatoes, mushrooms, green onions and cayenne pepper. Remove from heat.

Cook macaroni according to package directions; drain. Combine hot macaroni and cheese mixture in large bowl; toss until well coated. Spoon into greased 2-quart casserole dish. Cover and bake 15 to 20 minutes. Stir; sprinkle with Parmesan cheese. Bake, uncovered, 5 minutes more. Let stand 10 minutes before serving. Refrigerate leftovers.

Makes 6 to 8 servings

Mushroom and Tuna Bake

1 can (10¾ ounces) cream of celery soup
1 cup milk
1 jar (4 ounces) sliced mushrooms, drained
½ cup grated Parmesan cheese, divided
1 teaspoon dried Italian herb blend
½ teaspoon seasoned salt
⅛ to ¼ teaspoon garlic powder
1 can (12 ounces) STARKIST® Solid White or Chunk Light Tuna, drained and chunked
3 cups cooked egg noodles
1 cup crispy rice cereal

In medium saucepan, combine soup and milk; blend well. Add mushrooms, ¼ cup cheese, Italian herb blend, seasoned salt, garlic powder and tuna; cook over low heat until heated through. Remove from heat; stir in egg noodles. Transfer mixture to lightly greased 11×7-inch baking dish. Top with remaining ¼ cup Parmesan cheese and cereal. Bake in 350°F oven 30 minutes.

Makes 6 servings

Prep Time: 40 minutes

Country Sausage Macaroni and Cheese

Pad Thai (Thai Fried Noodles)

7¼ cups water, divided
12 ounces dried thin rice stick noodles
4 tablespoons vegetable oil, divided
3 tablespoons light brown sugar
3 tablespoons soy sauce
2 tablespoons lime juice
1 tablespoon anchovy paste
2 eggs, lightly beaten
12 ounces medium shrimp, peeled and deveined
2 cloves garlic, minced
1 tablespoon paprika
¼ to ½ teaspoon ground red pepper
8 ounces fresh bean sprouts, divided
½ cup coarsely chopped unsalted dry-roasted peanuts
4 green onions with tops, cut into 1-inch lengths
½ lime, cut lengthwise into 4 wedges, for garnish

1. Place 6 cups water in wok; bring to a boil over high heat. Add noodles; cook 2 minutes or until tender but still firm, stirring frequently. Drain and rinse under cold running water to stop cooking. Drain again and place noodles in large bowl. Add 1 tablespoon oil; toss lightly to coat. Set aside.

2. Combine remaining 1¼ cups water, brown sugar, soy sauce, lime juice and anchovy paste in small bowl; set aside.

3. Heat wok over medium heat about 30 seconds or until hot. Drizzle 1 tablespoon oil into wok and heat 15 seconds. Add eggs and cook 1 minute or just until set on bottom. Turn eggs over and stir to scramble until cooked but not dry. Transfer to medium bowl; set aside.

4. Heat wok over high heat until hot. Drizzle 1 tablespoon oil into wok and heat 15 seconds. Add shrimp and garlic; stir-fry 2 minutes or until shrimp begin to turn pink and opaque. Add shrimp to eggs.

5. Heat wok over medium heat until hot. Drizzle remaining 1 tablespoon oil into wok and heat 15 seconds. Stir in paprika and red pepper. Add cooked noodles and anchovy mixture; cook and stir about 5 minutes or until noodles are softened. Stir in ¾ of bean sprouts. Add peanuts and green onions; toss and cook about 1 minute or until onions begin to wilt.

6. Add eggs and shrimp; stir-fry until heated through. Transfer to serving plate and garnish with remaining bean sprouts and lime wedges. *Makes 4 servings*

Quickest Chicken Cacciatore

4 BUTTERBALL® Boneless Skinless Chicken Thighs
2 tablespoons butter or margarine
1 jar (14 ounces) chunky-style meatless spaghetti sauce
1 jar (2½ ounces) sliced mushrooms, drained
½ cup chopped green bell pepper
¼ cup dry red wine
1 package (9 ounces) refrigerated fettuccine, cooked and drained

Cut each chicken thigh lengthwise into 3 pieces. Melt butter in large skillet over medium heat. Add chicken; cook 8 to 10 minutes or until no longer pink in center. Add remaining ingredients except fettuccine. Cook and stir until heated through. Serve over fettuccine.

Makes 4 servings

Preparation Time: 15 minutes

Pad Thai (Thai Fried Noodles)

Chicken Asparagus Casserole

2 teaspoons vegetable oil
1 cup seeded and chopped green
    and/or red bell peppers
1 medium onion, chopped
2 cloves garlic, minced
1 can (10¾ ounces) condensed cream
    of asparagus soup
2 eggs
1 container (8 ounces) ricotta cheese
2 cups (8 ounces) shredded Cheddar
    cheese, divided
1½ cups chopped cooked chicken, cut
    into ½-inch pieces
1 package (10 ounces) frozen chopped
    asparagus,* thawed and drained
8 ounces egg noodles, cooked
    Ground black pepper (optional)

*Or, substitute ½ pound fresh asparagus cut into ½-inch pieces. Bring 6 cups water to a boil over high heat in large saucepan. Add fresh asparagus. Reduce heat to medium. Cover and cook 5 to 8 minutes or until crisp-tender. Drain.

1. Preheat oven to 350°F. Grease 13×9-inch casserole; set aside.

2. Heat oil in small skillet over medium heat. Add bell peppers, onion and garlic; cook and stir until crisp-tender.

3. Mix soup, eggs, ricotta cheese and 1 cup Cheddar cheese in large bowl until well blended. Add onion mixture, chicken, asparagus and noodles; mix well. Season with pepper, if desired.

4. Spread mixture evenly in prepared casserole. Top with remaining 1 cup Cheddar cheese.

5. Bake 30 minutes or until center is set and cheese is bubbly. Let stand 5 minutes before serving. Garnish as desired.

Makes 12 servings

Turkey Tetrazzini

2 tablespoons cornstarch
1¼ cups skim milk
¾ cup turkey broth or chicken bouillon
½ teaspoon salt
½ teaspoon garlic powder
⅛ teaspoon pepper
¼ cup grated Parmesan cheese
2 tablespoons dry white wine
1 can (4 ounces) mushrooms, drained
1 jar (2 ounces) chopped pimiento,
    drained
4 ounces spaghetti, cooked according
    to package instructions and
    drained
2 cups cooked turkey, cut into ½-inch
    cubes
2 tablespoons sliced almonds

1. Preheat oven to 375°F.

2. In 3-quart saucepan, over medium heat, combine cornstarch, milk, broth, salt, garlic powder and pepper. Bring mixture to boil, stirring constantly. Remove from heat and stir in cheese, wine, mushrooms, pimiento, spaghetti and turkey.

3. Pour turkey mixture into lightly greased 9-inch square casserole dish. Top with almonds. Bake 25 minutes or until mixture bubbles and top is browned.

Makes 4 servings

*Favorite recipe from **National Turkey Federation***

Chicken Asparagus Casserole

Pasta with Salmon and Dill

6 ounces uncooked mafalda pasta
1 tablespoon olive oil
2 ribs celery, sliced
1 small red onion, chopped
1 can (10¾ ounces) condensed cream of celery soup, undiluted
¼ cup reduced-fat mayonnaise
¼ cup dry white wine
3 tablespoons chopped fresh parsley
1 teaspoon dried dill weed
1 can (7½ ounces) pink salmon, drained
½ cup dry bread crumbs
1 tablespoon margarine or butter, melted
Fresh dill sprigs (optional)

Preheat oven to 350°F. Spray 1-quart square baking dish with nonstick cooking spray.

Cook pasta according to package directions until al dente; drain and set aside.

Meanwhile, heat oil in medium skillet over medium-high heat until hot. Add celery and onion; cook and stir 2 minutes or until vegetables are tender. Set aside.

Combine soup, mayonnaise, wine, parsley and dill weed in large bowl. Stir in pasta, vegetables and salmon until pasta is well coated. Pour salmon mixture into prepared dish.

Combine bread crumbs and margarine in small bowl; sprinkle evenly over casserole.

Bake, uncovered, 25 minutes or until hot and bubbly. Garnish with dill sprigs, if desired. *Makes 4 servings*

Chicken Paprikash

2 tablespoons margarine or butter
1 pound skinless, boneless chicken breasts or thighs, cut into 1-inch pieces
½ cup chopped onion
1 clove garlic, minced
1 tablespoon paprika
½ cup milk
1 package (4.7 ounces) PASTA RONI® Fettuccine Alfredo
1 medium green bell pepper, cut into strips
½ cup sour half-and-half or sour cream

1. In large skillet, melt margarine over medium heat. Add chicken, onion and garlic; cook 1 minute, stirring occasionally. Add paprika; continue cooking 2 minutes.

2. Add 1½ cups water, milk, pasta, contents of seasoning packet and green pepper. Bring just to a boil. Reduce heat to medium-low.

3. Boil, uncovered, stirring frequently, 9 to 11 minutes or until pasta is desired tenderness and chicken is no longer pink inside. Sauce will thicken upon standing. Stir in sour half-and-half before serving.
Makes 4 servings

Pasta with Salmon and Dill

Double Spinach Bake

8 ounces uncooked spinach fettuccine noodles
1 cup fresh mushroom slices
1 green onion with top, finely chopped
1 clove garlic, minced
4 to 5 cups fresh spinach, coarsely chopped *or* 1 package (10 ounces) frozen spinach, thawed and drained
1 tablespoon water
1 container (15 ounces) nonfat ricotta cheese
¼ cup skim milk
1 egg
½ teaspoon ground nutmeg
½ teaspoon ground black pepper
¼ cup (1 ounce) shredded reduced-fat Swiss cheese

1. Preheat oven to 350°F. Cook pasta according to package directions. Drain; set aside.

2. Spray medium skillet with nonstick cooking spray. Add mushrooms, green onion and garlic. Cook and stir over medium heat until mushrooms are softened. Add spinach and water. Cover; cook until spinach is wilted, about 3 minutes.

3. Combine ricotta cheese, milk, egg, nutmeg and black pepper in large bowl. Gently stir in noodles and vegetables; toss to coat evenly.

4. Lightly coat shallow 1½-quart casserole with nonstick cooking spray. Spread noodle mixture in casserole. Sprinkle with Swiss cheese.

5. Bake 25 to 30 minutes or until knife inserted halfway into center comes out clean. *Makes 6 (1-cup) servings*

Broccoli Chicken Pasta Casserole

2 teaspoons CRISCO® Vegetable Oil
⅔ cup chopped onion
2 large cloves garlic, minced
1 pound boneless, skinless chicken breasts, cut into 1-inch pieces
2 cans (14½ ounces each) whole tomatoes, undrained and coarsely chopped
1 can (8 ounces) tomato sauce
¼ cup ketchup
1¼ teaspoons dried basil leaves
¾ teaspoon dried oregano leaves
¼ teaspoon salt
1 package (10 ounces) frozen broccoli cuts, thawed and well drained
5 ounces uncooked small macaroni, cooked (without salt or fat) and well drained
½ cup grated Parmesan cheese, divided

1. Heat oven to 350°F.

2. Heat Crisco Oil® in large skillet on medium-high heat. Add onion and garlic. Cook and stir until tender. Add chicken. Cook and stir just until chicken is no longer pink in center. Stir in tomatoes, tomato sauce, ketchup, basil, oregano and salt. Bring to a boil. Reduce heat to low. Simmer 5 minutes, stirring occasionally.

3. Combine broccoli, macaroni, chicken mixture and ¼ cup cheese in large bowl. Stir well. Spoon into 13×9×2-inch baking dish. Sprinkle with remaining ¼ cup cheese.

4. Bake at 350°F for 20 minutes.
Makes 8 servings

Double Spinach Bake

Pizza Chicken Bake

3½ cups uncooked bow tie pasta
1 tablespoon vegetable oil
1 cup sliced mushrooms
1 jar (26 ounces) herb-flavored
    spaghetti sauce
1 teaspoon pizza seasoning blend
3 boneless skinless chicken breast
    halves (about ¾ pound), quartered
1 cup (4 ounces) shredded mozzarella
    cheese

Preheat oven to 350°F. Spray 2-quart round casserole with nonstick cooking spray.

Cook pasta according to package directions until al dente. Drain and place in prepared dish.

Meanwhile, heat oil in large skillet over medium-high heat until hot. Add mushrooms; cook and stir 2 minutes. Remove from heat. Stir in spaghetti sauce and pizza seasoning.

Pour half of spaghetti sauce mixture into casserole; stir until pasta is well coated. Arrange chicken on top of pasta. Pour remaining spaghetti sauce mixture evenly over chicken.

Bake, covered, 50 minutes or until chicken is no longer pink in centers. Remove from oven; sprinkle with cheese. Cover and let stand 5 minutes before serving.

Makes 4 servings

Creamy Pasta Primavera

1 bag (16 ounces) BIRDS EYE® frozen
    Pasta Secrets Primavera
½ cup 1% milk
2 packages (3 ounces each) cream
    cheese, cubed
1 cup cubed ham
¼ cup grated Parmesan cheese

• In large skillet, heat Pasta Secrets in milk over medium heat to a simmer; cover and simmer 7 to 9 minutes or until vegetables are tender.

• Add cream cheese; reduce heat to low and cook until cream cheese is melted, stirring often.

• Stir in ham and cheese; cover and cook 5 minutes more.
Makes 4 servings

Prep Time: 10 minutes

Cook Time: 20 minutes

Pork Pasta Fazool

½ pound lean ground pork
1 small onion, diced
1 clove garlic, minced
1 can (15 ounces) cannellini beans,
    drained
1 can (14½ ounces) chicken broth
1 can (14½ ounces) Italian-style
    chopped tomatoes
½ cup small pasta shells or macaroni
1 teaspoon dried oregano leaves
½ teaspoon salt
½ teaspoon crushed fennel seed
½ teaspoon coarsely ground black
    pepper
¼ teaspoon crushed red pepper flakes

In large heavy saucepan brown and crumble ground pork. Stir in onion and garlic; cook and stir until onion is soft, about 3 minutes. Stir in remaining ingredients; bring to a boil, reduce heat and simmer 10 to 12 minutes or until pasta is tender.

Makes 6 (1-cup) servings

Prep Time: 20 minutes

*Favorite recipe from **National Pork Producers Council***

Pizza Chicken Bake

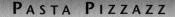

Tacos in Pasta Shells

1 package (3 ounces) cream cheese with chives
18 jumbo pasta shells
1¼ pounds ground beef
1 teaspoon salt
1 teaspoon chili powder
2 tablespoons butter, melted
1 cup prepared taco sauce
1 cup (4 ounces) shredded Cheddar cheese
1 cup (4 ounces) shredded Monterey Jack cheese
1½ cups crushed tortilla chips
1 cup dairy sour cream
3 green onions, chopped
Leaf lettuce, small pitted ripe olives and cherry tomatoes for garnish

1. Cut cream cheese into ½-inch cubes. Let stand at room temperature until softened.

2. Cook pasta according to package directions. Place in colander and rinse under warm running water. Drain well. Return to saucepan.

3. Preheat oven to 350°F. Butter 13×9-inch baking pan.

4. Cook beef in large skillet over medium-high heat until brown, stirring to separate meat; drain drippings.

5. Reduce heat to medium-low. Add cream cheese, salt and chili powder; simmer 5 minutes.

6. Toss shells with butter. Fill shells with beef mixture using spoon. Arrange shells in prepared pan. Pour taco sauce over each shell. Cover with foil.

7. Bake 15 minutes. Uncover; top with Cheddar cheese, Monterey Jack cheese and chips. Bake 15 minutes more or until bubbly. Top with sour cream and onions. Garnish, if desired. *Makes 4 to 6 servings*

Tomato Pesto Lasagna

8 ounces lasagna noodles (2 inches wide)
1 pound crumbled sausage or ground beef
1 can (14½ ounces) DEL MONTE® Diced Tomatoes with Garlic & Onion, undrained
1 can (6 ounces) DEL MONTE® Tomato Paste
8 ounces ricotta cheese
1 package (4 ounces) pesto sauce*
2 cups (8 ounces) shredded mozzarella cheese

Pesto sauce is available frozen or refrigerated at the supermarket.

1. Cook noodles according to package directions; rinse, drain and separate noodles.

2. Meanwhile, brown meat in large skillet; drain. Stir in tomatoes, tomato paste and ¾ cup water.

3. Layer ⅓ meat sauce, then half each of noodles, ricotta cheese, pesto and mozzarella cheese in 2-quart casserole or 9-inch square baking dish; repeat layers. Top with remaining sauce. Sprinkle with grated Parmesan cheese, if desired.

4. Bake at 350°F, 30 minutes or until heated through. *Makes 6 servings*

Microwave Directions: Assemble lasagna in 9-inch square microwavable dish as directed. Cover with vented plastic wrap; microwave on HIGH 10 minutes, rotating dish after 5 minutes.

Prep Time: 20 minutes

Cook Time: 30 minutes

Microwave Cook Time: 10 minutes

Tacos in Pasta Shells

Creamy Chicken and Pasta with Spinach

6 ounces uncooked egg noodles
1 tablespoon olive oil
¼ cup chopped onion
¼ cup chopped red bell pepper
1 package (10 ounces) frozen spinach, thawed and drained
2 boneless skinless chicken breast halves (¾ pound), cooked and cut into 1-inch pieces
1 can (4 ounces) sliced mushrooms, drained
2 cups (8 ounces) shredded Swiss cheese
1 container (8 ounces) sour cream
¾ cup half-and-half
2 eggs, slightly beaten
½ teaspoon salt
   Red onion and fresh spinach for garnish

Preheat oven to 350°F. Prepare egg noodles according to package directions; set aside.

Heat oil in large skillet over medium-high heat. Add onion and bell pepper; cook and stir 2 minutes or until onion is tender. Add spinach, chicken, mushrooms and cooked noodles; stir to combine.

Combine cheese, sour cream, half-and-half, eggs and salt in medium bowl; blend well.

Add cheese mixture to chicken mixture; stir to combine. Pour into 13×9-inch baking dish coated with nonstick cooking spray. Bake, covered, 30 to 35 minutes or until heated through. Garnish with red onion and fresh spinach, if desired. *Makes 8 servings*

Serving Suggestion: Serve with orange slices sprinkled with coconut.

Thai Peanut Noodle Stir-Fry

1 cup COLLEGE INN® Chicken Broth or Lower Sodium Chicken Broth
½ cup GREY POUPON® Dijon Mustard
⅓ cup creamy peanut butter
3 tablespoons firmly packed light brown sugar
2 tablespoons soy sauce
1 clove garlic, crushed
½ teaspoon minced fresh ginger
1 tablespoon cornstarch
4 cups cut-up vegetables (red pepper, carrot, mushrooms, green onions, pea pods)
1 tablespoon vegetable oil
1 pound linguine, cooked
   Chopped peanuts and scallion brushes for garnish

In medium saucepan, combine chicken broth, mustard, peanut butter, sugar, soy sauce, garlic, ginger and cornstarch. Cook over medium heat until mixture thickens and begins to boil; reduce heat and keep warm.

In large skillet, over medium-high heat, sauté vegetables in oil until tender, about 5 minutes. In large serving bowl, combine hot cooked pasta, vegetables and peanut sauce, tossing until well coated. Garnish with chopped peanuts and scallion brushes. Serve immediately. *Makes 4 to 6 servings*

Creamy Chicken and Pasta with Spinach

Baked Ziti with Three Cheeses

8 ounces uncooked ziti
8 ounces sweet Italian sausage
1½ cups part-skim ricotta cheese
¾ cup (3 ounces) shredded ALPINE LACE® Fat Free Pasteurized Process Skim Milk Cheese Product—For Parmesan Lovers, divided
¼ cup 2% low fat milk
1 large egg white
2 teaspoons minced garlic
3 cups chunky marinara sauce (in jar or refrigerator section)
1½ cups (6 ounces) shredded ALPINE LACE® Reduced Fat Mozzarella Cheese

1. Preheat the oven to 375°F. Spray a 14-inch oval au gratin pan or a 13×9×3-inch baking dish with nonstick cooking spray. Spray a medium-size skillet with the cooking spray. Cook the ziti until al dente, according to package directions.

2. Meanwhile, prepare the sausage: Remove the sausage meat from its casing and crumble. Heat the skillet for 1 minute over medium-high heat. Add the crumbled sausage and sauté for 5 minutes or until browned. Transfer to paper towels to drain.

3. In a medium-size bowl, combine the ricotta cheese, ½ cup of the Parmesan, the milk, egg white and garlic.

4. Spread one third of the sauce in the baking dish. Layer with: one half of the ziti, one third of the sauce, all of the ricotta mixture, one half of the sausage, then the remaining ziti, sausage and sauce. Sprinkle with the mozzarella cheese and the remaining ¼ cup of Parmesan.

5. Cover with foil and bake for 45 minutes. Uncover and bake 10 minutes more or until hot and bubbly.

Makes 12 first-course servings or
6 main-dish servings

Pasta with Roasted Vegetables

1 (2-pound) butternut squash, peeled, seeded and cut into 1-inch cubes
1 (10-ounce) container fresh Brussels sprouts, each cut into halves
1 small bulb fennel (about 8 ounces), trimmed, halved and thinly sliced
¼ cup olive oil
3 large cloves garlic, peeled and halved lengthwise
¾ teaspoon salt
½ teaspoon dried oregano leaves
8 ounces penne or ziti pasta
¼ cup pumpkin seeds
1½ teaspoons TABASCO® Pepper Sauce
½ cup grated Parmesan cheese

Preheat oven to 450°F. In roasting pan, combine squash, Brussels sprouts, fennel, olive oil, garlic, salt and oregano. Bake 20 minutes, stirring occasionally.

Meanwhile, prepare penne according to package directions. During last 2 minutes of roasting vegetables, add pumpkin seeds to vegetables. Continue cooking until seeds are lightly toasted.

To serve, toss cooked, drained pasta with roasted vegetables, TABASCO® Sauce and Parmesan cheese to mix well.

Makes 4 servings

Skillet Spaghetti and Sausage

¼ pound mild or hot Italian sausage links, sliced
½ pound ground beef
¼ teaspoon dried oregano, crushed
4 ounces spaghetti, broken in half
1 can (14½ ounces) DEL MONTE® Pasta Style Chunky Tomatoes
1 can (8 ounces) DEL MONTE® Tomato Sauce
1½ cups sliced fresh mushrooms
2 stalks celery, sliced

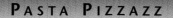

1. Brown sausage in large skillet over medium-high heat. Add beef and oregano; season to taste with salt and pepper, if desired.

2. Cook, stirring occasionally, until beef is browned; drain.

3. Add pasta, 1 cup water, tomatoes, tomato sauce, mushrooms and celery. Bring to boil, stirring occasionally.

4. Reduce heat; cover and simmer 12 to 14 minutes or until spaghetti is tender. Garnish with grated Parmesan cheese and chopped parsley, if desired. Serve immediately.

Makes 4 to 6 servings

Prep Time: 5 minutes

Cook Time: 30 minutes

Tortellini Vegetable Soup

1 package (14 ounces) turkey or pork breakfast sausage, crumbled
2 quarts water
6 HERB-OX® Beef Bouillon cubes*
½ teaspoon garlic powder
1 package (9 ounces) fresh tortellini cheese pasta
1 package (16 ounces) frozen vegetable combination (broccoli, cauliflower, red pepper), thawed

*1 bouillon cube = 1 teaspoon instant bouillon = 1 packet instant broth and seasoning.

In Dutch oven over medium-high heat, cook sausage until browned; drain. Add water, bouillon and garlic powder; bring to a boil. Add pasta; boil 5 minutes. Stir in vegetables. Simmer, uncovered, 10 minutes until vegetables and pasta are tender.

Makes 8 servings

Foolproof Clam Fettucine

1 package (6 ounces) fettucine-style noodles with creamy cheese sauce mix
¾ cup milk
1 can (6½ ounces) chopped clams, undrained
¼ cup (1 ounce) grated Parmesan cheese
1 teaspoon parsley flakes
1 can (4 ounces) mushroom stems and pieces, drained
2 tablespoons diced pimiento
1⅓ cups FRENCH'S® French Fried Onions, divided

Preheat oven to 375°F. In large saucepan, cook noodles according to package directions; drain. Return hot noodles to saucepan; stir in sauce mix, milk, undrained clams, Parmesan cheese, parsley flakes, mushrooms, pimiento and ⅔ cup French Fried Onions. Heat and stir 3 minutes or until bubbly. Pour into 10×6-inch baking dish. Bake, covered, at 375°F for 30 minutes or until thickened. Place remaining ⅔ cup onions around edges of casserole; bake, uncovered, 3 minutes or until onions are golden brown. *Makes 4 servings*

Microwave Directions: Prepare noodle mixture as above; pour into 10×6-inch microwave-safe dish. Cook, covered, on HIGH 4 to 6 minutes or until heated through. Stir noodle mixture halfway through cooking time. Top with remaining onions as above; cook, uncovered, 1 minute. Let stand 5 minutes.

Easy Tuna & Pasta Pot Pie

1 tablespoon margarine or butter
1 large onion, chopped
1½ cups cooked small shell pasta or
    elbow macaroni
1 can (10¾ ounces) condensed cream
    of celery or mushroom soup,
    undiluted
1 cup frozen peas, thawed
1 can (6 ounces) tuna in water,
    drained and broken into pieces
½ cup sour cream
½ teaspoon dried dill weed
¼ teaspoon salt
1 package (7.5 ounces) refrigerated
    buttermilk or country biscuits

1. Preheat oven to 400°F. Melt margarine in medium ovenproof skillet over medium heat. Add onion; cook 5 minutes, stirring occasionally.

2. Stir in pasta, soup, peas, tuna, sour cream, dill and salt; mix well. Cook 3 minutes or until hot. Press mixture down in skillet to form even layer.

3. Unwrap biscuit dough; arrange individual biscuits over tuna mixture. Bake 15 minutes or until biscuits are golden brown and tuna mixture is bubbly. *Makes 5 servings*

Prep and Cook Time: 28 minutes

Colorful Turkey Pasta Bake

2 cups (about 8 ounces) uncooked
    mixed vegetable rotini pasta*
1 tablespoon margarine
1 tablespoon all-purpose flour
¼ teaspoon salt
⅛ teaspoon pepper
1⅓ cups skim milk
2 cups cubed cooked turkey
1 cup (4 ounces) shredded natural
    Swiss cheese, divided

*If desired, substitute elbow macaroni, rotelle, small shells or ziti for rotini.

1. Cook pasta according to package directions; drain. In 2-quart saucepan, melt margarine over medium heat. Stir in flour, salt and pepper. Blend in milk; cook, stirring constantly, until thickened and bubbly. Add ¾ cup cheese; stir until melted. Stir in turkey and pasta.

2. Spray 8-inch square baking dish with nonstick vegetable spray. Add pasta mixture; sprinkle with remaining ¼ cup cheese. Bake at 350°F until heated through, about 30 minutes. To serve, cut into squares.
Makes 4 servings

*Favorite recipe from **National Turkey Federation***

Ham-Noodle Casserole

1 can (10¾ ounces) condensed
    Cheddar cheese soup, undiluted
½ cup milk
½ cup sour cream
½ cup sliced celery
1 can (2½ ounces) sliced mushrooms,
    drained
2 cups diced HILLSHIRE FARM® Ham
3 ounces uncooked medium-size
    noodles, cooked and drained
¾ cup crushed rich round crackers
1 tablespoon butter or margarine,
    melted

Preheat oven to 375°F.

Combine soup, milk and sour cream in large bowl. Add celery and mushrooms. Stir in Ham and noodles. Pour mixture into medium casserole. Combine cracker crumbs and butter in small bowl; sprinkle over ham mixture. Bake, uncovered, 30 minutes or until hot and bubbly. *Makes 6 servings*

Easy Tuna & Pasta Pot Pie

Baked SPAM™ & Tortellini Casserole

1 (30-ounce) jar spaghetti sauce
1 (12-ounce) can SPAM® Luncheon Meat, cubed
1 (10-ounce) package refrigerated cheese tortellini
½ cup chopped onion
1 cup (4 ounces) shredded mozzarella cheese

Heat oven to 375°F. In 2½-quart casserole combine all ingredients except cheese; mix gently. Bake, covered, stirring halfway through baking, 50 to 60 minutes or until tortellini are tender. During last 5 minutes of baking, uncover and top with cheese.

Makes 6 servings

Cheeseburger Macaroni

1 cup mostaccioli or elbow macaroni, uncooked
1 pound ground beef
1 medium onion, chopped
1 can (14½ ounces) DEL MONTE® Diced Tomatoes with Basil, Garlic & Oregano
¼ cup DEL MONTE® Tomato Ketchup
1 cup (4 ounces) shredded Cheddar cheese

1. Cook pasta according to package directions; drain.

2. Brown meat with onion in large skillet; drain. Season with salt and pepper, if desired. Stir in tomatoes, ketchup and pasta; heat through.

3. Top with cheese. Garnish, if desired.

Makes 4 servings

Prep Time: 8 minutes

Cook Time: 15 minutes

Orzo Risotto with Shrimp and Vegetables

1 zucchini, sliced and halved
2 teaspoons grated lemon peel
1 cup sliced mushrooms
½ cup chopped onion
2 cloves garlic
¾ teaspoon dried sage leaves
¼ to ½ teaspoon dried thyme leaves
1¼ cups uncooked orzo
2 cans (14½ ounces each) fat-free reduced-sodium chicken broth
8 ounces shrimp, peeled and deveined
¾ cup frozen peas, thawed
¼ cup grated Parmesan cheese
Salt and black pepper

1. Spray large saucepan with cooking spray. Heat over medium heat until hot. Add zucchini and lemon peel; cook and stir 2 to 3 minutes or until zucchini is tender. Remove from saucepan; set aside.

2. Add mushrooms, onion, garlic, sage and thyme to saucepan; cook and stir 2 to 3 minutes or until onion is tender. Stir in orzo; cook and stir until browned.

3. Bring chicken broth to a boil in medium saucepan. Add broth to orzo mixture, ½ cup at a time, stirring constantly until broth is absorbed before adding next ½ cup. Continue cooking 10 to 15 minutes or until orzo is tender.

4. Stir shrimp and peas into orzo mixture during last half of cooking time; stir in zucchini mixture last 2 to 3 minutes of cooking time. Stir in cheese; season to taste with salt and pepper.

Makes 4 main-dish servings

Orzo Risotto with Shrimp and Vegetables

THE BOUNTIFUL
BRUNCH

Classic Spinach Soufflé

1 pound fresh spinach leaves
¼ cup butter or margarine
2 tablespoons finely chopped onion
¼ cup all-purpose flour
¼ teaspoon salt
¼ teaspoon ground nutmeg
⅛ teaspoon black pepper
1 cup milk
4 eggs, separated
1 cup (4 ounces) shredded sharp
  Cheddar cheese

1. Preheat oven to 375°F. Grease 1½- or 2-quart soufflé dish; set aside.

2. Bring 1 quart salted water in 2-quart saucepan to a boil over high heat. Add spinach. Return to a boil and cook 2 to 3 minutes or until spinach is crisp-tender. Drain spinach and immediately plunge into cold water. Drain and let stand until cool enough to handle. Squeeze spinach to remove excess moisture. Finely chop spinach.

3. Melt butter in large saucepan over medium heat. Add onion; cook and stir 2 to 3 minutes. Stir in flour, salt, nutmeg and pepper. Gradually stir in milk. Cook and stir until mixture comes to a boil and thickens. Remove from heat.

4. Stir egg yolks into saucepan until well blended. Add spinach and cheese; mix well.

5. Beat egg whites in clean large bowl with electric mixer at high speed until stiff peaks form. Fold egg whites into spinach mixture until egg whites are evenly incorporated. Pour into prepared dish.

6. Bake 35 to 40 minutes or until puffed and wooden skewer inserted in center comes out clean. Garnish, if desired. Serve immediately.

Makes 4 servings

Classic Spinach Soufflé

Breakfast in a Loaf

Scrambled Eggs (recipe follows)
1 round loaf bread (8- to 9-inch
    diameter)
4 ounces sliced ham
½ red bell pepper, thinly sliced
    crosswise
½ cup (2 ounces) shredded Monterey
    Jack cheese, divided
½ cup (2 ounces) shredded Cheddar
    cheese, divided
½ cup sliced pitted ripe olives
1 medium tomato, thinly sliced
8 ounces mushrooms, sliced and
    cooked

1. Prepare Scrambled Eggs. Remove from heat; cover to keep warm.

2. Preheat oven to 350°F. Cut 2-inch slice from top of loaf; set aside for lid. Remove soft interior of loaf, leaving a 1-inch-thick wall and bottom.

3. Place ham on bottom of loaf. Top with bell pepper rings; sprinkle with half of cheeses. Layer Scrambled Eggs, olives and tomato over cheeses. Top with remaining cheeses and mushrooms.

4. Place lid on loaf. Wrap in foil. Place on baking sheet. Bake about 30 minutes or until heated through. Cut into 8 wedges.

Makes 8 servings

Scrambled Eggs

1 tablespoon butter or margarine
6 eggs, lightly beaten
½ teaspoon salt
¼ teaspoon ground pepper

1. Melt butter in 10-inch skillet over medium heat.

2. Season eggs with salt and pepper. Add eggs to skillet; cook, stirring gently and lifting to allow uncooked eggs to flow under cooked portion. Do not overcook; eggs should be soft with no liquid remaining.

Makes 4 servings

Crunchy Ranch-Style Eggs

2 cans (10 ounces each) tomatoes and
    green chilies, drained
1⅓ cups FRENCH'S® French Fried Onions,
    divided
2 tablespoons FRANK'S® Original
    REDHOT® Cayenne Pepper Sauce
2 tablespoons FRENCH'S®
    Worcestershire Sauce
6 eggs
1 cup (4 ounces) shredded Cheddar
    cheese

Preheat oven to 400°F. Grease 2-quart shallow baking dish. Combine tomatoes, ⅔ cup French Fried Onions, RedHot® sauce and Worcestershire in prepared dish. Make 6 indentations in mixture. Break 1 egg into each indentation.

Bake, uncovered, 15 to 20 minutes or until eggs are set. Top with cheese and remaining ⅔ cup onions. Bake 1 minute or until onions are golden. *Makes 6 servings*

Tip: Recipe may be prepared in individual ramekin dishes. Bake until eggs are set.

Prep Time: 5 minutes

Cook Time: 16 minutes

Breakfast in a Loaf

Broccoli & Cheese Quiche

2 cups zwieback crumbs
½ teaspoon ground nutmeg
⅓ cup honey
2 cups fresh broccoli florets or frozen broccoli florets, thawed and drained
½ tablespoon unsalted butter substitute
1 cup chopped yellow onion
1 cup (4 ounces) shredded ALPINE LACE® Reduced Fat Swiss Cheese
1 cup (4 ounces) shredded ALPINE LACE® Reduced Fat Colby Cheese
1 cup chopped red bell pepper
¾ cup egg substitute or 3 large eggs
2 large egg whites
¾ cup 2% low fat milk
½ teaspoon dry mustard
½ teaspoon salt
¼ teaspoon freshly ground white pepper

1. Preheat the oven to 400°F. Spray a 10-inch pie plate with nonstick cooking spray. To make the crumb crust: Toss the crumbs and nutmeg with the honey until the crumbs are thoroughly coated. Press onto the bottom and up the side of the pie plate.

2. To make the filling: Coarsely chop the broccoli. Half-fill a medium-size saucepan with water and bring to a boil over medium-high heat. Add the broccoli and cook, uncovered, for 5 minutes or just until crisp-tender. Drain.

3. In a small nonstick skillet, melt the butter over medium-high heat. Add the onion and sauté for 5 minutes or until soft. Layer both of the cheeses, then the onion, bell pepper and broccoli in the crust.

4. In a medium-size bowl, whisk the egg substitute (or the whole eggs), the egg whites, milk, mustard, salt and pepper together until blended. Pour evenly over the vegetables in the crust.

5. Bake for 10 minutes. Reduce the oven temperature to 350°F. Bake 20 minutes longer or until golden brown and puffy and a knife inserted in the center comes out clean. *Makes 8 servings*

Hearty Breakfast Custard Casserole

1 pound (2 medium-large) Colorado baking potatoes
Salt and pepper
8 ounces low-fat bulk pork sausage, cooked and crumbled *or* 6 ounces finely diced lean ham *or* 6 ounces turkey bacon, cooked and crumbled
⅓ cup julienne-sliced roasted red pepper *or* 1 jar (2 ounces) sliced pimientos, drained
3 eggs
1 cup low-fat milk
3 tablespoons chopped fresh chives or green onion tops *or* ¾ teaspoon dried thyme or oregano leaves
Salsa and low-fat sour cream or plain yogurt (optional)

Heat oven to 375°F. Grease 8- or 9-inch square baking dish or other small casserole. Peel potatoes and slice very thinly; arrange half of potatoes in baking dish. Sprinkle with salt and pepper. Cover with half of sausage. Arrange remaining potatoes on top; sprinkle with salt and pepper. Top with remaining sausage and red pepper. Beat eggs, milk and chives until blended. Pour over potatoes. Cover baking dish with foil and bake 35 to 45 minutes or until potatoes are tender. Uncover and bake 5 to 10 minutes more. Serve with salsa and sour cream, if desired. *Makes 4 to 5 servings*

Favorite recipe from **Colorado Potato Administrative Committee**

Broccoli & Cheese Quiche

Cheesy Country Spam™ Puff

6 slices white bread, torn into small pieces
1¼ cups milk
3 eggs
1 tablespoon spicy mustard
½ teaspoon garlic powder
½ teaspoon paprika
1 (12-ounce) can SPAM® Luncheon Meat, cubed
2 cups (8 ounces) shredded sharp Cheddar cheese, divided
½ cup chopped onion
½ cup (2 ounces) shredded Monterey Jack cheese

Heat oven to 375°F. In large bowl, combine bread, milk, eggs, mustard, garlic powder and paprika. Beat at medium speed of electric mixer 1 minute or until smooth. Stir in SPAM®, 1 cup Cheddar cheese and onion. Pour into greased 12×8-inch baking dish. Bake 25 minutes. Top with remaining 1 cup Cheddar cheese and Monterey Jack cheese. Bake 5 minutes longer or until cheese is melted. Let stand 10 minutes before serving.

Makes 6 servings

Betty Jo's Sausage and Cheese Grits

WESSON® No-Stick Cooking Spray
1 pound mild or hot cooked sausage, crumbled and drained
1½ cups grits
2½ cups shredded Cheddar cheese
3 tablespoons WESSON® Vegetable Oil
1½ cups milk
3 eggs, slightly beaten

Preheat oven to 350°F. Lightly spray a 13×9×2-inch baking dish with Wesson® Cooking Spray. Evenly spread crumbled sausage on bottom of dish; set aside. Bring 4½ cups water to a boil in a large saucepan. Stir in grits and lower heat. Cook 5 minutes until thickened, stirring occasionally. Add cheese and Wesson® Oil; stir until cheese has melted. Stir in milk and eggs; blend well. Evenly spoon mixture over sausage; bake, uncovered, 1 hour or until grits have set.

Makes 6 to 8 servings

Parmesan and Roasted Red Pepper Strata

1 loaf (16 ounces) French bread, cut into ½-inch-thick slices
2 jars (7½ ounces each) roasted red peppers, drained and cut into ½-inch pieces
1 cup grated Parmesan cheese
1 cup sliced green onions
3 cups (12 ounces) shredded mozzarella cheese
8 eggs
¾ cup reduced-fat (2%) milk
1 container (7 ounces) prepared pesto
2 teaspoons minced garlic
¾ teaspoon salt

1. Grease 13×9-inch baking dish. Arrange half of bread slices in single layer on bottom of prepared baking dish. Top bread with half of red peppers, ½ cup Parmesan cheese, ½ cup green onions and 1½ cups mozzarella cheese. Repeat layers with remaining bread, red peppers, Parmesan cheese, green onions and mozzarella cheese.

2. Combine eggs, milk, pesto, garlic and salt in medium bowl; whisk to combine. Pour egg mixture evenly over strata. Cover and refrigerate overnight.

3. Preheat oven to 375°F. Bake, uncovered, 30 minutes or until hot and bubbly.

Makes 6 servings

Cheesy Country Spam™ Puff

Italian Baked Frittata

1 cup broccoli flowerettes
½ cup sliced mushrooms
½ red pepper, cut into rings
2 green onions, sliced into 1-inch pieces
1 tablespoon margarine
8 eggs
¼ cup GREY POUPON® Dijon or COUNTRY DIJON® Mustard
¼ cup water
½ teaspoon Italian seasoning
1 cup (4 ounces) shredded Swiss cheese

In 10-inch ovenproof skillet, over medium-high heat, cook broccoli, mushrooms, red pepper and green onions in margarine until tender-crisp, about 5 minutes. Remove from heat.

In small bowl, with electric mixer at medium speed, beat eggs, mustard, water and Italian seasoning until foamy; stir in cheese. Pour mixture into skillet over vegetables. Bake at 375°F for 20 to 25 minutes or until set. Serve immediately.   *Makes 4 servings*

Brunch Eggs Olé

8 eggs
½ cup all-purpose flour
1 teaspoon baking powder
¾ teaspoon salt
2 cups (8 ounces) shredded Monterey Jack cheese with jalapeño peppers
1½ cups (12 ounces) small curd cottage cheese
1 cup (4 ounces) shredded sharp Cheddar cheese
1 jalapeño pepper, seeded, chopped*
½ teaspoon hot pepper sauce
Fresh Salsa (recipe follows)

Jalapeño peppers can sting and irritate the skin; wear rubber gloves when handling peppers and do not touch eyes. Wash hands after handling.

1. Preheat oven to 350°F. Grease 9-inch square baking pan.

2. Beat eggs in large bowl at high speed with electric mixer 4 to 5 minutes or until slightly thickened and lemon colored.

3. Combine flour, baking powder and salt in small bowl. Stir flour mixture into eggs until blended.

4. Combine Monterey Jack cheese, cottage cheese, Cheddar cheese, jalapeño and hot pepper sauce in medium bowl; mix well. Fold into egg mixture until well blended. Pour into prepared pan.

5. Bake 45 to 50 minutes or until golden brown and firm in center. Let stand 10 minutes before cutting into squares to serve. Serve with Fresh Salsa. Garnish as desired.
Makes 8 servings

Fresh Salsa

3 medium plum tomatoes, seeded and chopped
2 tablespoons chopped onion
1 small jalapeño pepper, stemmed, seeded and minced
1 tablespoon chopped fresh cilantro
1 tablespoon lime juice
¼ teaspoon salt
⅛ teaspoon black pepper

Stir together tomatoes, onion, jalapeño pepper, cilantro, lime juice, salt and black pepper in small bowl. Refrigerate until ready to serve.   *Makes 1 cup*

Brunch Eggs Olé

Ranch Quiche Lorraine

2 cups crushed butter-flavored crackers
6 tablespoons butter or margarine, melted
2 cups shredded Swiss cheese
4 eggs
2 cups heavy cream
1 package (1.2 ounces) HIDDEN VALLEY® Original Ranch® with Bacon salad dressing mix
1 tablespoon dehydrated minced onion

Preheat oven to 375°F. In medium bowl, combine crackers and butter. Press crumb mixture evenly into 10-inch pie pan or quiche dish. Bake until golden, about 7 minutes. Remove and cool pan on wire rack.

Increase oven temperature to 425°F. Sprinkle cheese over cooled pie crust. In medium bowl, whisk eggs until frothy. Add cream, salad dressing mix and onion. Pour egg mixture over cheese. Bake 15 minutes; reduce temperature to 350°F and continue baking until knife inserted in center comes out clean, about 20 minutes longer. Cool on wire rack 10 minutes before slicing.

Makes 8 servings

Ham Scramble

2 tablespoons vegetable oil or butter
1 pound HILLSHIRE FARM® Ham, cut into bite-size pieces
2 onions, thinly sliced
2 apples, cored and sliced

Heat oil in large skillet over medium-high heat. Sauté Ham, onions and apples until onions and apples are tender, stirring constantly. *Makes 4 to 6 servings*

Ham and Cheese Bread Pudding

1 small loaf (8 ounces) sourdough, country French or Italian bread, cut into 1-inch-thick slices
3 tablespoons butter or margarine, softened
8 ounces ham or smoked ham, cubed
2 cups (8 ounces) shredded Cheddar cheese
3 eggs
2 cups milk
1 teaspoon dry mustard
½ teaspoon salt
⅛ teaspoon white pepper

1. Grease 11×7-inch baking dish. Spread 1 side of each bread slice with butter. Cut into 1-inch cubes; place on bottom of prepared dish. Top with ham; sprinkle with cheese.

2. Beat eggs in medium bowl. Whisk in milk, mustard, salt and pepper. Pour egg mixture evenly over bread mixture. Cover; refrigerate at least 6 hours or overnight.

3. Preheat oven to 350°F.

4. Bake bread pudding uncovered 45 to 50 minutes or until puffed and golden brown, and knife inserted in center comes out clean. Garnish, if desired. Cut into squares. Serve immediately. *Makes 8 servings*

Ham and Cheese Bread Pudding

Spinach Sensation

½ pound bacon slices
1 cup (8 ounces) sour cream
3 eggs, separated
2 tablespoons all-purpose flour
⅛ teaspoon black pepper
1 package (10 ounces) frozen chopped
  spinach, thawed and squeezed dry
½ cup (2 ounces) shredded sharp
  Cheddar cheese
½ cup dry bread crumbs
1 tablespoon margarine or butter,
  melted

Preheat oven to 350°F. Spray 2-quart round baking dish with nonstick cooking spray.

Place bacon in single layer in large skillet; cook over medium heat until crisp. Remove from skillet; drain on paper towels. Crumble and set aside.

Combine sour cream, egg yolks, flour and pepper in large bowl; set aside. Beat egg whites in medium bowl with electric mixer at high speed until stiff peaks form. Stir ¼ of egg whites into sour cream mixture; fold in remaining egg whites.

Arrange half of spinach in prepared dish. Top with half of sour cream mixture. Sprinkle ¼ cup cheese over sour cream mixture. Sprinkle bacon over cheese. Repeat layers, ending with remaining ¼ cup cheese.

Combine bread crumbs and margarine in small bowl; sprinkle evenly over cheese.

Bake, uncovered, 30 to 35 minutes or until egg mixture is set. Let stand 5 minutes before serving.   *Makes 6 servings*

Oven Breakfast Hash

2 pounds baking potatoes, unpeeled
  (5 or 6 medium)
1 pound BOB EVANS® Original Recipe
  Roll Sausage
1 (12-ounce can) evaporated milk
⅓ cup chopped green onions
1 tablespoon Worcestershire sauce
½ teaspoon salt
¼ teaspoon black pepper
¼ cup dried bread crumbs
1 tablespoon melted butter or
  margarine
½ teaspoon paprika

Cook potatoes in boiling water until fork-tender. Drain and coarsely chop or mash. Preheat oven to 350°F. Crumble and cook sausage in medium skillet until browned. Drain and transfer to large bowl. Stir in potatoes, milk, green onions, Worcestershire sauce, salt and pepper. Pour into greased 2½- or 3-quart casserole dish. Sprinkle with bread crumbs; drizzle with melted butter. Sprinkle with paprika. Bake, uncovered, 30 to 35 minutes or until casserole bubbles and top is browned. Refrigerate leftovers.

Makes 6 to 8 servings

Spinach Sensation

Puffy Orange Omelets

5 eggs, separated
2 tablespoons all-purpose flour
1 tablespoon grated orange peel
4 tablespoons sugar, divided
¾ cup orange juice
2 tablespoons butter or margarine
2 tablespoons brown sugar

1. Preheat oven to 375°F. Whisk together egg yolks, flour and orange peel in large bowl until well blended.

2. Combine egg whites and 2 tablespoons sugar in medium bowl; cover and refrigerate overnight. Beat egg white mixture on high speed of electric mixer 3 to 5 minutes or until stiff, but not dry, peaks form. Fold into egg yolk mixture. Set aside.

3. Combine orange juice, butter and brown sugar in small saucepan. Cook and stir over medium heat 3 to 5 minutes or until butter melts and sauce is heated through.

4. Grease 6 (5-ounce) soufflé dishes or custard cups; lightly sprinkle with remaining 2 tablespoons sugar, shaking out excess. Place 1 tablespoon orange sauce in bottom of each soufflé dish, reserving remaining sauce. Spoon egg mixture equally into dishes.

5. Place soufflé dishes in shallow baking pan. Bake 15 to 20 minutes or until tops are golden brown. Serve immediately with reserved warm orange sauce.

Makes 6 servings

Breakfast Bread Pudding with Berry Sauce

8 slices cinnamon raisin bread, cubed
2 cups skim milk
1 cup EGG BEATERS® Healthy Real Egg Substitute
¼ cup sugar
1 teaspoon vanilla extract
½ teaspoon ground nutmeg
½ cup maple-flavored syrup
2 tablespoons FLEISCHMANN'S® Original Margarine
1 cup sliced strawberries
½ cup blueberries
1 teaspoon lemon juice
1 teaspoon lemon peel

Evenly divide bread cubes between 8 greased heatproof (6-ounce) custard cups or ramekins. In medium bowl, combine milk, Egg Beaters®, sugar, vanilla and nutmeg. Evenly pour mixture over bread cubes. Place cups in roasting pan filled with 1-inch depth hot water. Bake at 325°F for 35 to 45 minutes or until set. Let stand for 5 minutes.

In small saucepan, heat syrup and margarine until blended. Stir in fruit, lemon juice and peel; heat through. Unmold puddings onto individual serving plates; serve with berry sauce.

Makes 8 servings

Prep Time: 15 minutes

Cook Time: 45 minutes

Puffy Orange Omelet

Cheddar and Leek Strata

8 eggs, lightly beaten
2 cups milk
½ cup ale or beer
2 cloves garlic, minced
¼ teaspoon salt
¼ teaspoon black pepper
1 loaf (16 ounces) sourdough bread,
    cut into ½-inch cubes
2 small leeks, coarsely chopped
1 red bell pepper, chopped
1½ cups (6 ounces) shredded Swiss
    cheese
1½ cups (6 ounces) shredded sharp
    Cheddar cheese
Fresh sage (optional)

1. Combine eggs, milk, ale, garlic, salt and black pepper in large bowl. Beat until well blended.

2. Place ½ of bread cubes on bottom of greased 13×9-inch baking dish. Sprinkle ½ of leeks and ½ of bell pepper over bread cubes. Top with ¾ cup Swiss cheese and ¾ cup Cheddar cheese. Repeat layers with remaining ingredients, ending with Cheddar cheese.

3. Pour egg mixture evenly over top. Cover tightly with plastic wrap or foil. Weight top of strata down with slightly smaller baking dish. Refrigerate strata at least 2 hours or overnight.

4. Preheat oven to 350°F. Bake uncovered 40 to 45 minutes or until center is set. Garnish with fresh sage, if desired. Serve immediately.   *Makes 12 servings*

Baked Ham & Cheese Monte Cristo

6 slices bread, divided
2 cups (8 ounces) shredded Cheddar
    cheese
1⅓ cups FRENCH'S® French Fried Onions,
    divided
1 package (10 ounces) frozen broccoli
    spears, thawed, drained and cut
    into 1-inch pieces
2 cups (10 ounces) cubed cooked ham
5 eggs
2 cups milk
½ teaspoon ground mustard
½ teaspoon seasoned salt
¼ teaspoon coarsely ground black
    pepper

Preheat oven to 325°F. Cut 3 bread slices into cubes; place in greased 12×8-inch baking dish. Top bread with 1 cup cheese, ⅔ cup French Fried Onions, the broccoli and ham. Cut remaining bread slices diagonally into halves. Arrange bread halves down center of casserole, overlapping slightly, crusted points all in one direction. In medium bowl, beat eggs, milk and seasonings; pour evenly over casserole. Bake, uncovered, at 325°F for 1 hour or until center is set. Top with remaining cheese and ⅔ cup onions; bake, uncovered, 5 minutes or until onions are golden brown. Let stand 10 minutes before serving.

Makes 6 to 8 servings

Cheddar and Leek Strata

Low Fat Turkey Bacon Frittata

- 1 package (12 ounces) BUTTERBALL® Turkey Bacon, heated and chopped
- 6 ounces uncooked angel hair pasta, broken
- 2 teaspoons olive oil
- 1 small onion, sliced
- 1 red bell pepper, cut into thin strips
- 4 containers (4 ounces each) egg substitute
- 1 container (5 ounces) fat free ricotta cheese
- 1 cup (4 ounces) shredded fat free mozzarella cheese
- 1 cup (4 ounces) shredded reduced fat Swiss cheese
- ½ teaspoon salt
- ½ teaspoon black pepper
- 1 package (10 ounces) frozen spinach, thawed and squeezed dry

Cook and drain pasta. Heat oil in large skillet over medium heat until hot. Cook and stir onion and bell pepper until tender. Combine egg substitute, cheeses, salt, pepper and cooked pasta in large bowl. Add vegetables, spinach and turkey bacon. Spray 10-inch quiche dish with nonstick cooking spray; pour mixture into dish. Bake in preheated 350°F oven 30 minutes. Cut into wedges. Serve with spicy salsa, if desired.

Makes 8 servings

Preparation Time: 15 minutes plus baking time

Chile Cheese Puff

- ¾ cup all-purpose flour
- 1½ teaspoons baking powder
- 9 eggs
- 1 pound (16 ounces) shredded Monterey Jack cheese
- 2 cups (1 pint) 1% milkfat cottage cheese
- 2 cans (4 ounces each) diced green chiles, drained
- 1½ teaspoons sugar
- ¼ teaspoon salt
- ⅛ teaspoon hot pepper sauce
- 1 cup salsa

Preheat oven to 350°F. Spray 13×9-inch baking dish with nonstick cooking spray.

Combine flour and baking powder in small bowl.

Whisk eggs in large bowl until blended; add Monterey Jack cheese, cottage cheese, chiles, sugar, salt and hot pepper sauce. Add flour mixture; stir just until combined. Pour into prepared dish.

Bake, uncovered, 45 minutes or until egg mixture is set. Let stand 5 minutes before serving. Serve with salsa.

Makes 8 servings

Low Fat Turkey Bacon Frittata

Onion, Cheese and Tomato Tart

Parmesan-Pepper Dough (recipe follows)
1 tablespoon butter
1 medium onion, thinly sliced
1 cup (4 ounces) shredded Swiss cheese
2 to 3 ripe tomatoes, sliced
Black pepper
2 tablespoons snipped fresh chives

1. Make Parmesan-Pepper Dough.

2. Melt butter in large skillet over medium heat. Add onion; cook and stir 20 minutes or until tender.

3. Spread onion over prepared dough. Sprinkle with cheese. Let rise in warm place 20 to 30 minutes or until edges are puffy.

4. Preheat oven to 400°F. Top dough with tomatoes. Sprinkle with pepper. Bake 25 minutes or until edges are deep golden and cheese is melted. Let cool 10 minutes. Transfer to serving platter. Sprinkle with chives. Cut into wedges.

Makes 6 to 8 servings

Parmesan-Pepper Dough

1 package (¼ ounce) active dry yeast
1 tablespoon sugar
⅔ cup warm water (105° to 115°F)
2 cups all-purpose flour, divided
¼ cup grated Parmesan cheese
1 teaspoon salt
½ teaspoon black pepper
1 tablespoon olive oil

1. Sprinkle yeast and sugar over warm water in small bowl; stir until yeast is dissolved. Let stand 5 minutes or until mixture is bubbly.

2. Combine 1¾ cups flour, cheese, salt and pepper in large bowl. Pour yeast mixture and oil over flour mixture and stir until mixture clings together.

3. Turn out dough onto lightly floured surface. Knead 8 to 10 minutes or until smooth and elastic, adding remaining ¼ cup flour if necessary. Shape dough into a ball; place in large greased bowl. Turn dough so that top is greased. Cover with towel; let rise in warm place 1 hour or until doubled in bulk.

4. Punch down dough. Knead on lightly floured surface 1 minute or until smooth. Flatten into disc. Roll dough to make 11-inch round. Press into bottom and up side of buttered 9- or 10-inch tart pan with removable bottom.

Scalloped Eggs and Bacon

2 tablespoons butter or margarine
¼ cup chopped onion
2 tablespoons all-purpose flour
1½ cups milk
½ cup (2 ounces) shredded American cheese
½ cup (2 ounces) shredded Swiss cheese
6 hard-cooked eggs, sliced
10 to 12 slices HILLSHIRE FARM® Bacon, crisp-cooked and crumbled
1½ cups packaged fried onions

Preheat oven to 350°F.

Melt butter in medium skillet over medium heat. Add chopped onion; sauté until tender. Whisk in flour until thoroughly combined. Add milk; continue stirring until thick. Add cheeses; stir until melted. Place ½ of eggs in bottom of small baking dish; pour ½ of cheese mixture over eggs. Sprinkle with ½ of Bacon and ½ of fried onions. Repeat layers. Bake, uncovered, 15 to 20 minutes or until heated through.

Makes 6 servings

Onion, Cheese and Tomato Tart

Asparagus-Swiss Soufflé

¼ cup unsalted butter substitute
½ cup chopped yellow onion
¼ cup all-purpose flour
½ teaspoon salt
¼ teaspoon cayenne pepper
1 cup 2% low fat milk
1 cup (4 ounces) shredded ALPINE
   LACE® Reduced Fat Swiss Cheese
1 cup egg substitute or 4 large eggs
1 cup coarsely chopped fresh
   asparagus pieces, cooked, or
   frozen asparagus pieces, thawed
   and drained
3 large egg whites

1. Preheat the oven to 325°F. Spray a 1½-quart soufflé dish with nonstick cooking spray.

2. In a large saucepan, melt the butter over medium heat, add the onion and sauté for 5 minutes or until soft. Stir in the flour, salt and pepper and cook for 2 minutes or until bubbly. Add the milk and cook, stirring constantly, for 5 minutes or until the sauce thickens. Add the cheese and stir until melted.

3. In a small bowl, whisk the egg substitute (or the whole eggs). Whisk in a little of the hot cheese sauce, then return this egg mixture to the saucepan and whisk until well blended. Remove from the heat and fold in the drained asparagus.

4. In a medium-size bowl, using an electric mixer set on high, beat the egg whites until stiff peaks form. Fold the hot cheese sauce into the whites, then spoon into the soufflé dish.

5. Place the soufflé on a baking sheet and bake for 50 minutes or until golden brown and puffy.   *Makes 8 servings*

Egg & Sausage Casserole

½ pound pork sausage
3 tablespoons margarine or butter,
   divided
2 tablespoons all-purpose flour
¼ teaspoon salt
¼ teaspoon black pepper
1¼ cups milk
2 cups frozen hash brown potatoes
4 eggs, hard-boiled and sliced
½ cup cornflake crumbs
¼ cup sliced green onions

Preheat oven to 350°F. Spray 2-quart oval baking dish with nonstick cooking spray.

Crumble sausage into large skillet; brown over medium-high heat until no longer pink, stirring to separate meat. Drain sausage on paper towels. Discard fat and wipe skillet with paper towel.

Melt 2 tablespoons margarine in same skillet over medium heat. Stir in flour, salt and pepper until smooth. Gradually stir in milk; cook and stir until thickened. Add sausage, potatoes and eggs; stir to combine. Pour into prepared dish.

Melt remaining 1 tablespoon margarine. Combine cornflake crumbs and melted margarine in small bowl; sprinkle evenly over casserole.

Bake, uncovered, 30 minutes or until hot and bubbly. Sprinkle with onions.

Makes 6 servings

Asparagus-Swiss Soufflé

Country Skillet Hash

2 tablespoons butter or margarine
4 pork chops (¾ inch thick), diced
¼ teaspoon black pepper
¼ teaspoon cayenne pepper (optional)
1 medium onion, chopped
2 cloves garlic, minced
1 can (14½ ounces) DEL MONTE®
    FreshCut™ Brand Whole New
    Potatoes, drained and diced
1 can (14½ ounces) DEL MONTE®
    FreshCut™ Diced Tomatoes,
    undrained
1 medium green bell pepper, chopped
½ teaspoon thyme, crushed

1. Melt butter in large skillet over medium heat. Add meat; cook, stirring occasionally, until no longer pink in center. Season with black pepper and cayenne pepper, if desired.

2. Add onion and garlic; cook until tender. Stir in potatoes, tomatoes, green pepper and thyme. Cook 5 minutes, stirring frequently. Season with salt, if desired.

Makes 4 servings

Tip: The hash may be topped with a poached or fried egg.

Prep Time: 10 minutes

Cook Time: 15 minutes

Ham & Cheese Grits Soufflé

3 cups water
¾ cup quick-cooking grits
½ teaspoon salt
½ cup (2 ounces) shredded mozzarella
    cheese
2 ounces ham, finely chopped
2 tablespoons minced chives
2 eggs, separated
    Dash hot pepper sauce

1. Preheat oven to 375°F. Grease 1½-quart soufflé dish or deep casserole.

2. Bring water to a boil in medium saucepan. Stir in grits and salt. Cook, stirring frequently, about 5 minutes or until thickened. Stir in cheese, ham, chives, egg yolks and hot pepper sauce.

3. In small clean bowl, beat egg whites until stiff but not dry; fold into grits mixture. Pour into prepared dish. Bake about 30 minutes or until puffed and golden. Serve immediately.

Makes 4 to 6 servings

Spinach-Cheese Strata

6 slices whole wheat bread
2 tablespoons butter or margarine,
    softened
1 cup (4 ounces) shredded Cheddar
    cheese
½ cup (2 ounces) shredded Monterey
    Jack cheese
1¼ cups milk
6 eggs, lightly beaten
1 package (10 ounces) frozen spinach,
    thawed and well drained
¼ teaspoon salt
⅛ teaspoon pepper

1. Spread bread with butter; arrange in single layer in greased 13×9-inch baking dish. Sprinkle with cheeses.

2. Combine milk, eggs, spinach, salt and pepper in large bowl; stir well. Pour over bread and cheese. Cover; refrigerate at least 6 hours or overnight.

3. Bake, uncovered, at 350°F about 1 hour or until puffy and lightly golden.

Makes 4 to 6 servings

Country Skillet Hash

Sausage and Potato Bake

1 pound small red new potatoes, cut
  into halves or quarters
1½ cups sliced onions
½ pound baby carrots
2 tablespoons vegetable oil
1 envelope (1¼ ounces) savory herb
  with garlic flavor dry soup mix
1 pound HILLSHIRE FARM® Gourmet
  Cooked Sausage—Chicken and
  Turkey with Apples and Spice,
  diagonally cut into ⅓-inch slices

Preheat oven to 400°F.

Spray 13×9-inch baking pan with nonstick
cooking spray. Combine potatoes, onions,
carrots, oil and soup mix in large bowl. Stir
until evenly coated.

Place potato mixture into prepared pan;
bake, uncovered, 30 minutes. Add Gourmet
Sausage to potato mixture; stir well. Return
pan to oven; bake 15 to 20 minutes or until
potatoes are tender and golden brown.

Makes 5 to 6 servings

Farm Fresh Tip: Did you know?—You can
avoid tears from cutting onions. Cut the
ends off the onions, peel and rinse them
under cold water, then wrap and refrigerate
them for at least an hour or two. When you
are ready to use the onions, simply remove
the wrap and chop with a sharp knife.

Vegetable Cheese Frittata

½ cup fresh green beans, cut into
  1-inch pieces
1 small onion, chopped
3 tablespoons butter or margarine
¼ red bell pepper, chopped
¼ cup sliced fresh mushrooms
¼ cup dry bread crumbs
½ cup prepared HIDDEN VALLEY®
  Original Ranch® salad dressing
6 eggs, beaten
⅓ cup shredded Cheddar cheese
¼ cup grated Parmesan cheese

Preheat oven to 350°F. In medium saucepan,
steam green beans over boiling water until
crisp-tender, about 4 minutes. In medium
skillet, sauté onion in butter until onion is
softened; stir in beans, red pepper and
mushrooms. Fold vegetables, bread crumbs
and salad dressing into eggs. Pour into
buttered quiche dish. Sprinkle with cheeses.
Bake until set, about 25 minutes.

Makes 6 servings

Note: Substitute chopped tomatoes, diced
green chili peppers, sliced black olives,
chopped zucchini or any vegetable
combination for green beans, onion and
mushrooms.

Sausage and Potato Bake

Cheesy Broccoli Soufflé

    2 tablespoons unsalted butter
        substitute
    ¼ cup all-purpose flour
    ½ teaspoon salt
    ¼ teaspoon cayenne pepper
  1½ cups 2% low fat milk
    ¾ cup (3 ounces) shredded ALPINE
        LACE® Fat Free Pasteurized Process
        Skim Milk Cheese Product—For
        Cheddar Lovers
    ¾ cup (3 ounces) shredded ALPINE
        LACE® Fat Free Pasteurized Process
        Skim Milk Cheese Product—For
        Mozzarella Lovers
    1 cup egg substitute or 4 large eggs,
        separated
    1 cup diced, cooked broccoli florets,
        well drained
    3 large egg whites

1. Preheat the oven to 325°F. Spray a 1-quart soufflé dish with nonstick cooking spray.

2. In a large saucepan, melt the butter over medium heat. Stir in the flour, salt and pepper and cook for 2 minutes or until bubbly. Add the milk and cook, stirring constantly, for 5 minutes or until the sauce thickens. Add both of the cheeses and stir until melted.

3. In a small bowl, whisk the egg substitute (or the 4 egg yolks). Pour in a little of the hot cheese sauce, then return all to the saucepan and whisk until blended. Remove from the heat and fold in the broccoli.

4. In a medium-size bowl, using an electric mixer set on high, beat the 3 egg whites (or the 7 whites if using whole eggs) until stiff peaks form. Fold the hot cheese sauce into the whites, then spoon into the dish. Place the soufflé on a baking sheet and bake for 50 minutes or until golden brown and puffy.

Makes 6 servings

Baked Eggs Florentine

    2 packages (10 ounces each) frozen
        creamed spinach
    4 slices (⅛ inch thick) deli ham, about
        5 to 6 ounces
    4 eggs
        Salt
        Black pepper
    ⅛ teaspoon ground nutmeg
    ½ cup (2 ounces) shredded provolone
        cheese
    2 tablespoons chopped roasted red
        pepper

1. Preheat oven to 450°F. Make small cut in each package of spinach. Microwave on HIGH 5 to 6 minutes, turning packages halfway through cooking time.

2. Meanwhile, grease 8-inch square baking pan. Place ham slices on bottom of prepared pan, overlapping slightly. Spread spinach mixture over ham slices.

3. Make 4 indentations in spinach. Carefully break 1 egg in each. Season to taste with salt and black pepper. Sprinkle with nutmeg.

4. Bake 16 to 19 minutes or until eggs are set. Remove from oven. Sprinkle cheese and red pepper over top. Return to oven and bake 1 to 2 minutes longer or until cheese is melted. Serve immediately.

Makes 4 servings

Serving Suggestion: Serve with toasted English muffin halves and fresh pineapple pieces.

Prep and Cook Time: 28 minutes

Cheesy Broccoli Soufflé

Feta Brunch Bake

1 medium red bell pepper
2 bags (10 ounces each) fresh spinach, washed and stemmed
6 eggs
6 ounces crumbled feta cheese
⅓ cup chopped onion
2 tablespoons chopped fresh parsley
¼ teaspoon dried dill weed
Dash ground black pepper

Preheat broiler. Place bell pepper on foil-lined broiler pan. Broil, 4 inches from heat, 15 to 20 minutes or until blackened on all sides, turning every 5 minutes with tongs. Place in paper bag; close bag and set aside to cool about 15 to 20 minutes. To peel pepper, cut around core, twist and remove. Cut in half and peel off skin with paring knife; rinse under cold water to remove seeds. Cut into ½-inch pieces.

To blanch spinach, heat 1 quart water in 2-quart saucepan over high heat to a boil. Add spinach. Return to a boil; boil 2 to 3 minutes until crisp-tender. Drain and immediately plunge into cold water. Drain; let stand until cool enough to handle. Squeeze spinach to remove excess water. Finely chop with chef's knife.

Preheat oven to 400°F. Grease 1-quart baking dish. Beat eggs in large bowl with electric mixer at medium speed until foamy. Stir in bell pepper, spinach, cheese, onion, parsley, dill weed and black pepper. Pour egg mixture into prepared dish. Bake 20 minutes or until set. Let stand 5 minutes before serving. Garnish as desired.

Makes 4 servings

South-of-the-Border Quiche Squares

1 pound BOB EVANS® Zesty Hot Roll Sausage
1 (8-ounce) package refrigerated crescent dinner roll dough
1 cup (4 ounces) shredded Monterey Jack cheese, divided
1 cup (4 ounces) shredded Cheddar cheese, divided
½ cup diced green chiles
½ cup chopped green onions
1 cup diced fresh or drained canned tomatoes
8 eggs, beaten
1 cup half-and-half
1 cup milk
2 tablespoons Dijon mustard
1 tablespoon chopped fresh parsley
½ teaspoon chili powder

Preheat oven to 350°F. Crumble and cook sausage in medium skillet over medium heat until browned. Drain well on paper towels. Unroll dough and press perforations together. Press dough on bottom and 1 inch up sides of greased 13×9×2-inch baking pan. Bake 8 minutes or until light golden. Remove from oven; sprinkle with half of cheeses. Top with chiles, onions, tomatoes, sausage and remaining cheeses. Blend eggs, half-and-half, milk, mustard, parsley and chili powder in medium bowl. Pour mixture evenly over cheese layer. Bake 25 to 30 minutes or until set. Cool 5 minutes before cutting into 8 (4-inch) squares. Serve hot. Refrigerate leftovers.   *Makes 8 servings*

Feta Brunch Bake

Potato and Egg Pie

1 (20-ounce) package frozen O'Brien
    hash brown potatoes, thawed
⅓ cup WESSON® Vegetable Oil
1½ tablespoons chopped fresh parsley,
    divided
¾ cup shredded pepper-jack cheese
¾ cup shredded Swiss cheese
1 (12-ounce) package bulk breakfast
    sausage, cooked, crumbled and
    drained
1 (4-ounce) can sliced mushrooms,
    drained
½ cup milk
4 eggs, beaten
1 teaspoon garlic salt
¼ teaspoon pepper
4 to 6 thin tomato slices

Preheat oven to 425°F. In a medium bowl,
combine potatoes and Wesson® Oil; blend to
coat. Press mixture into a 10-inch pie dish.
Bake for 30 minutes or until golden brown;
remove from oven. *Reduce oven temperature
to 350°F.* Meanwhile, in a large bowl,
combine 1 tablespoon parsley and *remaining*
ingredients *except* tomato slices; blend well.
Pour into potato crust. Bake for 25 minutes
or until eggs are set. Place tomato slices over
pie and top with *remaining* parsley. Bake 5
to 7 minutes longer.   *Makes 6 servings*

Lit'l Links Soufflé

8 slices white bread
2 cups (8 ounces) shredded Cheddar
    cheese
1 pound HILLSHIRE FARM® Lit'l Polskas
6 eggs
2¾ cups milk
¾ teaspoon dry mustard

Spread bread in bottom of greased 13×9-
inch baking pan. Sprinkle cheese over top of
bread.

Arrange Lit'l Polskas on top of cheese. Beat
eggs with milk and mustard in large bowl;
pour over links. Cover pan with aluminum
foil; refrigerate overnight.

Preheat oven to 300°F. Bake egg mixture
1½ hours or until puffy and brown.
    Makes 4 to 6 servings

Double Onion Quiche

3 cups thinly sliced yellow onions
3 tablespoons butter or margarine
1 cup thinly sliced green onions
3 eggs
1 cup heavy cream
½ cup grated Parmesan cheese
¼ teaspoon hot pepper sauce
1 package (1 ounce) HIDDEN VALLEY®
    Milk Recipe Original Ranch® salad
    dressing mix
1 (9-inch) deep-dish pastry shell,
    baked, cooled
Fresh oregano sprig for garnish

Preheat oven to 350°F. In medium skillet,
cook and stir yellow onions in butter, stirring
occasionally, about 10 minutes. Add green
onions; cook 5 minutes. Remove from heat;
cool.

In large bowl, whisk eggs until frothy. Whisk
in cream, cheese, pepper sauce and salad
dressing mix. Stir in cooled onion mixture.
Pour egg and onion mixture into cooled
pastry shell. Bake until top is browned and
knife inserted in center comes out clean, 35
to 40 minutes. Cool on wire rack 10 minutes
before slicing. Garnish with oregano.
    Makes 8 servings

Potato and Egg Pie

Garden Frittata

1 tablespoon extra-virgin olive oil
1 cup sliced, unpeeled, small red-skinned potatoes (about 4 ounces)
½ cup chopped red onion
½ cup chopped red bell pepper
1 teaspoon minced garlic
1 cup chopped fresh asparagus
½ cup fresh corn kernels or frozen corn, thawed and drained
1 cup diced ALPINE LACE® Boneless Cooked Ham (4 ounces)
¾ cup egg substitute or 3 large eggs
3 large egg whites
1 cup (4 ounces) shredded ALPINE LACE® Reduced Fat Lightly Smoked Provolone Cheese
¼ cup slivered fresh basil leaves or 1 tablespoon dried basil
½ teaspoon salt
¼ teaspoon freshly ground black pepper

1. Preheat the broiler. In a large broilerproof nonstick skillet, heat the oil over medium-high heat. Add the potatoes, onion, bell pepper and garlic. Cook, stirring occasionally, for 7 minutes or until the potatoes are almost tender. Stir in the asparagus, corn and ham and cook 3 minutes more or until the vegetables are crisp-tender.

2. In a medium-size bowl, whisk the egg substitute (or the whole eggs), the egg whites, cheese, basil, salt and black pepper together until blended. Pour over the vegetables. Reduce the heat and cook, uncovered, for 8 minutes or just until the egg mixture is set around the edges.

3. Slide the skillet under the broiler for 1 minute or until the eggs are set in the center. Serve immediately.

Makes 4 servings

Dixie Casserole

White Sauce (recipe follows)
1 pound HILLSHIRE FARM® Gourmet Cooked Sausage—Chicken and Turkey with Wild Rice and Herbs, sliced
1 can (17 ounces) corn, drained
4 hard-cooked eggs, sliced
¾ cup soft bread crumbs
1 tablespoon butter or margarine, melted

Preheat oven to 350°F.

Prepare White Sauce; set aside. Lightly brown Gourmet Sausage in large skillet over medium-high heat. Combine sausage, corn and eggs in large bowl; add White Sauce and stir together. Pour sausage mixture into small casserole. Toss bread crumbs with butter in small bowl; sprinkle over top of sausage mixture. Bake, uncovered, 30 minutes or until heated through.

Makes 6 servings

White Sauce

¼ cup butter or margarine
¼ cup all-purpose flour
½ teaspoon salt
2 cups milk

Melt butter in small saucepan over medium heat; stir in flour and salt. Add milk; cook and stir until mixture is thickened and bubbly. Cook and stir 1 to 2 minutes more.

Makes about 2½ cups

Dixie Casserole

Ham and Egg Enchiladas

2 tablespoons butter or margarine
1 small red bell pepper, chopped
3 green onions with tops, sliced
½ cup diced ham
8 eggs
8 (7- to 8-inch) flour tortillas
2 cups (8 ounces) shredded Colby-Jack cheese or Monterey Jack cheese with jalapeño peppers, divided
1 can (10 ounces) enchilada sauce
½ cup prepared salsa
Sliced avocado, fresh cilantro and red pepper slices for garnish

1. Preheat oven to 350°F.

2. Melt butter in large nonstick skillet over medium heat. Add bell pepper and onions; cook and stir 2 minutes. Add ham; cook and stir 1 minute.

3. Lightly beat eggs with wire whisk in medium bowl. Add eggs to skillet; cook until eggs are set, but still soft, stirring occasionally.

4. Spoon about ⅓ cup egg mixture evenly down center of each tortilla; top with 1 tablespoon cheese. Roll tortillas up and place seam side down in shallow 11×7-inch baking dish.

5. Combine enchilada sauce and salsa in small bowl; pour evenly over enchiladas.

6. Cover enchiladas with foil; bake 20 minutes. Uncover; sprinkle with remaining cheese. Continue baking 10 minutes or until enchiladas are hot and cheese is melted. Garnish, if desired. Serve immediately.

Makes 4 servings

Acapulco Eggs

3 corn tortillas, cut into 2-inch strips
3 tablespoons butter or margarine
½ cup chopped onion
1 can (14½ ounces) DEL MONTE® Mexican Recipe Stewed Tomatoes
1 cup cooked ham, cut into thin strips or shredded turkey
½ cup green pepper strips
6 eggs, beaten
¾ cup shredded Monterey Jack cheese

1. Cook tortilla strips in butter in large skillet until golden. Remove and set aside.

2. Cook onion in same skillet until tender. Drain tomatoes, reserving liquid. Add reserved liquid to skillet; cook over high heat 3 minutes, stirring frequently.

3. Stir in tomatoes, meat and green pepper; heat through. Reduce heat to low; add tortillas and eggs.

4. Cover and cook 4 to 6 minutes or until eggs are set. Sprinkle with cheese; cover and cook 1 minute or until cheese is melted. Garnish with chopped cilantro or parsley, if desired.

Makes 4 to 6 servings

Prep Time: 10 minutes

Cook Time: 15 minutes

Ham and Egg Enchiladas

Mini Vegetable Quiches

2 cups cut-up vegetables (bell peppers,
    broccoli, zucchini and/or carrots)
2 tablespoons chopped green onions
2 tablespoons FLEISCHMANN'S®
    Original Margarine
4 (8-inch) flour tortillas, each cut into
    8 triangles
1 cup EGG BEATERS® Healthy Real Egg
    Substitute
1 cup skim milk
½ teaspoon dried basil leaves

In medium nonstick skillet, over medium-high heat, sauté vegetables and green onions in margarine until tender.

Arrange 4 tortilla pieces in each of 8 (6-ounce) greased custard cups or ramekins, placing points of tortilla pieces at center of bottom of cup and pressing lightly to form shape of cup. Divide vegetable mixture evenly among cups. In small bowl, combine Egg Beaters®, milk and basil. Pour evenly over vegetable mixture. Place cups on baking sheet. Bake at 375°F for 20 to 25 minutes or until puffed and knife inserted into centers comes out clean. Let stand 5 minutes before serving. *Makes 8 servings*

Spaghetti & Egg Casserole

12 ounces uncooked spaghetti
 3 tablespoons FILIPPO BERIO® Olive Oil
¾ cup sliced onion
 4 eggs, beaten
 3 tablespoons grated Parmesan cheese
    Additional grated Parmesan cheese
    (optional)
    Additional beaten egg (optional)

Preheat oven to 350°F. Cook pasta according to package directions until al dente (tender but still firm). Drain. Meanwhile, in medium skillet, heat olive oil over medium heat until hot. Add onion;

cook and stir 5 minutes or until softened. Remove with slotted spoon to large bowl. When oil is cool, grease 9-inch square baking pan with a portion of oil from skillet.

Add 4 beaten eggs and 3 tablespoons Parmesan cheese to onion; mix well. Add pasta; toss until lightly coated. Pour into prepared pan. Bake 10 to 20 minutes or until egg is firm.

Sprinkle with additional Parmesan cheese or brush with additional beaten egg, if desired. Broil, 4 to 5 inches from heat, until golden brown. *Makes 6 servings*

Tuna and Pasta Frittata

1 tablespoon olive oil
2 cups cooked spaghetti
4 large eggs
¼ cup prepared pesto sauce
2 tablespoons milk
1 can (6 ounces) STARKIST® Solid
    White or Chunk Light Tuna,
    drained and flaked
½ cup shredded mozzarella cheese

Preheat broiler. In medium ovenproof skillet, heat oil over medium-high heat; sauté spaghetti. In bowl, combine eggs, pesto sauce and milk; blend well. Add tuna; pour mixture over hot spaghetti. Cook over medium-low heat, stirring occasionally until eggs are almost completely set. Sprinkle cheese over cooked eggs; place under broiler until cheese is bubbly and golden. Serve hot or at room temperature.
Makes 2 to 4 servings

Prep Time: 8 minutes

Mini Vegetable Quiches

Savory Bread Pudding

8 slices thick-cut, day-old white bread, crusts trimmed
2 tablespoons unsalted butter substitute, softened
2 cups (8 ounces) shredded ALPINE LACE® Reduced Fat Swiss Cheese, divided
1 cup grated peeled apple
½ cup egg substitute or 2 large eggs
2 large egg whites
2 cups 2% low fat milk
½ teaspoon salt
¼ teaspoon freshly ground black pepper

1. Preheat the oven to 400°F. Spray a 13×9×2-inch rectangular or 3-quart oval baking dish with nonstick cooking spray. Thinly spread the bread slices with the butter. Cut each bread slice into 4 triangles, making a total of 32. In a small bowl, toss 1¾ cups of the cheese with the grated apple.

2. In a medium-size bowl, using an electric mixer set on high, beat the egg substitute (or the whole eggs), the egg whites, milk, salt and pepper together until frothy and light yellow.

3. To assemble the pudding: Line the bottom of the dish with 16 of the bread triangles. Cover with the apple-cheese mixture, then pour over half the egg mixture. Arrange the remaining 16 triangles around the edge and down the center of the dish, overlapping slightly as you go.

4. Pour the remaining egg mixture over the top, then sprinkle with the remaining ¼ cup of cheese. Bake, uncovered, for 35 minutes or until crisp and golden brown.

Makes 8 servings

Hearty Spam™ Breakfast Skillet

2 cups frozen diced or shredded potatoes, thawed
½ cup chopped onion
¼ medium green bell pepper, cut into 1-inch thin strips
¼ medium red or yellow bell pepper, cut into 1-inch thin strips
2 teaspoons vegetable oil
1 (12-ounce) can SPAM® Luncheon Meat, cut into julienne strips
1 (8-ounce) carton frozen fat-free egg product, thawed *or* 4 eggs
¼ teaspoon dried basil leaves
⅛ teaspoon salt
⅛ teaspoon black pepper
6 drops hot pepper sauce
¼ cup (1 ounce) shredded Cheddar cheese

In large nonstick skillet over medium-high heat, cook potatoes, onion and bell peppers in oil 5 minutes, stirring constantly. Add SPAM®; cook and stir 5 minutes. In small bowl, combine egg product, basil, salt, black pepper and hot pepper sauce; blend well. Pour over mixture in skillet. Cover. Cook over medium-low heat 8 to 12 minutes or until set. Sprinkle with cheese; remove from heat.

Makes 6 servings

Savory Bread Pudding

Denver Spoonbread

3 tablespoons butter or margarine, divided
2 tablespoons grated Parmesan cheese
½ cup chopped onion
¼ cup chopped green bell pepper
¼ cup chopped red bell pepper
2½ cups milk
1 cup yellow cornmeal
1 teaspoon salt
1½ cups (6 ounces) shredded Cheddar cheese
4 eggs, separated*

Egg whites must be free from any yolk to reach proper volume when beaten.

1. Preheat oven to 350°F.

2. Grease 1½-quart soufflé dish with 1 tablespoon butter. Sprinkle bottom and side of dish evenly with Parmesan cheese.

3. Melt remaining 2 tablespoons butter in medium, heavy saucepan over medium heat. Add onion and bell peppers; cook 5 to 7 minutes or until tender, stirring occasionally. Transfer mixture to small bowl; set aside.

4. Combine milk, cornmeal and salt in same saucepan. Bring to a boil over high heat. Reduce heat to medium; cook and stir 5 minutes or until mixture thickens. Remove from heat. Stir in Cheddar cheese until cheese is melted. Stir in onion mixture.

5. Beat egg whites in clean large bowl using clean beaters with electric mixer at high speed until stiff but not dry; set aside.

6. Beat egg yolks in separate large bowl. Stir into cornmeal mixture. Stir ⅓ of egg whites into cornmeal mixture. Fold remaining egg whites into cornmeal mixture until evenly incorporated. Pour into prepared soufflé dish.

7. Bake about 50 minutes or until puffed and golden brown. Serve immediately. Garnish, if desired.   *Makes 6 servings*

Mexican Strata Olé

4 (6-inch) corn tortillas, halved, divided
1 cup chopped onion
½ cup chopped green bell pepper
1 clove garlic, crushed
1 teaspoon dried oregano leaves
½ teaspoon ground cumin
1 teaspoon FLEISCHMANN'S® Original Margarine
1 cup dried kidney beans, cooked in unsalted water according to package directions
½ cup (2 ounces) shredded reduced-fat Cheddar cheese
1½ cups skim milk
1 cup EGG BEATERS® Healthy Real Egg Substitute
1 cup thick and chunky salsa

Arrange half the tortilla pieces in bottom of greased 12×8×2-inch baking dish; set aside.

In large nonstick skillet, over medium-high heat, sauté onion, bell pepper, garlic, oregano and cumin in margarine until tender; stir in beans. Spoon half the mixture over tortillas; repeat layers once. Sprinkle with cheese.

In medium bowl, combine milk and Egg Beaters®; pour evenly over cheese. Bake at 350°F for 40 minutes or until puffed and golden brown. Let stand 10 minutes before serving. Serve topped with salsa.

Makes 8 servings

Denver Spoonbread

Summer Sausage 'n' Egg Wedges

    4 eggs, beaten
    ⅓ cup milk
    ¼ cup all-purpose flour
    ½ teaspoon baking powder
    ⅛ teaspoon garlic powder
    2½ cups (10 ounces) shredded Cheddar
        or mozzarella cheese, divided
    1½ cups diced HILLSHIRE FARM®
        Summer Sausage
    1 cup cream-style cottage cheese with
        chives

Preheat oven to 375°F.

Combine eggs, milk, flour, baking powder and garlic powder in medium bowl; beat until combined. Stir in 2 cups Cheddar cheese, Summer Sausage and cottage cheese. Pour into greased 9-inch pie plate. Bake, uncovered, 25 to 30 minutes or until golden and knife inserted into center comes out clean. To serve, cut into 6 wedges. Sprinkle wedges with remaining ½ cup Cheddar cheese.   *Makes 6 servings*

Chili-Walnut Egg Puff

    1¼ cups low-cholesterol egg substitute
    ¼ cup all-purpose flour
    ½ teaspoon baking powder
    1 cup fat-free cottage cheese
    ½ cup (2 ounces) grated reduced-fat
        Monterey Jack or Cheddar cheese
    ½ cup (2 ounces) chopped California
        Walnuts, toasted if desired
    ¼ cup (2 ounces) diced mild green
        chilies

Preheat oven to 350°F. Coat 8-inch square baking dish with nonstick cooking spray.

Pour egg substitute into large bowl. In small cup, stir together flour and baking powder. Sift over egg substitute and beat until completely blended. Beat in cheeses,

walnuts and chilies. Pour into prepared pan and bake for about 35 minutes or until puffy and knife inserted slightly off center comes out clean. Serve with pineapple or melon and corn muffins.   *Makes 4 servings*

*Favorite recipe from **Walnut Marketing Board***

Spinach & Egg Casserole

    1 box (10 ounces) BIRDS EYE® frozen
        Chopped Spinach
    1 can (15 ounces) Cheddar cheese
        soup
    1 tablespoon mustard
    ½ pound deli ham, cut into ¼-inch
        cubes
    4 hard-boiled eggs, chopped or sliced

• Preheat oven to 350°F.

• In large saucepan, cook spinach according to package directions; drain well.

• Stir in soup, mustard and ham.

• Pour into 9×9-inch baking pan. Top with eggs.

• Bake 15 to 20 minutes or until heated through.   *Makes 4 servings*

Serving Suggestion: Sprinkle with paprika for added color.

Birds Eye Idea: Cook eggs the day before and refrigerate. They will be much easier to peel.

Prep Time: 10 minutes

Cook Time: 15 to 20 minutes

Summer Sausage 'n' Egg Wedge

French Toast Strata

4 ounces day-old French or Italian
   bread, cut into ¾-inch cubes
   (4 cups)
⅓ cup golden raisins
1 package (3 ounces) cream cheese,
   cut into ¼-inch cubes
3 eggs
1½ cups milk
½ cup maple-flavored pancake syrup
1 teaspoon vanilla
2 tablespoons sugar
1 teaspoon ground cinnamon
   Additional maple-flavored pancake
   syrup (optional)

Spray 11×7-inch baking dish with nonstick
cooking spray.

Place bread cubes in even layer in prepared
dish; sprinkle raisins and cream cheese
evenly over bread.

Beat eggs in medium bowl with electric
mixer at medium speed until blended. Add
milk, ½ cup pancake syrup and vanilla; mix
well. Pour egg mixture evenly over bread
mixture. Cover; refrigerate at least 4 hours
or overnight.

Preheat oven to 350°F. Combine sugar and
cinnamon in small bowl; sprinkle evenly over
strata.

Bake, uncovered, 40 to 45 minutes or until
puffed, golden brown and knife inserted in
center comes out clean. Cut into squares
and serve with additional pancake syrup, if
desired.   *Makes 6 servings*

Sausage Scramble

1 (12-ounce) package BOB EVANS®
   Original Links
¼ cup chopped onion
1 tablespoon butter or margarine
1 medium tomato, seeded and coarsely
   chopped
½ cup (2 ounces) diced processed
   American cheese
2 tablespoons chopped fresh parsley
2 to 3 drops hot pepper sauce
   (optional)
¼ teaspoon salt
⅛ teaspoon black pepper
8 eggs
1 tablespoon water
   Buttered toast or toasted English
   muffins

Cook sausage in medium skillet until
browned; drain off any drippings. Cut each
link into 6 or 7 pieces and set aside. Cook
onion in butter in medium nonstick skillet
over medium heat until tender. Add tomato;
cook 2 to 3 minutes. Add cheese, parsley,
hot pepper sauce, salt and black pepper;
remove skillet from heat and stir to melt
cheese. Beat eggs and water lightly in
medium bowl. Whisk small amount of warm
cheese mixture into egg mixture, then add
egg mixture back into skillet. Stir in sausage;
cook until eggs are scrambled but still moist.
Serve over toast or English muffins.
Refrigerate leftovers.   *Makes 6 servings*

French Toast Strata

Ham and Cheese Frittata

1 tablespoon vegetable oil
1 cup chopped red onion
½ cup chopped green bell pepper
1 teaspoon minced garlic
1 cup (6 ounces) slivered ALPINE LACE®
    Boneless Cooked Ham
1 cup egg substitute *or* 4 large eggs
3 large egg whites
1 cup (4 ounces) shredded ALPINE
    LACE® Reduced Fat Cheddar
    Cheese, divided
¼ cup whole fresh tarragon leaves *or*
    2 teaspoons dried tarragon
½ teaspoon salt
¼ teaspoon cracked black pepper
2 large plum tomatoes, thinly sliced

1. Preheat the broiler. In a large broilerproof skillet, heat the oil over medium-high heat. Add the onion, bell pepper and garlic and sauté for 5 minutes or until soft. Stir in the ham and cook 3 minutes more.

2. In a medium-size bowl, whisk the egg substitute (or the 4 whole eggs) with the egg whites until foamy; fold in ½ cup of the cheese, the tarragon, salt and black pepper. Pour over the vegetable-ham mixture.

3. Reduce the heat and cook, uncovered, for 6 minutes or just until the egg mixture is set around the edges. Arrange the tomato slices on top of the frittata, in a circle around the edge and in a cluster in the center. Sprinkle with the remaining ½ cup of cheese.

4. Slide the skillet under the broiler for 1 minute or until the frittata is set in the center. Serve immediately right from the skillet! *Makes 4 servings*

Enchilada Breakfast Spam™ Casserole

8 (8-inch) flour tortillas
1 (12-ounce) can SPAM® Luncheon
    Meat, cubed
1 cup chopped onions
1 cup chopped green bell pepper
1 tomato, chopped
2 cups (8 ounces) shredded Cheddar
    cheese, divided
4 eggs
2 cups whipping cream
1 (4.25-ounce) jar CHI-CHI'S® Diced
    Green Chilies
CHI-CHI'S® Picante Sauce

In center of each tortilla, place about ¼ cup SPAM®, 1 tablespoon onion, 1 tablespoon bell pepper, 1 tablespoon tomato and 1 tablespoon cheese. Roll up tightly. Repeat procedure to make 8 enchiladas. Place enchiladas seam side down in greased 13×9-inch baking dish. In medium bowl, beat together eggs, cream and green chilies. Pour over enchiladas. Cover. Refrigerate overnight. Heat oven to 350°F. Bake, uncovered, 40 to 50 minutes or until egg mixture is set. Sprinkle with remaining cheese. Bake 5 minutes longer or until cheese is melted. Serve with picante sauce. *Makes 8 servings*

Ham and Cheese Frittata

Pizza for Breakfast

1 (6½-ounce) package pizza crust mix
1 pound BOB EVANS® Original Recipe
    Roll Sausage
1 cup diced fresh or drained canned
    tomatoes
8 ounces fresh mushrooms, sliced
1½ cups (6 ounces) shredded mozzarella
    cheese, divided
1½ cups (6 ounces) shredded sharp
    Cheddar cheese, divided
4 eggs
    Salt and pepper to taste
    Salsa (optional)

Preheat oven to 350°F. Prepare crust mix according to package directions. Spread pizza dough into greased 13×9-inch baking dish, making sure dough evenly covers bottom and 2 inches up sides of dish. Crumble and cook sausage in medium skillet until browned; drain well on paper towels. Top crust with sausage, tomatoes, mushrooms, 1 cup mozzarella cheese and 1 cup Cheddar cheese. Bake 8 to 10 minutes or until crust is golden brown at edges. Remove from oven. Whisk eggs, salt and pepper in small bowl; pour over pizza. Return to oven; bake 7 to 9 minutes more or until eggs are set. Immediately sprinkle with remaining cheeses. Serve hot with salsa, if desired. Refrigerate leftovers.

Makes 8 to 10 servings

Note: Refrigerated crescent roll dough may be used instead of pizza crust mix. Seal edges together and stretch to fit baking dish.

Spinach-Cheddar Squares

1½ cups EGG BEATERS® Healthy Real Egg
    Substitute
¾ cup skim milk
1 tablespoon dried onion flakes
1 tablespoon grated Parmesan cheese
¼ teaspoon garlic powder
⅛ teaspoon ground black pepper
¼ cup plain dry bread crumbs
¾ cup shredded fat-free Cheddar
    cheese, divided
1 (10-ounce) package frozen chopped
    spinach, thawed and well drained
¼ cup diced pimentos

In medium bowl, combine Egg Beaters®, milk, onion flakes, Parmesan cheese, garlic powder and pepper; set aside.

Sprinkle bread crumbs evenly onto bottom of lightly greased 8×8×2-inch baking dish. Top with ½ cup Cheddar cheese and spinach. Pour egg mixture evenly over spinach; top with remaining Cheddar cheese and pimentos.

Bake at 350°F for 35 to 40 minutes or until knife inserted in center comes out clean. Let stand 10 minutes before serving.

Makes 16 appetizer servings

Prep Time: 15 minutes

Cook Time: 40 minutes

Pizza for Breakfast

Sausage & Apple Quiche

1 unbaked (9-inch) pastry shell
½ pound bulk spicy pork sausage
½ cup chopped onion
¾ cup shredded, peeled tart apple
1 tablespoon lemon juice
1 tablespoon sugar
⅛ teaspoon red pepper flakes
1 cup (4 ounces) shredded Cheddar
  cheese
3 eggs
1½ cups half-and-half
¼ teaspoon salt
  Ground black pepper

1. Preheat oven to 425°F.

2. Place piece of foil inside pastry shell; partially fill with uncooked beans or rice. Bake 10 minutes. Remove foil and beans; continue baking pastry 5 minutes or until lightly browned. Let cool.

3. *Reduce oven temperature to 375°F.*

4. Crumble sausage into large skillet; add onion. Cook over medium heat until meat is browned and onion is tender. Spoon off and discard pan drippings.

5. Add apple, lemon juice, sugar and red pepper flakes to skillet. Cook on medium-high, stirring constantly, 4 minutes or until apple is just tender and all liquid is evaporated. Let cool.

6. Spoon sausage mixture into pastry shell; top with cheese. Whisk eggs, half-and-half, salt and dash of black pepper in medium bowl. Pour over sausage mixture.

7. Bake 35 to 45 minutes or until filling is puffed and knife inserted in center comes out clean. Let stand 10 minutes before cutting. *Makes 6 servings*

Apple & Raisin Oven Pancake

1 large baking apple, cored and thinly
  sliced
⅓ cup golden raisins
2 tablespoons packed brown sugar
½ teaspoon ground cinnamon
4 eggs
⅔ cup milk
⅔ cup all-purpose flour
2 tablespoons butter or margarine,
  melted
  Powdered sugar (optional)

Preheat oven to 350°F. Spray 9-inch pie plate with nonstick cooking spray.

Combine apple, raisins, brown sugar and cinnamon in medium bowl. Transfer to prepared pie plate.

Bake, uncovered, 10 to 15 minutes or until apple begins to soften. Remove from oven. Increase oven temperature to 450°F.

Meanwhile, whisk eggs, milk, flour and butter in medium bowl until blended. Pour batter over apple mixture.

Bake 15 minutes or until pancake is golden brown. Invert onto serving dish. Sprinkle with powdered sugar, if desired.

Makes 6 servings

Apple & Raisin Oven Pancake

Skillet Sausage with Potatoes and Rosemary

1 tablespoon vegetable oil
3 cups diced red skin potatoes
1 cup diced onion
1 pound BOB EVANS® Original Recipe
   Roll Sausage
½ teaspoon dried rosemary
¼ teaspoon rubbed sage
   Salt and black pepper to taste
2 tablespoons chopped fresh parsley

Heat oil in large skillet over medium-high heat 1 minute. Add potatoes; cook 5 to 10 minutes or until slightly brown, stirring occasionally. Add onion; cook until tender. Add crumbled sausage; cook until browned. Add rosemary, sage, salt and pepper; cook and stir until well blended. Transfer to serving platter and garnish with parsley. Refrigerate leftovers.

Makes 4 to 6 servings

Vegetable Strata

2 slices white bread, cubed
¼ cup shredded reduced-fat Swiss
   cheese
½ cup sliced carrots
½ cup sliced mushrooms
¼ cup chopped onion
1 clove garlic, crushed
1 teaspoon FLEISCHMANN'S® Original
   Margarine
½ cup chopped tomato
½ cup snow peas
1 cup EGG BEATERS® Healthy Real Egg
   Substitute
¾ cup skim milk

Place bread cubes evenly on bottom of greased 1½-quart casserole dish. Sprinkle with cheese; set aside.

In medium nonstick skillet, over medium heat, sauté carrots, mushrooms, onion and garlic in margarine until tender. Stir in tomato and snow peas; cook 1 to 2 minutes more. Spoon over cheese. In small bowl, combine Egg Beaters® and milk; pour over vegetable mixture. Bake at 375°F for 45 to 50 minutes or until knife inserted in center comes out clean. Let stand 10 minutes before serving.   *Makes 6 servings*

Prep Time: 15 minutes

Cook Time: 55 minutes

Spinach-Cheese Pasta Casserole

8 ounces uncooked pasta shells
2 eggs
1 cup ricotta cheese
1 package (10 ounces) frozen chopped
   spinach, thawed and squeezed dry
1 jar (26 ounces) marinara sauce
1 teaspoon salt
1 cup (4 ounces) shredded mozzarella
   cheese
¼ cup grated Parmesan cheese

Preheat oven to 350°F. Spray 1½-quart round casserole with nonstick cooking spray.

Cook pasta according to package directions until al dente. Drain.

Meanwhile, whisk eggs in large bowl until blended. Add ricotta and spinach to eggs; stir until combined. Stir in pasta, marinara sauce and salt until pasta is well coated. Pour into prepared dish. Sprinkle mozzarella and Parmesan evenly over casserole.

Bake, covered, 30 minutes. Uncover and bake 15 minutes or until hot and bubbly.

Makes 6 to 8 servings

Vegetable Strata

Bacon and Maple Grits Puff

8 slices bacon
2 cups milk
1¼ cups water
1 cup quick-cooking grits
½ teaspoon salt
½ cup pure maple syrup
4 eggs
Fresh chives (optional)

1. Preheat oven to 350°F. Grease 1½-quart round casserole or soufflé dish; set aside.

2. Cook bacon in large skillet over medium-high heat about 7 minutes or until crisp. Remove bacon to paper towel; set aside. Reserve 2 tablespoons bacon drippings.

3. Combine milk, water, grits and salt in medium saucepan. Bring to a boil over medium heat, stirring frequently. Simmer 2 to 3 minutes or until mixture thickens, stirring constantly. Remove from heat; stir in syrup and reserved 2 tablespoons bacon drippings.

4. Crumble bacon; reserve ¼ cup for garnish. Stir remaining crumbled bacon into grits mixture.

5. Beat eggs in medium bowl. Gradually stir small amount of grits mixture into eggs, then stir back into remaining grits mixture. Pour into prepared casserole.

6. Bake 1 hour and 20 minutes or until knife inserted in center comes out clean. Top with reserved ¼ cup bacon. Garnish with fresh chives, if desired. Serve immediately.

Makes 6 to 8 servings

Note: Puff will fall slightly after removing from oven.

Bratwurst Skillet Breakfast

1½ pounds red potatoes
3 bratwurst links (about ¾ pound)
2 tablespoons butter or margarine
1½ teaspoons caraway seed
4 cups shredded red cabbage

1. Cut potatoes into ¼- to ½-inch pieces. Place in microwavable casserole. Microwave, covered, on HIGH 3 minutes; stir. Microwave 2 minutes more or until just tender; set aside.

2. While potatoes are cooking, slice sausage into ¼-inch pieces. Place in large skillet. Heat over medium-high heat. Cook, stirring occasionally, 8 minutes or until browned and no longer pink in center. Remove sausage from pan with slotted spoon; set aside. Pour off drippings.

3. Melt butter in skillet. Add potatoes and caraway. Cook, stirring occasionally, 6 to 8 minutes or until potatoes are golden and tender. Return sausage to skillet; stir in cabbage. Cook, covered, 3 minutes or until cabbage is slightly wilted. Uncover and stir 3 to 4 minutes more or until cabbage is just tender yet still bright red.

Makes 4 servings

Serving Suggestion: Serve with fresh fruit.

Prep and cook time: 30 minutes

Bacon and Maple Grits Puff

Spinach and Cheese Brunch Squares

1 box (11 ounces) pie crust mix
⅓ cup cold water
1 package (10 ounces) frozen chopped spinach, thawed and well drained
1⅓ cups FRENCH'S® French Fried Onions
1 cup (4 ounces) shredded Swiss cheese
1 container (8 ounces) low-fat sour cream
5 eggs
1 cup milk
1 tablespoon FRENCH'S® Deli Brown Mustard
½ teaspoon salt
⅛ teaspoon ground black pepper

Preheat oven to 450°F. Line 13×9×2-inch baking pan with foil; spray with nonstick cooking spray. Combine pie crust mix and water in large bowl until moistened and crumbly. Using floured bottom of measuring cup, press mixture firmly into bottom of prepared pan. Prick with fork. Bake 20 minutes or until golden. *Reduce oven temperature to 350°F.*

Layer spinach, French Fried Onions and cheese over crust. Combine sour cream, eggs, milk, mustard, salt and pepper in medium bowl; mix until well blended. Pour over vegetable and cheese layers. Bake 30 minutes or until knife inserted in center comes out clean. Let stand 10 minutes. Cut into squares* to serve.

Makes 8 main-course servings

*To serve as appetizers, cut into 2-inch squares.

Prep Time: 20 minutes

Cook Time: 50 minutes

Stand Time: 10 minutes

SPAM™ Hash Brown Bake

1 (32-ounce) package frozen hash brown potatoes, thawed slightly
½ cup butter or margarine, melted
1 teaspoon salt
1 teaspoon black pepper
½ teaspoon garlic powder
2 cups (8 ounces) shredded Cheddar cheese
1 (12-ounce) can SPAM® Luncheon Meat, cubed
1 (10¾-ounce) can cream of chicken soup
1½ cups sour cream
½ cup milk
½ cup chopped onion
1 (4.25-ounce) jar CHI-CHI'S® Diced Green Chilies, drained
2 cups crushed potato chips

Heat oven to 350°F. In large bowl, combine potatoes, melted butter, salt, pepper and garlic powder. In separate large bowl, combine cheese, SPAM®, soup, sour cream, milk, onion and green chilies. Add SPAM™ mixture to potato mixture; mix well. Pour into 2-quart baking dish. Sprinkle with potato chips. Bake 45 to 60 minutes or until thoroughly heated. *Makes 8 servings*

Spinach and Cheese Brunch Square

Quiche Lorraine Florentine

1 (10-ounce) package frozen chopped
   spinach, thawed and well drained
1 cup shredded Swiss cheese
   (4 ounces)
4 slices bacon, cooked and crumbled
2 tablespoons chopped green onions
1 (9-inch) unbaked pastry shell
3 eggs, slightly beaten
1 cup light cream or half-and-half
¼ cup GREY POUPON® Dijon Mustard

Combine spinach, cheese, bacon and green onions. Spoon mixture evenly into pastry shell.

In small bowl, blend eggs, cream and mustard. Pour evenly over spinach mixture. Bake at 375°F for 35 to 40 minutes or until knife inserted in center comes out clean. Let stand 10 minutes before serving. To serve, cut into wedges.   *Makes 8 servings*

Sunny Day Casserole

1 jar (8 ounces) pasteurized processed
   cheese spread, melted
¾ cup milk
4 cups diced potatoes, partially cooked
2 cups diced HILLSHIRE FARM® Ham
1 package (16 ounces) frozen mixed
   vegetables, thawed
½ cup chopped onion
1 cup (4 ounces) shredded Swiss,
   Cheddar or Monterey Jack cheese
1 cup rich round cracker crumbs

Preheat oven to 350°F.

Combine cheese spread and milk in large bowl. Stir in potatoes, Ham, mixed vegetables and onion. Pour into medium casserole. Bake, covered, 45 minutes, stirring

occasionally. Sprinkle Swiss cheese and cracker crumbs over top. Bake, uncovered, until Swiss cheese is melted.
          Makes 6 servings

Asparagus Frittata Casserole

3 large eggs
1½ cups 1% milk
1 teaspoon salt
1 box (10 ounces) BIRDS EYE® frozen
   Deluxe Asparagus Spears, thawed
½ cup shredded Monterey Jack or
   Cheddar cheese

• Preheat oven to 400°F.

• In medium bowl, beat eggs. Add milk and salt; blend well.

• Pour mixture into greased 9×9-inch baking pan; top with asparagus.

• Sprinkle with cheese.

• Bake 15 minutes or until egg mixture is set.   *Makes 4 servings*

Prep Time: 5 to 7 minutes
Cook Time: 15 minutes

ACKNOWLEDGMENTS

The publisher would like to thank the companies and organizations listed below for the use of their recipes and photographs in this publication.

A.1.® Steak Sauce
Birds Eye®
Blue Diamond Growers®
Bob Evans®
Butterball® Turkey Company
Chef Paul Prudhomme's Magic Seasoning Blends®
COLLEGE INN® Broth
Colorado Potato Administrative Committee
Del Monte Corporation
Delmarva Poultry Industry, Inc.
Dole Food Company, Inc.
Egg Beaters® Healthy Real Egg Substitute
Equal® sweetener
Filippo Berio Olive Oil
Florida Department of Agriculture and Consumer Services, Bureau of Seafood and Aquaculture
Golden Grain®
GREY POUPON® Mustard
Guiltless Gourmet®
Healthy Choice®
Heinz U.S.A.
Hillshire Farm®
Hormel Foods Corporation
Hunt-Wesson, Inc.
The HV Company
The J.M. Smucker Company
Kikkoman International Inc.

Kraft Foods, Inc.
Land O' Lakes, Inc.
Lawry's® Foods, Inc.
Lipton®
McIlhenny Company (TABASCO® Pepper Sauce)
Minnesota Cultivated Wild Rice Council
MOTT'S® Inc., a division of Cadbury Beverages Inc.
National Honey Board
National Pork Producers Council
National Turkey Federation
Nestlé USA, Inc.
Norseland, Inc.
North Dakota Beef Commission
North Dakota Wheat Commission
Perdue Farms Incorporated
The Procter & Gamble Company
Reckitt & Colman Inc.
Riviana Foods Inc.
Southeast United Dairy Industry Association, Inc.
StarKist® Seafood Company
USA Dry Pea & Lentil Council
USA Rice Federation
Veg-All®
Walnut Marketing Board
Wisconsin Milk Marketing Board

INDEX